American Democratic Theory

American Democratic Theory

PLURALISM AND ITS CRITICS

William Alton Kelso

 *Contributions in Political Science, Number 1*

GREENWOOD PRESS
WESTPORT, CONNECTICUT • LONDON, ENGLAND

Library of Congress Cataloging in Publication Data

Kelso, William Alton.
    American democratic theory.

    (Contributions in political science ; no. 1, ISSN 0147-1066)
    Includes bibliographical references.
    1. Democracy. 2. Pluralism (Social sciences). 3. Political participa-
tion—United States. 4. United States—Politics and government—
1945-   . I. Title. II. Series: Contributions in political science ; no. 1.
JC423.K379   321.8   77-83894
ISBN 0-8371-9825-9

Library of Congress Catalog Card Number: 77-83894
ISBN: 0-8371-9825-9
ISSN: 0147-1066

First published in 1978

Greenwood Press, Inc.
51 Riverside Avenue, Westport, Connecticut 06880

Printed in the United States of America

10 9 8 7 6 5 4 3 2 1

Acknowledgments

Chapter 2 is adapted from William Kelso, "Public Pluralism: A New Defense of an Old Doctrine," *Social Science*, Winter 1977, Vol. 52, No. 1, pp. 16-30, and is reprinted with permission of the publisher.

Part of chapter 6 is from William Kelso, "Organizing the Poor: Reexamining the OEO Data," *The Bureaucrat*, October 1977, Vol. 6, No. 3, and is reprinted with permission of the publisher.

Table 1 is from Robert Dahl, *A Preface to Democratic Theory*. Copyright © 1956 by The University of Chicago. Used with permission of the University of Chicago Press.

Table 3 is adapted from *Public Finance* by Richard Musgrave and Peggy Musgrave. Copyright © 1973 by McGraw-Hill, Inc. Used with permission of McGraw-Hill Book Company.

To Linda

Contents

Preface

My reasons for writing a book on democratic theory are essentially threefold. First of all, this piece is intended as a defense of a pluralistic form of democracy. In recent years textbooks on American government and more specialized monographs on democratic theory have been extremely hostile to pluralistic forms of politics. Many of the criticisms seem unwarranted for they fail to distinguish among different types of pluralism and they often overlook considerable evidence that pluralistic patterns of participation can work well if properly structured. While many readers will undoubtedly reject a number of my conclusions, this book will serve some purpose if it causes them to reconsider the merits of pluralistic government.

Besides defending an often maligned form of government, this book also attempts to identify and analyze the major assumptions underlying competing theories of democracy. In many cases the debate over democratic theory seems muddled because commentators use the same label to refer to what are analytically different forms of government. Quite frequently, people mistakenly equate pluralistic democracy with polyarchal, or elitist, forms of democratic rule even though the two systems of government entail radically different conceptions of what democracy means. As a means of clarifying some of this confusion, this study analytically identifies and then compares four types of democratic theory: (a) polyarchy, which sees the essence of democracy as competition among political elites, (b) pluralism, which conceives of democratic government as a twofold process involving competition among elites and bargaining among interest groups, (c) populism, which equates democracy with maximizing the power of the majority to decide substantive political issues, and (d) participatory democracy, which views democratic government as a form of community decision making in which all citizens can actively participate on a day-to-day basis.

Finally, this book is an attempt to synthesize recent findings in the fields of voting behavior, participation, decision making, and public administration. More often than not, specialized studies in these fields have larger ramifications for democratic theory that have never been fully discussed or developed. As the discipline of political science has become more specialized, there has been a tendency for scholars to ignore the larger consequences of their own work. While this study is a normative defense of one type of democratic theory, it also attempts to offer a new perspective for analyzing and understanding recent developments in the various subfields of political science.

In preparing this manuscript I have received generous help from numerous friends and colleagues whom I would like to thank. I am especially endebted to Booth Fowler, my graduate advisor at the University of Wisconsin, who originally got me interested in the subject of democratic theory. As innumerable other students will testify, he is a very gifted teacher. His encouragement as well as his numerous critical comments greatly improved the quality of this manuscript. Nobutaka Ike also read the book in its entirety and made many helpful suggestions. David Colburn, Manning Dauer, Mark Kann, Brian Peckham, Richard Scher, and Dan Siminoski provided much needed assistance and encouragement during the actual writing. Thanks are also due to Molly Loughlin and Adrienne Turner, who cheerfully typed the completed manuscript. Finally, I should like to thank my wife, Linda, who is in reality almost a coauthor of this book. She patiently read and reread the various drafts of the manuscript, pointing out instances where the logic of an argument seemed weak or the evidence substantiating a point appeared inadequate. Her excellent editing also improved the clarity and readability of the book. And, as a respite from democratic theory, she willingly spent many an evening at the movies with me. While such behavior delayed the completion of the work, it greatly improved the morale of the author.

William Alton Kelso

PART I

Alternative Types of Democratic Theory

Chapter

1

Introduction

This study is primarily a response to recent attacks on a pluralistic theory of democracy. In the 1950s and 1960s, scholars like Robert Dahl and David Truman articulated and defended a model of politics that viewed democracy as a two-fold process involving competition among political elites and bargaining among interest groups. As the term *pluralism* implies, the underlying assumption of the doctrine was that political power is and ought to be wielded by a number of groups rather than any single set of interests. In recent years, however, this model of democracy has been subject to intense attack from a wide spectrum of critics. Robert Paul Wolff, among others, has insisted that the disparity in power and resources between established and marginal groups is so great in a pluralistic system that there is little genuine possibility of initiating reform from below.[1] In contrast, critics like Theodore Lowi have argued that a pluralistic dispersion of political power makes it impossible for public officials to deal with pressing social issues in any sort of centralized, purposeful fashion.[2] Still other commentators, like Michael Harrington, have charged that pluralism so caters to the needs of special interest groups that the welfare of the larger public suffers as a result.[3]

The critics not only disagree on their diagnosis of pluralism's problems but also are at odds as to the measures necessary to remedy its alleged defects. In the debate over how the political system should be structured, three rivals to pluralism have been proposed.

First, participatory democrats like Robert Paul Wolff, Alan Altshuler, and Milton Kotler have advocated the creation of small units of government that will allow people to participate more intensely in the day-to-day affairs of the community.[4] Traditional communitarian democrats like Wolff have justified decentralization of political power on the grounds that the individual will be likely to develop his capabilities to their fullest only when he has an opportunity to participate in the deliberation of important social issues. They believe that regardless of the instrumental advantages a person may secure, he will emotionally and morally benefit from immersing himself in the social affairs of his community. More recently, advocates of community control like Altshuler and Kotler have also argued that political decentralization is necessary in order to increase the ability of minority members to shape their own lives. In their view, unless a centralized political system devolves more power to local neighborhoods, blacks and other minority groups will lack the leverage to control those policies which directly affect their communities.

On the other hand, polyarchal democrats like Theodore Lowi, Robert Crain, and Joseph Schumpeter have called for the concentration of power in the hands of political elites.[5] Lowi in particular maintains that a pluralistic system of decision making so fragments political power that it renders the government incapable of dealing quickly and comprehensively with the numerous problems that beset it. Other polyarchists like Schumpeter contend that consolidation of authority is necessary because the vast majority of citizens are incapable of rational, competent behavior in the political realm. Rejecting the notion of intensive citizen participation, they insist that democratic government entails the right of the public to hold its elites accountable for their actions. In the polyarchal view, government officials can be made to exercise their enhanced power in a beneficent and responsible fashion so long as there are periodic elections in which the public can hold them accountable for their behavior.

Thirdly, populist democrats like Michael Harrington have called both for increasing participation from the bottom up and for strengthening government power from the top down.[6] Populists contend that policy should be determined by a majority of citizens rather than a handful of elites or a small coterie of interest groups, and they therefore advocate periodic referendums as the major means of arriving at public decisions. But because they believe that the pluralistic interplay of groups can often frustrate the wishes of the majority, they maintain that referendum voting should be accompanied by a consolidation of government authority. If the political system is to be made responsive to the needs of the majority, the state must have sufficient power to block small minorities that seek to thwart the wishes of the larger public.

The Need for a Comparative Focus

In order to respond to the above criticisms, this book will look in a more analytical fashion at both the alleged defects of pluralism and the limitations of competing theories of democracy. Unfortunately, many critics have failed to examine the strengths and weaknesses of pluralism from this sort of comparative perspective. When opponents maintain that an interest-group theory of democracy works to the disadvantage of minority groups, they overlook the fact that marginal interests have often fared less well under alternative forms of decision making. Similarly, when commentators insist that a pluralistic system of power makes it impossible to get anything done, they fail to take account of the evidence indicating that pluralistic forms of decision making lead to more policy innovations than do either more centralized or more decentralized patterns of policy making. All too often critics have faulted pluralism for one reason or another but have neglected to show how polyarchy or populism or participatory democracy would rectify the defects they attribute to an interest-group theory of politics.

Recent attacks on pluralism are also deficient because they often fail to distinguish among different varieties of the doctrine. While many commentators assume that there is a single form of pluralistic democracy, I wish to suggest that there are several different analytic types and that many of the complaints leveled against pluralism are actually problems that trouble only certain varieties of the theory.[7] The type of interest-group democracy that I shall call *laissez-faire pluralism* posits a self-regulating political system made up of a multitude of private interests that bargain among themselves and check one another's advances. The advocates of this model—including Robert Dahl, David Truman, and Charles Lind-blom—contend that powerful interest groups will precipitate the emergence of countervailing groups to restrain the monopolistic exercise of power by any single element in society. They also argue that interest-group competition will lead to rational and innovative policy making, since a mulititude of participants can compensate for the limitations in knowledge and ability of any single decision maker. Like its counterpart in economics, laissez-faire pluralism regards competition as the mechanism that maintains the system in working order without any need for outside regulation.

An alternative form of pluralism, which I shall call *corporate pluralism,* minimizes the benefits that accrue from the clash of interests and instead stresses the importance of cooperation be-tween interest groups and government agencies. This model, which is embodied in programs like the NRA of the New Deal, envisions a political system broken down into a series of autonomous fief-doms presided over by small coteries of interest groups. In each separate domain, government authorities have conferred the ability to make public decisions upon private groups, thereby blurring the boundaries between private interests and public power. The basic assumption is that enhanced decision making will result when the public and private sectors cooperate in resolving problems common to both.

Finally, it is possible to identify a third type of interest-group democracy, which I shall call *public pluralism.* It is this third type of the doctrine that I will defend in this study as the most viable alternative among all the competing models of democracy. The efforts of the Johnson administration to organize the poor under OEO and to coordinate federal policies under the Model Cities program are forms of organizational behavior most closely approx-imating this variety of pluralism. Like its laissez-faire counterpart, public pluralism regards competition among groups as the mecha-nism that will produce the optimal set of public policies. But be-cause various elements in society lack the resources to organize or to gain access to government decision makers, and because interest groups and agencies often agree to refrain from competing with one another in specific policy areas, public pluralism calls upon the government to undertake measures that will guarantee that the political arena remains competitive. More specifically, it envisions public supervision of the bargaining process, increased centralization of the decision-making arena on both regional and national levels, and stepped-up government action to organize marginal elements in society that lack the resources for bargaining effectively with competing interest groups. In this latter sense public pluralism is similar to corporate pluralism, for it seeks to erase the distinction between public and private authority; but in calling for public agencies to share their resources with private groups, it seeks to foster competition rather than to discourage it.

The Issue of Participation

In defending pluralism against rival theories of democracy, this study will focus on two perennial issues of democratic theory, the scope and limits of popular participation and the consequences of such participation for public decision making. The reason for focusing on these two problems is that on the most basic level democracy has been defined in terms of popular participation in government decision making. Beyond this general level, however, alternative theories of democracy have very different conceptions of what popular participation should involve. While all forms of democratic theory see the public as playing a crucial role in politics, they disagree on three fundamental issues: (1) what the scope of the public's power should be, (2) how the public should be defined and how it should express its views, and (3) what purpose should be served by popular participation in politics.

Polyarchal democrats have usually wanted to confine the public's involvement in politics to choosing among competing elites at election time. By contrast, pluralists and populists have argued that the citizenry should have a voice in deciding many of the substantive issues confronting the political system, while participatory democrats have gone even further and insisted that the public should participate in all the daily decisions that face the political community. Pluralists, populists, and participatory democrats contend that elitist versions of democracy underestimate the citizenry's ability to make informed decisions in crucial policy matters. Despite their common agreement that the public should play a prominent role in politics, these three versions of democracy have often strongly disagreed over who constitutes the public and how it should express its sentiments on important issues. Pluralists have tended to conceive of the relevant constituency as the numerous issue publics that make up society, while populists have envisaged the people as the numerical majority existing on any one particular issue and participatory democrats have insisted that the public includes all members of the community. In addition, both populists and pluralists have differed over how policy decisions should be formulated. While populists have wanted to rely on referendums to decide major issues confronting the political system, pluralists have maintained that public welfare can be maximized if decisions are made through political bargaining. Finally, alternative theories of democracy often have very different conceptions of the benefits that accrue to the individual from becoming involved in political affairs. Polyarchists, populists, and pluralists have usually tended to visualize political participation as a utilitarian device for realizing the interests of the public. In contrast, participatory democrats have argued that participation fosters the intellectual and emotional development of the individual and that it should therefore be viewed as an end in and of itself and not as a means for the accomplishment of other substantive ends.

To demonstrate that the pluralist theory of participation is preferable to the above alternatives, this study will argue with opposing democratic theories on both empirical and normative grounds. If, as populists insist, the wishes of the majority ought to prevail, it will be essential to look at the empirical evidence to see whether a majority interest actually exists on most issues. And if it is possible to identify a majoritarian position, it will then be imperative to debate on normative grounds whether the intensity of interests or the majority of interests should be the determining factor in arriving at public decisions. Likewise, to respond to the claim of participatory democrats that pluralism fails to provide adequate opportunities for individual participation, it will be necessary to determine whether there is adequate empirical evidence for the assumption that people are able to sustain an intense involvement in communitarian politics.

The Issue of Decision Making

After comparing their contrasting views of participation, this book will examine how alternative theories of democracy attempt to deal with the problem of decision making. In many respects participation and decision making are corollary problems, for individuals participate in politics in order to influence the content of public decisions. However, as the modern state has assumed increasing responsibility for the welfare of its citizens, the question has arisen whether popular participation and rational, innovative policy making are compatible goals. Many commentators have argued that the complexities of social planning require a trade-off between citizen involvement and effective policy making. Since so many of the attacks on pluralism have focused on the subject of decision making, it is essential that we examine this issue in more detail. More specifically, it will be necessary to study alternative forms of democratic theory in terms of (1) what kinds of decision-making procedures will be most effective in generating rational policy solutions and (2) what kinds of institutional or administrative procedures will be most likely to succeed in translating publicly determined goals into operating policy. While polyarchists like Lowi maintain that effective, long-range policies will be developed only when political elites have sufficient power to act in a decisive, comprehensive manner, I will argue that public pluralism's adversary style of decision making constitutes a more effective method of social planning since bargaining and competition among a multitude of groups and agencies can offset the limitations in knowledge and ability of any single set of decision makers. Likewise, while advocates of community control like Kotler contend that decentralized, neighborhood forms of government will maximize responsiveness to constituent needs, I will argue that a pluralistic style of policy making can better meet public demands since it can deal with complex issues, like pollution, which transcend the boundaries and the problem-solving capabilities of local jurisdictions.

Besides analyzing pluralism's doubts about both highly centralized and highly decentralized forms of decision making, I will also show how pluralism questions the rationality and effectiveness of bureaucratic behavior. Polyarchal democrats like Lowi tend to see bureaucracies in Weberian terms as rational instruments for neutrally implementing predetermined social goals, but students of the administrative process have long argued that bureaucratic behavior can often be inefficient and even pathological in nature. By drawing on the work of Mathew Holden and Philip Selznick, among others, I hope to demonstrate how the political constituents of organizations often inhibit agencies from translating publicly determined goals into operating policy. [8] Likewise, I hope to show how a system of public pluralism can mitigate this type of bureaucratic goal displacement by encouraging agencies and interest groups to monitor one another's activities.

Finally, in a related fashion, I wish to question Lowi's argument that government bureaus should be granted only limited discretion in the implementation of their organizational responsibilities. Lowi maintains that because of our pluralistic system of administration, in which government agencies have considerable leeway in interpreting their obligations, the public has lost faith in the legitimacy and inherent justice of our political institutions. As I shall argue in more detail, it is questionable whether Lowi's explanation for the existence of widespread cynicism about government institutions is completely accurate. And even more importantly, I shall show there is considerable evidence to indicate that if Lowi's call for "juridical democracy" were ever implemented and government bureaus were forced to behave in a highly legalistic, nondiscretionary manner, the ability of public officials to act effectively might be drastically curtailed. In pursuit of what he believes is a just administrative state, Lowi has proposed administrative reforms that may severely hamper the successful delivery of public services.

However, before taking up these issues, it is necessary to deal in more detail with the doctrine of pluralism itself. Although many critics talk as if there were a single form of interest-group democracy, it is possible to identify several different analytic types. Chapter 2 will therefore be devoted to the delineation of three different models of pluralism. In parts II and III I will defend pluralism against rival theories of democracy, arguing that a public form of pluralism can meet many of the objections raised by alternative theories of democracy.

NOTES

1. Robert Paul Wolff, Barrington Moore, Jr., and Herbert Marcuse, *A Critique of Pure Tolerance*, pp. 3-53.

2. Theodore J. Lowi, *The End of Liberalism*.

3. Michael Harrington, *Toward a Democratic Left*.

4. Alan Altshuler, *Community Control*; Milton Kotler, *Neighborhood Government*; Wolff, Moore, and Marcuse, *Critique of Pure Tolerance*.

5. Lowi, *End of Liberalism*; Robert L. Crain, Elihu Katz, and Donald Rosenthal, *The Politics of Community Conflict*; Joseph A. Schumpeter, *Capitalism, Socialism and Democracy*.

6. Harrington, *Toward a Democratic Left*; See also Jack Newfield and Jeff Greenfield, *A Populist Manifesto*.

7. It should be stressed that this book is not intended to be a history of pluralism. In delineating three types of pluralistic government I have focused primarily on the works of contemporary American political scientists and ignored the writings of English pluralists at the turn of the century. In the early 1900s Frederick Maitland and John Neville Figgis and later Harold Laski, R. H. Tawney, and G. D. H. Cole formulated the doctrine of pluralism as an attack on continental idealism and British liberalism. They rejected both the Hegelian notion that the modern state has a virtual monopoly on legitimate authority and the nineteenth-century liberal belief that the individual exists in a social vacuum. Since these concerns have been of only peripheral interest to American pluralists, I have refrained from dealing with the above authors. For similar reasons I have spent no space discussing Arthur Bentley's classic work, *The Process of Government*. While many people might be inclined to call him a pluralist, his interests were very different from those explored in this book. Rather than offering an empirical description of American politics or a normative defense of a style of decision making, Bentley was primarily concerned with fashioning a tool to analyze political phenomena. Revolting against the "formalism" of the political thought of his day, he proposed the use of group analysis as a means of capturing the very process of governmental activity. While he maintained that group analysis was a useful device to apply to political behavior, he did not necessarily conclude that the interplay of groups was either empirically important or normatively desirable in resolving policy disputes.

8. Mathew Holden "Imperialism in Bureaucracy," pp. 943-51; Philip Selznick, *TVA and the Grass Roots*.

Chapter

2

Three Types of Pluralism

In recent years the debate over pluralistic democracy has elicited intense comment from detractors as well as defenders of the doctrine. While supporters of a group theory of democracy contend that the interplay of interests enhances individual freedom and promotes rational decision making, critics claim that it retards comprehensive planning and works to the disadvantage of marginal interests in society. The purpose of this chapter is to argue that the debate has often been somewhat beside the point since the antagonists have failed to realize that there are distinct varieties of pluralism. The pattern of policy making that Robert Dahl and David Truman have described as pluralism has little in common with that form of politics Theodore Lowi has called "interest group liberalism" or Grant McConnell has termed "a group theory of politics." Because of their failure to recognize the existence of different kinds of interest-group democracy, many commentators have not always realized that their criticisms may apply only to specific forms of the doctrine. As we shall soon see, it is analytically possible to identify three distinct varieties: laissez-faire, corporate, and public pluralism. These alternative types make not only very different empirical assumptions about the openness of the present political system, but also very different normative assumptions about the most desirable pattern of group interaction.

Laissez-faire Pluralism

The form of pluralism I have labeled laissez-faire finds its clearest expression in the works of Robert Dahl, David Truman, Wallace Sayre, Herbert Kaufman, Edward Banfield, Charles Lindblom, and William Kornhauser.[1] Despite some variations in their respective views, these authors conceive of democracy as essentially a twofold process involving competition among political elites and bargaining among interest groups. They insist that whenever members of the public are concerned about a particular issue, they can bring about political change either directly through the process of group bargaining or indirectly through the mechanism of elections. Laissez-faire pluralists reject the argument that the political system is dominated by a single ruling elite and instead insist that it is responsive to a variety of interests with divergent policy preferences. Like their laissez-faire counterparts in economics, they view the political arena as a competitive marketplace in which any entrepreneur can gain entry to merchandise his views. Politics is seen as an open, fluid process in which responsibility for formulating decisions is shared by a diverse array of groups and public officials who constantly bargain and negotiate with one another.

According to Dahl, whose case study of New Haven politics constitutes the classic example of the laissez-faire model, this openness represents the major distinguishing characteristic of the American political system.

When one looks at American political institutions in their entirety and compares them with institutions in other democracies, what stands out as a salient feature is the extraordinary variety of opportunities these institutions provide for an organized minority to block, modify, or delay a policy which the minority opposes. Consequently, it is a rarity for any coalition to carry out its policies without having to bargain, negotiate, and compromise with its opponents.[2]

In New Haven, the process of bargaining and negotiation has made it possible for such diverse groups as wealthy businessmen, old-time patricians, and working-class ethnics to wield considerable control over those policies which happen to concern them.[3] Since these groups have a variety of resources at their disposal as well as a number of points at which to influence policy, they cannot be denied access to the bargaining table for any prolonged period of time. Given the decentralized nature of the decision-making process, no single party can succeed in permanently excluding interests that hold opposing views. If a group feels intensely about an issue and is skillful in using its resources, it can win a favorable hearing of its demands even though it may not wield any preponderant strength in terms of wealth, social standing, or the like. [4]

Secondly, laissez-faire pluralists contend that the political system is self-regulating and self-correcting. If particular groups do start to accumulate excessive amounts of power, countervailing forces are likely to become active, which will check or limit their actions. Dahl argues that the phenomenon of unused resources, or what he terms "political slack," constitutes the chief brake on the decision-making process. [5] Since all groups possess some sort of resources, whether they be numbers, skill, or wealth, and since on most occasions groups do not expend all of their available assets to influence the deliberations of the political system, they have a certain amount of political slack on which they can draw when they perceive a threat to their interests. If a group starts to abuse its power or to deny access to other interests, opposing groups can tap previously unused resources in order to counterbalance these developments.

While Dahl speaks of political slack, Truman regards the phenomenon of "potential groups" as the chief restraint on monopoly power. Truman points out that individuals who are concerned with a particular issue do not necessarily need to use their resources overtly in order to wield influence. Established interests that recognize that their actions may elicit hostile reactions from other parties often seek to moderate their demands in order to minimize political opposition to their programs.

The power of unorganized interests lies in the possibility that, if these wide, weak interests are too flagrantly ignored, they may be stimulated to organize for aggressive counteraction. In a society permitting wide freedom of association, access to power is not confined to the organized groups in the population. [6]

In a slightly different vein, Sayre and Kaufman argue that the self-regulating nature of the political system derives from the existence of multiple decision-making points.[7] In their case study of politics in New York City, they show how the decentralized nature of the city's government structure prevents any one group from monopolizing the political arena. Because there are so many points at which groups can voice their opinions, interests that lose out at one center of decision making can often seek redress of their grievances at another location.

Thirdly, because laissez-faire pluralists see the political system as both open and self-regulating, they believe that the power of the state to guide and regulate the political process is problematic at best. In a fluid political system in which decisions are reached through continual negotiation and compromise, the power of all parties, including that of political elites, is necessarily limited. Truman views government officials as playing primarily a mediative role, reconciling conflicting group demands when particular interests are unable to resolve their differences by themselves.[8] In contrast, Banfield recognizes that political officials can institute change if they want to, but he argues that they often feel the cost is too high. Banfield's case study of Chicago graphically illustrates the constraints political leaders face under a highly pluralistic system of decision making: "In a system in which the political head must continually 'pay' to overcome formal decentralization and to acquire the authority he needs, the stock of influence in his possession cannot all be 'spent' as he might wish."[9] Thus instead of supervising the policy-making arena and orchestrating support for particular issues, leaders like Mayor Daley often choose to play a passive role. "When there is disagreement . . . the rational strategy for the political head usually is to do nothing."[10]

However, if government officials are especially skillful at what Dahl calls "pyramiding resources,"[11] they may be able to initiate significant change. In a laissez-faire system, elites like Mayor Lee of New Haven may be able to have a significant impact on their community by employing previously unused resources. But even when government officials are prominent actors in the political arena and not just mediators or passive bystanders, their power is based more on their personal skills as negotiators than on the institutional authority of their office. Mayor Lee succeeded in initiating an extensive urban redevelopment program in New Haven, but he was able to do so because "he was a negotiator rather than a hierarchical executive." [12]

He rarely commanded. He negotiated, cajoled, exhorted, beguiled, charmed, pressed, appealed, reasoned, promised, insisted, demanded, even threatened, but he most needed support and acquiescence from other leaders who simply could not be commanded. Because the mayor could not command, he had to bargain. [13]

While the above authors have developed a model that is primarily an empirical theory of politics, their work is not without normative significance. The defenders of laissez-faire pluralism can easily be seen as the inheritors of eighteenth- and nineteenth-century liberalism's interest in the rights and liberties of the individual. Like James Madison before them, they recognize that in a large and diverse society men are prone to infringe on the liberties of those who espouse conflicting values. But as an article of faith, most laissez-faire pluralists insist that the presence of multiple centers of power will be sufficient to deter any party from abusing the rights of others. Instead of attacking what Madison called the cause of faction—the very diversity of human goals—they seek to control its consequences by dividing power among numerous groups. As Dahl argues, when "one center of power is set against another, power itself will be tamed, civilized, controlled and limited to decent human purposes, while coercion, the most evil form of power, will be reduced to a minimum." [14]

By dispersing power among many parties laissez-faire pluralists believe they will not only inhibit the misuse of government power but also retard the development of coercive mass movements. As William Kornhauser has shown in an important defense of pluralistic democracy, when individuals have no ties to secondary associations, they often lack standards for evaluating the appeals of various mass movements. [15] In such a state of anomie or normlessness, they are more likely to be receptive to movements with authoritarian characteristics. However, if people have an opportunity to participate in a rich and diverse group life, they acquire alternative sources of information and standards for assessing various points of view. A plurality of groups that can shield the individual from the machinations of the government can also protect him from the pressures of an intolerant majority.

Although many laissez-faire pluralists endorse the responsiveness of the political system because it enhances liberal values, they often raise troublesome questions about the rationality of pluralism as a form of decision making. Truman recognizes that the dispersal of political power among many groups protects individual freedom, but he nonetheless suggests that widespread participation might lead to what he calls "morbific" politics, a state in which the political system cannot act quickly enough to deal with pressing problems. [16] Even though Truman is supportive of a pluralistic system of politics, he suggests that it might have offsetting costs. But other laissez-faire pluralists—like Dahl, Banfield, and Kornhauser—overlook or ignore questions dealing with the policy consequences of a pluralistic system of decision making. The fact that it tames the use of power, whether by the government or by the mass public, seems to them reason enough to normatively defend the existence of multiple decision makers.

However, in what constitutes a major revision of laissez-faire pluralism, Charles Lindblom has criticized his fellow pluralists for failing to see that a system of multiple decision makers bargaining and competing with one another fosters the formulation of informed and creative policy decisions. [17] Lindblom argues that a laissez-faire form of pluralism not only enhances individual freedom but also results in better policy making. First of all, a competitive, pluralistic style of politics simplifies the burdens a political system has to bear in deciding among alternative policy choices. The interaction among a variety of parties—or what he prefers to call "partisan mutual adjustment"—is often a convenient device for identifying problems and acquiring reliable information on issues. Lindblom insists that the ability of any one individual to anticipate and plan for the contingencies associated with a set of programs is limited. While centralized planners may desire to analyze all possible ramifications surrounding a problem, the burden of weighing the evidence bearing on complex issues may prompt them to screen out important bits of information. The attempt to engage in long-range, comprehensive planning is thus likely to be frustrated by the complexity of events. However, a competitive, pluralistic form of decision making avoids these difficulties, since it "imposes on no one the heroic demands for information, intellectual competence, time, energy, and money that are required for an overview of interrelationships among decisions."[18] When decisions are made through the give-and-take of partisan mutual adjustment, numerous groups have responsibility for defending and analyzing a limited set of values.

Moreover, as Lindblom notes, in partisan mutual adjustment there are "powerful motives for groups to mobilize information and analysis on the relations among possible decisions."[19] When decisions are made in a competitive fashion, each party has a vested interest in finding information that will advance the policies it prefers while discrediting the programs it opposes. Thus any attempt by a group to suppress information harmful to a particular course of action is likely to be uncovered by opposing interests. While no one participant is motivated to undertake a comprehensive view of a problem, the bargaining and competition among numerous interests will develop more information bearing on the issue than will more centralized and unified forms of decision making. As in the operation of Adam Smith's marketplace, the "invisible hand" of group competition helps to transform limited, parochial views into much broader, public benefits.

Besides stimulating the production of more information, partisan mutual adjustment can also help soften the consequences of political disagreement. The give-and-take of the bargaining process at times results in various parties' reformulating or modifying their values and therefore helps to narrow, rather than widen, policy differences among groups. Through the process of bargaining and negotiation, individuals often come to a more precise definition of what goals they hope to achieve, since the rank ordering they would attach to particular values may not become clear to them until they are faced with making concrete choices. What at first may appear to be a serious point of disagreement may disappear when a plurality of interests must negotiate over the shape of a particular policy.[20]

While Lindblom often stresses aspects that other laissez-faire pluralists have ignored, taken together their work nonetheless adds up to a unified theory of pluralism. The terms vary from "political slack" to "multiple decision making points," from "the noncumulative distribution of resources" to "potential groups," but they suggest a common theme: whether we look at the operations of local politics or the federal government, we see an open and self-regulating political system. The competitive nature of the political marketplace inhibits the rise of monopolistic power, while the openness of the polity in turn promotes the advancement of both individual freedom and rational policy making. This division of power among many groups curtails the ability of the government or a majority to infringe on individual liberties while enhancing the capability of the political system to identify and respond to pressing social issues. When groups share responsibility for deciding issues, they have not only ample incentives for generating data on important issues confronting the polity but also sufficient reason for containing the worst consequences of partisan disagreement.

Corporate Pluralism

Although the laissez-faire model is the dominant view of pluralism in the academic literature today, analytically it is possible to identify another form, which I have chosen to call corporate pluralism. Its clearest description—albeit a hostile one—is found in Lowi's notion of interest group liberalism and McConnell's group theory of politics.[21] Empirically most laissez-faire pluralists have derived their model of interest-group interaction from the realm of urban politics, but Lowi and McConnell have examined the behavior of federal agencies and their clientele groups and argue that the notion of an open, competitive political arena does not apply. While laissez-faire pluralists envision a self-correcting system in which the invisible hand of political bargaining inevitably restrains the concentration of power, Lowi and McConnell see the fragmentation of the polity into a series of small, autonomous fiefdoms, all of which are independent of one another. Under a corporate form of pluralism, no single party has the ability to monopolize all decisions, but certain groups have been able to acquire controlling power within individual policy areas. Regardless of the political slack in the system or the existence of potential groups, various parties have been able to isolate their detractors and enjoy the luxury of making decisions without negotiating or bargaining with their competitors. Any self-correcting pressures that may once have been present in the political system have been overwhelmed by the organized power of selective interest groups.

The reasons for the breakdown of the laissez-faire model are varied, but critics like Lowi and McConnell usually point to three factors: (1) the capture of government power by interest groups, (2) the efforts of interest groups and agencies to narrow the size of the policy making arena, and (3) the tacit agreement among certain interests to refrain from competing with one another. By any criterion, the willingness of government officials to relinquish their power to interest groups has been the most distinctive characteristic of corporate pluralism. While laissez-faire pluralists have tended to view government officials as either neutral mediators of the group process or merely another party competing with private groups for political power, McConnell and others have recognized that public officials often become captured by constituents who use the authority of the state to enhance their own well-being. The process leads to a blurring of the distinction that laissez-faire pluralists have implicitly, if not explicitly, made between private interests and public authority. Private groups come to exercise the regulatory and rule-making powers that were once the exclusive responsibility of public officials, while public officials, having parcelled out their authority, become mere legitimizing agents, sanctioning the decisions agreed upon by private interests.* McConnell points to the

---

*While it is important to distinguish corporate pluralism from its laissez-faire counterpart, at the same time we must be careful not to confuse it with the doctrine of corporativism. Some of the examples of corporate pluralism, such as the NRA of the New Deal, have often been mistakenly called instances of corporativism. On a superficial level there is some degree of similarity, for both corporate pluralism as practiced in the United States and corporativism as practiced in fascist Italy involve a fusion of public and private authority. But aside from that similarity there are immense differences between the two approaches to government. In a corporativistic political system the government either sets up allegedly private groups or acquires control of private groups in order to advance its own specific objectives.

War Industries Board of World War I as a classic example involving this kind of surrender of government authority. The board was responsible for drawing up wartime mobilization plans for private industry, but instead of requiring business to implement government-decreed objectives, it allowed private industry to assume responsibility for setting prices and establishing production quotas. [22] A similar willingness to relinquish power to private groups underlay the National Recovery Administration of the New Deal, which sought to combat the economic disruption of the 1930s by encouraging business to draw up codes of fair competition regulating sales and production. As with the War Industries Board, the guiding assumption was that policy should be made through the cooperation and mutual agreement of business and government rather than through the competition of the economic and political arenas. [23]

Besides capturing government authority, interest groups have also managed to exercise semi-monopoly power by narrowing down and isolating the decision-making process. Established groups realize that the smaller the decision-making arena is, the easier it becomes for a few parties to shut out opposing interests and undermine the competitive nature of the political marketplace. As the decision-making sphere contracts, the advantages enjoyed by the most powerful interest become magnified, while the resources available to the least influential group become increasingly vulnerable. [24] Interest groups have often invoked the rhetoric of grassroots democracy in order to achieve this kind of narrowing of the decision-making arena. Farm groups have utilized such tactics to establish ten separate self-governing systems within the Department

---

In corporate pluralism, however, the situation is much more complex. Instead of the government attempting to assume exclusive control over the actions of private groups, it relinquishes much of its power to private groups seeking to advance their own special interests. Even when there is a common problem that government and private interest groups wish to resolve, public officials often turn their authority over to various interests to tackle the issue. Corporate pluralism involves the private capture of public agencies and the establishment of semipublic monopolies, while corporativism involves public domination of private groups. See W. Y. Elliot, *The Pragmatic Revolt in Politics,* for a theoretical discussion of the doctrine of corporativism.

of Agriculture, ranging from the soil conservation districts to the various price support districts. As Lowi has shown, each program is run as an independent fiefdom, with little or no interaction among them.[25] But even more importantly, on issues like price supports, commodity growers are able to exercise veto power over any policy recommendations public officials may wish to make. Rather than merely sharing power with government personnel, they have acquired full legal authority to approve or reject any changes that affect their interests.

Other groups, such as professional educators, have achieved similar objectives by calling for the depoliticization of certain policy areas. As Marilyn Gittell argues, once issues are removed from politics, it becomes much more difficult for groups with influence in the larger political realm to wield any appreciable degree of power in isolated decision-making arenas. Gittell's study of the New York school system describes how professional educators sought to limit the influence of local politicians and community groups by taking "politics out of education" and how this attempt served merely to remove educational policy from the influence of groups, like minorities, who relied on alliances with political officials to achieve their goals. By making school policy independent of the city commission, the educational bureaucracy succeeded in undercutting those opposing groups which might have been able to challenge its decisions in a larger political setting.[26]

If interest groups have not been able to capture public authority or narrow down the policy-making arena, they have often sought to build monopolistic empires through tacit agreements and collusion. As a case in point, McConnell notes that in the 1940s when Congress considered measures for controlling the Missouri River, the Army Corps of Engineers and its clientele groups of construction firms and navigation companies called for the construction of extensive flood levies, while the Bureau of Land Reclamation and its agricultural supporters were more interested in promoting the development of dams and irrigation canals. Rather than pointing out the deficiencies in each other's programs, the two agencies agreed to refrain from criticizing one another and recommended the implementation of both proposals. In place of partisan mutual adjustment, the two agencies agreed to restrain their competitive impulses in return for mutual noninterference in each other's domains. [27]

Whether we look at the country's past efforts to mobilize for war or to recover from a depression, or at its present efforts to manage agriculture, formulate educational policy, or regulate our rivers, there emerges a pattern of interest-group activity differing significantly from the laissez-faire picture of politics. As is true of the economic marketplace, a competitive political market is neither self-maintaining nor self-correcting. By either persuading political officials to surrender their decision-making power to various interests, or by narrowing down the size of the decision-making arena, or by implicitly or explicitly agreeing not to compete with one another, a variety of groups have been able to exert semi-monopolistic dominance over certain policy areas. Through deft use of the above tactics, many organized interests have succeeded in restraining the countervailing forces which laissez-faire pluralists have posited as the main deterrent to excessive monopoly power.

While McConnell and Lowi are extremely critical of what we have called corporate pluralism, the doctrine is not without its defenders. It is possible to piece together a normative defense of the corporate model from a variety of sources, including the writings of individuals like Herbert Hoover and Raymond Moley or the pronouncements of various interest groups. [28] Despite the rather unsystematic nature of these sources, certain themes reappear constantly. For instance, unlike laissez-faire pluralists, who see numerous benefits accruing to society from competition among interest groups, corporate pluralists attach value to making decisions in a cooperative, rather than a competitive, fashion. Both Hoover, an enthusiastic supporter of the War Industries Board, and Moley, a strong advocate of the National Recovery Administration, maintained that the nation's social problems could be solved through cooperative action between government and business. Neither Hoover nor Moley believed there were any significant differences in the goals that government and business sought to achieve and they therefore did not see any need to pit organizations against one another. Unlike laissez-faire pluralists, who have argued that competition is necessary to tame the misuse of power, corporate pluralists have contended that in turning power over to private groups, government officials need not worry that public authority will be used for parochial or illicit ends. As Hoover once argued, "there is a wide difference between the whole social conception of capital combinations against public interest and cooperative action between individuals which may be profoundly in the public interest."[29] Unfortunately, however, corporate pluralists have not always been clear as to how one distinguishes between beneficial and harmful monopolies.[30] While the overriding importance of winning a war or ending a depression has perhaps resulted in a certain degree of convergence among most interests in society, it has nonetheless left a host of other problems unresolved. Especially on more mundane issues like agriculture or education, the most desirable course of action to follow often resists easy definition.

Corporate pluralists have also contended that competition is an inherently wasteful and disorderly process of decision making. In a laissez-faire system, where there is competition among a variety of groups and agencies, government programs often overlap one another. Instead of a unified, coherent attack on a particular issue, there is likely to be considerable duplication of effort in the formulation of various programs. In addition, as the number of parties involved in a particular policy increases, problems of coordination arise and energy has to be expended to resolve divergences of opinion. However, as Hoover and many others have often argued, when decisions are made in self-contained centers, the problems of duplication and coordination are greatly diminished. By establishing independent centers of decision making, public authorities and the private groups they rely on for guidance can develop uniform standards for regulating each separate policy area.

Finally, many of the defenders of a corporate form of pluralism have insisted that the establishment of semi-monopolistic decision-making centers is necessary to guarantee the professional handling of important social issues. For example, the Interior Department has often justified the surrender of government oil policy to the Petroleum Council, a semiprivate group, on purely technical grounds. The problem of developing and processing natural resources is so complex that the agency has sought to tap the expertise of those companies directly involved in the production of the country's basic energy resources. Many professional groups have sought to restrict the decision-making arena for very similar reasons, arguing that the complexity of issues like education or welfare requires the establishment of independent, nonpartisan commissions to supervise these programs. In the corporate view, not all semipublic monopolies are undesirable: when issues are technical or complex in nature, professionals or technicians should have the decisive voice in setting policy.

Public Pluralism

Finally, it is analytically possible to identify a third form, which I call public pluralism. This doctrine, which will be defended in the remainder of this book, differs from its predecessors in that it is essentially a prescriptive model of decision making. Whereas both laissez-faire and corporate pluralists attempt to describe the give-and-take of American politics as well as to normatively justify the variety of politics they have empirically identified, I wish to advance public pluralism as a reform-oriented model of decision making for regulating the interplay of interests in society.

Public pluralism recognizes, as does corporate pluralism, that the competitive nature of the political marketplace may break down, but it does not share corporate pluralism's approbation of this phenomenon. In any society as diverse and heterogeneous as the United States, there are bound to be disagreements over both the methods and the goals that the political system seeks to realize. The hope of corporate pluralists to formulate public policy in a cooperative, rather than a competitive, fashion is thus likely to prove illusory. But even more importantly, by insisting that decisions be made in a cooperative fashion, corporate pluralism may inadvertently create a political system that ignores important segments of the population and represses dissenting views.[31] Likewise, its stress on efficiency and technical expertise raises this problem: efficient for what purposes or ends? If a variety of groups must constantly bargain with one another and settle their differences through negotiation, it is true that the process may involve a great deal of time and may even result in a duplication of effort; but a process that may be uneconomical in saving time may be very economical in insuring that many different interests have an opportunity to make their voices heard. Finally, a corporate form of decision making that emphasizes technical expertise may overlook the fact that a large number of policies are not technical at all. Even if issues like education involve questions of a highly specialized nature, we must recognize that most problems have a normative, as well as a technical, aspect to them. While the most successful reading method may be a technical decision that professional educators should determine, the larger purposes schools should serve or the amount of resources they should have at their disposal are political or normative questions that no one group should have the exclusive power to decide. Allocating resources among different segments of society is a political, and not a technical, process.

The doctrine of public pluralism thus represents a reaction to the establishment of cooperative, semi-independent centers of decision making. Like its laissez-faire counterpart, the public variety of pluralism believes that it is imperative to divide power among numerous groups and to pit one interest against another. But in embracing laissez-faire's normative faith in the beneficial results of partisan mutual adjustment, it does not necessarily accept laissez-faire's contention that the present political system represents an empirical fulfillment of the competitive model. On the contrary, the doctrine of public pluralism identifies three defects in the laissez-faire picture of American politics.

First, it recognizes, as laissez-faire pluralists often do not, that many constituencies, especially marginal groups like the poor or amorphous groups like consumers, lack either the resources or the incentives to defend their interests effectively against opposing elements in society. While Truman often seems to suggest that potential groups will become activated when their wishes are thwarted, the less than successful record of many marginal elements seems to suggest otherwise. Secondly, as we have already seen, public pluralism realizes that various interests often avoid competition with one another either by capturing government authority or by insulating part of the political process from outside pressure. Lindblom's argument that partisan mutual adjustment may enhance the ability of the political system to recognize pressing social issues is based on the assumption that agencies and their clientele groups actually bargain and compete with one another. Unfortunately, as Lowi and McConnell have shown, many groups have been able to shut out their rivals and formulate policy monopolistically in specific areas. Thirdly, as Truman himself points out, a laissez-faire system faces the additional problem of not being able to respond quickly enough to pressing social issues. While Lindblom makes a convincing case that the clash of competing groups will simplify the decison-making process, he fails to show that this same system can resolve problems with any degree of dispatch. A pattern of policy making that is rational in Lindblom's sense of exposing all facets of a problem may be ineffective in the sense that it cannot act expeditiously to resolve issues. Naturally, as more parties participate in the decision-making arena, it becomes increasingly more time consuming to forge acceptable agreements among all concerned interests.

Public pluralism seeks to deal with the above problems through a system of regulated interest-group activity. The operating assumption of the doctrine is that many of the values espoused by laissez-faire pluralism can in effect be achieved if the president and the executive branch adopt a dual policy of organizing marginal elements from the bottom up and regulating the give-and-take among interests from the top down. Even if many groups are not organized or engage in collusion or restraint of trade, judicious government action may mitigate, if not eliminate altogether, the worst defects of an unregulated form of pluralistic government.

Public pluralism thus differs from Lindblom's version in that it rejects a pure or free-market, bargaining style of decision making. Instead it relies heavily on central direction and management to insure that the competitive nature of the political arena remains intact. [32] On those occasions when the political marketplace is no longer self-correcting, it insists that public officials facilitate the process of group competition by playing what must first appear as three mutually antagonistic roles. First, the government can act as an advocate, defending and even organizing interests like the poor or consumers who presently lack political clout. In stimulating previously dormant elements to become more active, government bureaus can assist various potential groups to contest the actions of agencies or groups that are pursuing objectives detrimental to their interests. Such a course of action will necessarily lead to a blurring of the distinction between public and private power, but instead of fostering the development of semi-monopolies, as occurs under a corporate form of pluralism, it will serve to enhance the competitive nature of the political process. Rather than relinquishing their authority to semi-monopolies, public officials will assist potential groups to become mobilized so that the rise of concentrated power can be averted.

Secondly, in order to prevent newly activated groups from being denied access to the bargaining table, the executive branch must also assume the role of political custodian, structuring and arranging the formulation of policy decisions so that interest groups are forced to compete with one another. Just as the government has acquired responsibility in the economic arena for breaking up monopolies, so it must seek to restrain any concentration of power that threatens the openness of the political marketplace. When it appears that the competitive nature of the political system is threatened, the president or central government bureaus, such as the Office of Management and Budget, must intervene to hinder the development of semiclosed centers of decision making.

Finally, in order to focus the bargaining process among different groups, the executive branch must assume responsibility for one additional role, that of political manager. Besides fostering competition among different interests, elected public officials such as the president must at the same time act as arbitrators, mediating disputes and choosing among the proposals of contending groups. Under public pluralism, the numerous interests in society will have to compete against one another not only for specific advantages, as they would under a laissez-faire system, but also for the attention and approval of political elites and their staff agencies. In contrast to a laissez-faire system of politics, in which the power of public officials like Mayor Lee is dependent primarily on their personal negotiating skills, a public form of pluralism seeks to augment the institutional, and not merely the personal, power of elected officials so that they have the capacity to direct the outcome of the group process. If elites acquire these additional responsibilities, they will be in a position to significantly alter the environment in which groups and their allies interact by vetoing logrolling arrangements that attempt to shut out other interests in society. Similarly, if government officials acquire the power to manage negotiations among interest groups, they may be able to insure that the political system does not become mired down in endless bargaining. Under a decentralized system in which groups must negotiate with many different parties, gradual and even time-consuming incremental changes in policy can give way to fruitless periods of interminable bargaining; but under a centrally coordinated style of decision making, political officials and their staff agencies will be in a position to mediate disputes and force the settlement of issues.

Admittedly, initiating such political changes is bound to be a difficult task, but we must realize that the fragmentation of the political marketplace and the freezing out of weaker competition were often accomplished not in the face of government opposition but with the tacit, if not open, consent of many government agencies and officials. In contrast, if various agencies choose to play advocate, custodial, and managerial roles, the breakdown of the bargaining process can possibly be contained. The visible hand of government regulation may be able to achieve what laissez-faire's self-corrective, invisible hand of bargaining promised but failed to deliver.

While public pluralism is primarily a set of prescriptive principles for regulating the interplay of interest groups and agencies, the doctrine is not without historical precedent. On a variety of occasions the federal government has attempted to initiate policies that are certainly consistent with a public form of pluralism. For example, in establishing his war on poverty, President Johnson created a variety of government bureaus to perform an advocate role for those segments of society which were unorganized at the time. OEO programs such as Community Action and Vista have sought to mobilize the poor to apply pressure on units of government that are insensitive to the plight of low-income individuals. [33]

The actions of the Johnson administration are by no means unusual, for at various points in time federal officials have sought to organize other groups that seemed incapable of effectively defending their interests against opposing groups. For instance, the formation of the Chamber of Commerce was in large part initiated by Charles Nagel, Secretary of Commerce and Labor under President

Taft. At Nagel's invitation, representatives from a number of local business associations met at the Department of Commerce and Labor in 1912 and drew up a plan for a nationwide organization whose main purpose was to counteract the anti-business stance of militant Progressives. [34] Similarly, the creation of the Farm Bureau, the most powerful agricultural pressure group in the United States today, was a result of government attempts to disseminate information about improved agricultural methods. What began in 1914 as an effort to improve traditional farming practices eventually resulted in the formation of local, state, and national bureaus that became powerful lobby groups for agricultural interests. [35] The rise of industrial unions in the United States likewise owed its success to government advocacy of union demands. While the AFL met with substantial success in organizing craft unions, the CIO never made much headway in organizing industrial workers until the government forced business to recognize and bargain with unions under section 7a of the National Industrial Recovery Act. Above all, however, it was the creation of the National Labor Relations Board under the Wagner Act that greatly strengthened the ability of mass industrial unions to extract concessions from business. [36]

If the efforts of the government to act as an advocate for previously unorganized interests perhaps date further back in time, there are nonetheless many instances in which the government has played a custodial role in politics. On the one hand, political officials have often attempted to stimulate competition directly by assigning overlapping jurisdictions and incomplete grants of authority to various agencies. Perhaps the most dramatic example of such action can be found during the Second New Deal of the Roosevelt administration when FDR made it a point to blur the mandate given to various government agencies. In contrast to the corporate spirit of the First New Deal, in which private groups and agencies were allowed to establish self-contained centers of decision making, Roosevelt pursued an administrative policy of setting one agency against another. By assigning overlapping responsibilities to various government bureaus and by issuing only incomplete grants of authority to competing government officials, Roosevelt made it impossible for any one agency or interest to establish a monopoly over a particular issue. [37] Besides attempting to foster competition by such direct means, the federal government has also tried to stimulate competition indirectly by breaking down isolated patterns of decision making and expanding the policy-making arena. For instance, the Nixon administration indirectly increased the competitive pressures on bureaus and their clientele groups by standardizing the regional boundaries of most federal agencies. Prior to 1971 the regional offices and jurisdictions of many agencies were not conterminous with one another and the resultant haphazard, unstandardized nature of each agency's field operations enabled them to avoid direct comparisons of their respective programs by Congress or the OMB.

Finally, the efforts of Presidents Kennedy, Johnson, and Nixon to strengthen institutions like the Office of Management and Budget on a national level and to encourage the spread of planning on supra- and sub-state levels may serve to enhance the managerial role of government. Nixon increased the OMB's staff and sought to expand its activities so that it could more effectively guide and regulate the interplay of agencies and interests seeking divergent and often conflicting goals. While many members of his administration who supported such attempts to concentrate power in the hands of central staff organizations may have done so in the hopes of limiting, rather than expanding, the interplay of pluralistic groups and agencies, the power of these institutions need not be used for that purpose. The strengthening of bureaus like OMB may prove to be more successful in regulating the partisan mutual adjustment among various segments of society than in supplanting agency and group bargaining with more centralized direction.

However, it must be admitted that recent efforts by the federal government to oversee and regulate the interplay of agencies and groups on a suprastate level are still in a state of evolution. Since President Johnson's administration, a variety of organizational arrangements have been employed on a suprastate level to provide some central direction to the myriad number of regional programs presently being administered. [38] For example, Johnson tried designating certain agencies like HUD as "convener," or lead, agencies that were to be responsible for resolving differences among various government bureaus in particular regions. However, this institutional arrangement encountered difficulties in achieving its objectives. Because HUD has special interests of its own to advance, many other government agencies have been unwilling to accept it as a convener agency with the power to choose among alternative requests. Since 1971 the federal government has relied on collections of federal agencies known as regional councils to establish policy priorities for different sections of the country. Unlike lead agencies, regional councils initially lacked central directors to control and guide their deliberations, but in recent years the makeup of these bodies has been considerably revamped to correct this oversight. The president has insisted that political appointees, rather than civil servants, represent each agency on the councils, and he has also designated one agency representative as his chairperson of each council. Similarly, in the last several years, the chief executive has increased the OMB's power over the members of the councils so that it might steer these regional units of government in a more purposive direction. [39]

There have also been attempts on a substate level to develop administrative machinery that will foster competition as well as focus the bargaining process among different interests in society. In the 1964 Housing Act, or Model Cities program, Congress stipulated that all requests from municipalities for federal funds be reviewed and cleared by local area-wide review boards. Similarly, in 1968 the OMB issued its A-95 review guidelines, which spelled out the procedures communities had to follow if they wished to satisfy federal requirements for central review of policy. In response to this federal pressure, most municipalities have joined councils of government, or COGs, which serve as A-95 review boards for evaluating local government applications for federal funds. Whether COGs and regional councils are the final institutional arrangements that will be adopted is difficult to say, but these recent efforts of the Johnson and Nixon administrations indicate that the government is experimenting with ways of managing the give-and-take of the political system more effectively.

A question that must be asked, however, is whether such kinds of measures will result in a viable form of pluralistic decision making. Merely because the federal government has or is presently experimenting with programs that are consistent with an advocate, custodial, or managerial role is no guarantee that such programs have been or will be successful. It stands to reason that established groups who have isolated themselves from the demands of partisan mutual adjustment are likely to resist government efforts to organize the poor or to foster more competition in the political arena. Nevertheless, as we shall see, the record of the programs we have been reviewing holds out some promise of eventual success. (Chapter 6 will look in more detail at the literature on OEO and suggest that the poverty program often did improve the conditions of the poor in a significant fashion.) However, the results of government efforts to supervise the bargaining process on supra- and sub-state levels presently appear to be too inconclusive for us to judge their effectiveness. Because government attempts to develop lead agencies or COGs are still in a process of evolution it is difficult to speculate what their future role will be.

Nonetheless, it is possible to identify certain conditions that must be present before the doctrine of public pluralism has a chance to work. Obviously, the attitude of the president toward our reformed style of pluralistic decision making will be crucial. Unless the chief executive and his staff are willing to act as advocates and to build an alliance between their offices at the top and the poor at the bottom, it will be difficult for these groups to exercise any leverage in the political system. As Nixon so aptly demonstrated, when the president is not supportive of government programs to organize marginal groups, efforts to expand the number of participants in the decision-making arena may falter. If there is going to be a true redistribution of political power to groups on the lower rungs of society, the federal government must throw its prestige and resources behind those seeking to become mobilized.

Similarly, if we wish to see the government foster competition and mediate among the divergent interests in society, we would need to elect a president who is highly interested in administrative matters and able to tolerate disagreement and conflict. As many observers have noted, if the administrative reforms discussed earlier are going to work, the president or the OMB need to put pressure on regional councils and COGs to play a custodial and managerial role in the decision-making process. Public pluralism is not a self-executing set of decision-making rules. On the contrary, it requires the executive branch to devote a considerable amount of time to structuring the policy-making arena so that every concerned interest has the opportunity to point out the deficiencies or benefits of programs that affect it. However, as Richard Neustadt has shown, presidents often vary in their interest in administrative matters and their tolerance of institutional arrangements where disagreement is prevalent. [40] But such an aversion may often reflect more an intellectual blind spot to the benefits of a guided style of pluralistic decision making than any deep-seated hostility to a more open, yet contentious, form of policy making.

In either case, it would be naive to assume that a public form of pluralism could or would be implemented with no difficulty whatsoever. Moreover, it should be pointed out that the reforms suggested here are not a panacea leading instantaneously to a more just and equitable society. As we have already seen, many interest groups and agencies who have transformed a laissez-faire form of pluralism into a corporate style of decision making are likely to resist any change in the status quo. Yet if many of the government activities of the late 1960s—such as Community Action Programs, lead agencies, and COGs—are given a new lease on life, the benefits of a competitive, pluralistic style of decision making may still be realized and the establishment of semi-independent, noncompetitive centers of decision making arrested. But to accomplish such an objective, these agencies will require time to gain political strength and maturity and will need the support of a chief executive who favors more public participation as well as more central guidance of the policy making process.

NOTES

1. In the course of his academic career Robert Dahl has espoused a variety of positions. In *Who Governs?* and *Pluralistic Democracy in the United States* he proposes what we have called a laissez-faire system of pluralism. In contrast, in *A Preface to Democratic Theory* he seems to advocate a polyarchal view of democracy, while more recently in *After the Revolution* he has argued that the most appropriate form of democracy depends on the level of government. See also Wallace Sayre and Herbert Kaufman, *Governing New York City*; David Truman, *The Governmental Process*; Edward C. Banfield, *Political Influence*; Charles Lindblom, *The Intelligence of Democracy*; David Braybrooke and Charles Lindblom, *A*

Strategy of Decision Making; Charles Lindblom, "The Science of Muddling Through," pp. 79-88; William Kornhauser, *The Politics of Mass Society.*

2. Dahl,*Pluralistic Democracy,* p. 326.

3. Dahl, *Who Governs?,* pp. 89-168.

4. See chap. 6 for a more detailed treatment of the explanations laissez-faire pluralists give for the openness of the political system.

5. Dahl, *Who Governs?,* p. 310.

6. Truman, *Governmental Process,* p. 114.

7. Sayre and Kaufman, *Governing New York City,* p. 710.

8. Truman, *Governmental Process,* pp. 45-63, 352-437.

9. Banfield, *Political Influence,* p. 241.

10. Ibid., p. 252.

11. Dahl, *Who Governs?,* p. 308.

12. Ibid., p. 209.

13. Ibid., p. 204.

14. Dahl, *Pluralistic Democracy,* p. 24.

15. Kornhauser, *Politics of Mass Society,* pp. 65-75.

16. Truman, *Governmental Process,* pp. 516-24.

17. Lindblom has developed this thesis in a variety of places but the best statements are found in *The Intelligence of Democracy* and "The Science of Muddling Through."

18. Lindblom, *Intelligence of Democracy,* p. 171.

19. Ibid., p. 174.

20. Ibid., pp. 206-25.

21. Theodore J. Lowi, *The End of Liberalism;* Theodore J. Lowi, "The Public Philosophy: Interest Group Liberalism"; Grant McConnell, *Private Power and American Democracy.*

22. McConnell, *Private Power and American Democracy,* p. 64.

23. Hugh Johnson, *The Blue Eagle.*

24. McConnell, *Private Power and American Democracy,* pp. 91-110.

25. Lowi, *End of Liberalism,* pp. 102-15.

26. Marilyn Gittell, *Participants and Participation.*

27. McConnell, *Private Power and American Democracy,* p. 224.

28. U. S. Department of Commerce, *Annual Report of the Secretary of Commerce, 1922;* Raymond Moley, *The First New Deal.*

29. U. S Department of Commerce, *Annual Report of the Secretary,* p. 29.

30. See McConnell, *Private Power and American Democracy,* pp. 66-69, for a further discussion of Hoover's outlook on cooperation.

31. See Arthur M. Schlesinger, Jr., *The Age of Roosevelt,* Vol II: *The Coming of the New Deal,* pp. 165-75, for a description of how NRA worked to the benefit of large corporations.

32. See Alexander George's excellent article on foreign affairs, "The Case for Multiple Advocacy," pp. 751-86, for another treatment of possible government roles. His analysis of foreign policy has greatly influenced my conception of public pluralism.

33. See James L. Sundquist, *Making Federalism Work*, for a history of the Johnson OEO and Model Cities programs.

34. Truman, *Governmental Process*, pp. 66-74.

35. Philip Selznick, *TVA and the Grass Roots*.

36. See Schlesinger, *Age of Roosevelt*, Vol. II, pp. 385-422.

37. Ibid., p. 535.

38. Harold Seidman, *Politics, Position, and Power*, pp. 164-94.

39. Martha Derthick, *Between State and Nation*, pp. 157-81.

40. Richard Neustadt, *Presidential Power*.

PART II

The Issue of Participation

Having delineated three types of pluralistic democracy, we must now place the doctrine within the larger context of democratic theory. To properly evaluate the advantages or drawbacks of an interest-group model of politics, it is imperative to examine it from a comparative perspective, since the merits of a theory can never be fully appreciated or discounted until they have been measured against the advantages of competing theories of democracy. While pluralism may appear to confront serious difficulties in the abstract, its limitations may be rather insignificant in the light of the problems that trouble other models of democratic government.

The following six chapters will compare how pluralism and alternative theories of democracy define the role that the public should play in the decision-making process. Even though democracy has always been defined in terms of popular participation in government policy making, few studies have attempted to examine the ways in which different theories view the nature of this participation. To remedy this deficiency, chapter 3 will discuss what the scope of the electorate's power should be. In particular, I will critically analyze the argument advanced by polyarchal democrats that the public's role in politics should be confined to choosing among competing political elites. I will try to demonstrate that the polyarchal position is based on a misreading of the empirical evidence about the citizenry's political capabilities. After arguing that the public should play an important role in politics, chapter 4 will try to analyze how we should define who the public is, an issue providing one of the major points of contention between pluralists and populists. While pluralists believe that the relevant constituency consists of the interest groups that make up society, populists have tended to define the relevant public in terms of the sentiments of the majority. I will argue that the majority is in many cases a mythical entity, that on numerous issues it is difficult to identify anything resembling a majoritarian position. In chapter 5 I will take a more critical look at the pluralist view of the public, analyzing the argument often made against pluralism that very few people actually belong to interest groups. Chapter 6 will look at the charge that pluralism ignores the interests of marginal groups in society. If pluralism insists that the public is made up of what Philip Converse calls "interest publics," it is necessary to analyze whether all interests in society are fairly represented. Chapter 7 will deal with the contention made by Henry Kariel and others that interest groups often become unresponsive to the needs of their own members. If we wish to argue that the public not only is, but should be, made up of numerous interest groups, we must show that organized groups will not necessarily become elitist in nature.

Be reexamining my threefold typology of pluralism, I hope to demonstrate how public pluralism is better equipped to deal with these difficulties than its laissez-faire or corporate counterparts. Having attempted to show in chapters 3 and 4 how pluralism is preferable to polyarchal or populist forms of democracy, I will argue in chapters 5, 6, and 7 that public pluralism is superior to alternative varieties of pluralistic democracy. Finally, in chapter 8 I will examine the purpose that is served by popular participation in politics. Participatory democrats have often attacked pluralists for failing to realize that political involvement can be an ennobling process that contributes to the self-development of the individual. However, by examining the available evidence, I hope to show that intensive participation may not have uniformly beneficial consequences.

Chapter

3

Pluralism Vs. Polyarchy: The Scope of Public Participation

Over the past several decades an increasing number of political scientists have come to advocate what is now known as an elitist or polyarchal form of democracy. Joseph Schumpeter, who formulated the classical statement of polyarchal democracy, has argued that elite rule is necessary because "the typical citizen drops down to a lower level of mental performance as soon as he enters the political field."[1] In a similar vein Giovanni Sartori has maintained that polyarchal government is a means of restraining the "mediocrity" he fears to be an inevitable part of mass participation in politics.[2] Still other polyarchists, such as Herbert McClosky, have embraced such a theory of democracy because they fear that a politically active public may pose a threat to civil liberties,[3] while others, like Theodore Lowi, have argued that a strong and insulated political elite is necessary in order to develop long-range plans capable of dealing effectively with such pressing problems as poverty and urban redevelopment.[4]

Admittedly, individual polyarchists often do not share all the same assumptions nor support elite rule for identical reasons, but it is nonetheless possible to piece together from their work a model of democracy that revolves around two sets of concerns: the political ineptitude of the masses and the capabilities of elites. On the one hand, it is assumed that the masses at best are apathetic or ill-informed and at worst are guilty of genuinely undemocratic attitudes and behavior. On the other hand, it is implied that elites display a greater concern for democratic modes of conduct and have the rationality and expertise to engage in effective social planning. Hence it is argued that day-to-day political affairs should be left to the purview of government officials while members of the public should involve themselves in politics only to the extent of choosing among elites at election time. In the polyarchal view democratic government involves electoral accountability rather than extensive citizen participation: democracy is preserved so long as there are mechanisms, like elections, that allow the public to hold its leaders accountable and there are competing political elites from which the electorate can choose. While the public lacks the capability to assume full control over politics, it is to retain the residual power to check or restrain its leaders through the process of competitive elections. Or as Harold Lasswell once argued:

Government is always government by the few, whether in the name of the few, the one, or the many. But this fact does not settle the question of the degree of democracy . . . since a society may be democratic and express itself through a small leadership. The key question turns on account-ability.[5]

The objective of this chapter is to ascertain whether polyarchists are on solid ground in attempting to equate democracy with electoral accountability. I will maintain that the polyarchal model is based on assumptions about (1) the public, (2) elites, and (3) the mechanism of elections that are unwarranted from both empirical and theoretical standpoints. Research on public opinion and voting behavior indicates that the electorate is not as ill-informed or as anti-civil libertarian as polyarchists often make it out to be. More-over, the available empirical evidence suggests that political elites have been overrated as social planners and as defenders of demo-cratic norms. I will argue that polyarchists have underestimated the feasibility and desirability of public participation in the policy-making process and will attempt to show that the most suitable vehicle for such participation lies in the realm of interest-group activity.

Polyarchy's View of the Public

If we look in detail at polyarchy's view of the public, it immediately becomes apparent that elitist democrats make two very different and even contradictory assumptions about the ability of the electorate. On the one hand, polyarchists like Schumpeter and Sartori argue that the public is not rational enough to express a preference on the issues; on the other hand, they imply that the electorate is rational and informed when it must choose among competing political elites. However, if voters are actually as ill-informed or as irrational as Schumpeter and Sartori claim, it is unclear how they can be knowledgeable enough to hold their officials accountable for their actions. The doctrine of electoral accountability assumes an alert and informed electorate who will reward or punish political officials according to their conduct in office. It thus appears that the justification many polyarchists have advanced for limiting the public's role to choosing among competing political elites at the same time undermines the very effectiveness of their call for electoral accountability. However, since many polyarchists do insist that voters can rationally hold elected officials responsible for their actions, it is necessary to inquire why the public's insight must be limited to that one act alone. If people are capable of choosing among alternative sets of elites, it certainly seems possible that they might be able to play an informed role in deciding specific policy issues.

To escape from this seeming paradox, a polyarchal democrat could argue that it might be easier for individuals to assess the performance of their elected officials than it would be to express a reasoned preference on a particular policy question. However, this line of reasoning is also open to criticism. While it is certainly more time-consuming to become involved in the policy-making process, an individual might find it intellectually less demanding to participate in the formulation of a specific set of policies than he would to assess the behavior of his elected representatives. To evaluate the record of a political official, a person would have to (1) have some knowledge of the issues he felt were salient public problems, (2) know what stand the competing political elites took on each issue, and (3) decide if his own policy preferences were in harmony or disagreement with the actions taken by his representatives. In contrast, if an individual wanted to contribute to the formulation of public policy, he would have to meet only the first condition stated above.

But leaving aside for the moment the logical problems inherent in a polyarchal theory of democracy, we need to ask if the empirical evidence supports polyarchy's pessimistic view of the public's abilities. To know whether an electoral accountability model of democracy is feasible in American politics requires an examination of the voluminous literature on voting and public attitudes for evidence of voter interest and concern about issues. As every student of American government undoubtedly knows, the early research on voting behavior was decidedly pessimistic about the capabilities of the average citizen to be aware of—let alone understand—the issues being debated in the public arena.[6] *The American Voter*, one of the best-known voting studies to emerge from the 1950s, argued that the public's awareness of political issues was generally minimal and that even when voters could state an opinion on a particular policy, they were often unable to identify the stand taken by either of the two contesting parties. On sixteen different issues, the authors found that only 18 to 36 percent of the public could (1) offer a definite opinion as to what policy should be pursued, (2) perceive what actions the government was undertaking, and (3) identify differences on issues between parties.[7] In measuring the degree of conceptualization among the public, Campbell et al. argued that less than 15 percent of the electorate could be defined as ideologues or near ideologues.[8] A large segment of the population seemed to vote for reasons totally unrelated to the performance of the candidate in office.

Although confirming polyarchy's rather pessimistic view of the public's awareness of issues, studies like *The American Voter* seemed to undermine the polyarchal assumption that the electorate could effectively hold its officials accountable for their actions. The early research on voting behavior seemed to support two rather uncomplimentary propositions about the public: first, the average voter rarely appeared to engage in policy voting; secondly, his lack of interest in political issues seemed to be a result of his own shortcomings. The typical voter was depicted as an individual who was neither informed nor concerned about any matters of political consequence.

However, additional research has indicated that the public may be more rational than studies like *The American Voter* have led us to believe. In particular, there are two approaches to voting behavior that have portrayed the American electorate in a much more favorable light. The first of these, which we shall call the *Downsian model*, contends that the voter's lack of concern with issues may be a result, not of his own shortcomings, but of the tweedledum-tweedledee nature of our party system. Since Republicans and Democrats often advocate similar stands on major issues, it may be difficult for the electorate to cast their votes for policy reasons. Or as Anthony Downs has argued in his seminal work *An Economic Theory of Democracy*, it may be "rational" for an individual to vote for frivolous and non-issue-related reasons if there are no meaningful differences between electoral contestants. [9] If candidates refuse to advocate divergent policies, the public will not be able to reward or punish elected officials for their position on the issues even if it is capable of doing so.

Furthermore, if contestants deliberately seek to confuse their stands on controversial questions, it should be expected that the public will be unable to identify the position of the different parties. The extent to which policy voting occurs in an election may be determined more by the campaign strategy of the candidates than by the competence or rationality of the voter. For confirming evidence we need only look at John Field's and Ronald Anderson's study of the 1956 and 1964 elections. They found that the number of people who voted for ideological reasons rose from 9 percent in 1956 to 24 percent in 1964, when Barry Goldwater offered the American public a radical alternative to the policies being pursued by Lyndon Johnson. [10] Similarly, Benjamin Page and Richard Brody discovered in a study of the 1968 election that the electorate was more likely to take into consideration an individual's position on a highly salient issue like Viet Nam when there were candidates like George Wallace and Eugene McCarthy who differed radically on their policies toward the war. [11] And more recently Norman Nie, Sidney Verba, and John Petrocik found in a survey of American voting behavior between 1952 and 1972 that the public has grown more interested in policy questions, and they indicated that "the new role of issues in the elections since 1964 is, in good part, a reaction to the nature of the candidates offered." [12] "The political behavior of the electorate is not determined solely by psychological and sociological forces," they concluded, "but also by the issues of the day and by the way in which candidates present those issues." [13]

A second approach to public attitudes, which we shall call the *issue-specific model* of voting, argues that the public is interested and concerned about issues but that the relevant area of policy varies from one individual to the next. Gerald Pomper among others has argued that the electorate should be viewed in terms of a series of "issue publics":

Sophisticated understanding of issues is not widespread, but there are different "issue publics" scattered throughout the electorate. Whereas few voters have an interest in and understanding of the entire range of issues, many do have an interest and understanding of a small number of issues. If we examine these separate "issue publics," rather than concentrating on the total electorate we find considerable sophistication and a direct relationship between policy views and the vote. [14]

Unfortunately most previous studies of voting behavior have been unable to detect the presence of these many issue publics because they have relied on closed-end questions to elicit information from the electorate. As David RePass has argued, closed-end questions often fail to identify people's concern with issues because they do not necessarily mention the problems that the public itself considers to be most important. [15] However, when open-end questions are used, allowing the individual to personally state the issues he feels are salient, citizens appear to have definite, informed opinions on a variety of matters. In the data from the 1960 and 1964 elections, when the Survey Research Center began asking open-end questions, RePass found that different segments of the population cited over twenty-eight issues as important political problems that they felt needed attention. Rather than being apathetic, the public seemed very concerned about a great variety of issues, even though the area of concern varied from one citizen to the next. [16]

Although the Downsian and the issue-specific models of public behavior differ radically in their interpretations of the empirical data, both imply that under certain conditions the public is indeed highly concerned and informed about policy issues. While the authors associated with the two approaches have not explicitly dealt with this problem, their studies suggest (1) that polyarchy's negative assessment of the public is unwarranted and (2) that electoral accountability may not be the most suitable mechanism for the public to express its concern with issues. Contrary to the view of many polyarchists, the political apathy of the average citizen may merely reflect the fact that most elections fail to offer meaningful policy choices. The average person will demonstrate an informed concern with issues if he is given the opportunity to discuss those particular policy areas which he finds personally relevant. However, there is no guarantee that he would engage in policy voting even if candidates were to begin advocating conflicting stands on the issues. Since most individuals are interested in certain select policy areas, it is possible that they might not ever find candidates for office who would take a stand on those particular issues which happen to be significant to them. As Sidney Verba and Norman Nie have argued, "given the fact that [a person's] own agenda is quite individual, and may contain many and varied issues, it is unreasonable to expect that there will be a voting choice tailored to his own particular policy preferences at the moment."[17] Thus, it is only natural that citizens will appear uninterested or uninformed under a system that seeks to limit popular participation to the act of voting. The quality of an individual's participation will depend to a large extent on whether or not he has meaningful opportunities for political involvement.

For this reason a pluralistic, rather than polyarchal, form of democracy may provide the best mechanism for the public to express its preferences. As indicated above, individuals have the potential to act in an informed and constructive manner if their concerns with particular issues are treated in a rational fashion. But because citizens are often interested in only a limited range of policies, group bargaining is preferable to elite competition as a vehicle for them to express their sentiments. In contrast to a polyarchal form of democracy in which individuals must choose among competing elites on the basis of issues that elites elect to discuss, a pluralistic style of decision making enables citizens to participate on only those issues which happen to interest them. Naturally, to the extent that pluralism relies on elections, it too will be plagued by the lack of meaningful policy choice characteristic of a polyarchal form of democracy. However, in a pluralistic system elections are supplemented by group bargaining; an individual who is concerned about a particular policy outcome can participate in the lobbying activities of the relevant interest group instead of having to wait until he can find a candidate for office who takes the desired stand on the issue. By expanding the public's role in politics, pluralism increases an individual's opportunities to participate rationally since it allows him to focus his time and energy on those issues he personally feels are the most salient.

The polyarchist's assertion that the public is hostile to democratic or civil libertarian norms can also be questioned. Elitist democrats like Herbert McClosky argue that a majority of citizens in this country are not supportive of basic civil liberties and that the preservation of democracy therefore depends on keeping the public's involvement in politics at a minimum.[18] In comparing a national sample of political influentials and nearly fifteen hundred adults in the general population, McClosky finds that elites display considerably more commitment to civil rights than do the public at large. While there seems to be a general consensus on abstract statements of principle, only political elites appear willing to defend civil liberties on a concrete, individual level. The importance of these findings, at least to McClosky, is obvious:

The evidence suggests that it is the articulate class rather than the public who serve as the major repositories of the public conscience and as the carriers of the Creed. Responsibility for keeping the system falls most heavily upon them.[19]

In McClosky's mind political apathy serves a useful function. Since the public is hostile to important civil liberties, it is desirable that they do not participate actively in the affairs of the community.

While the above findings are certainly no cause for rejoicing, they need not be interpreted in the pessimistic light that McClosky views them. First of all, it is unclear from McClosky's figures whether his results reflect well-ingrained beliefs among the public at large or whether they can more easily be explained by situational factors. In the 1950s many political leaders of high standing sanctioned political witch-hunts that jeopardized important civil liberties. Richard Hamilton has argued:

> It seems likely that . . . [public] response involved little more than an acceptance of the official "sounds of alarm" and of the official position about a need for new "rules of the game." If this was the case, then the . . . [public's] response would not indicate "authoritarianism" but instead would indicate acceptance of the leads provided by governments and private "opinion leaders."[20]

As in the case of voting behavior, the alleged faults of the average citizen may very easily be traced to the irresponsible behavior of public officials. The political appeals of government leaders who sanctioned the disregard of civil liberties may have stimulated and reinforced public attitudes that were hostile to the country's basic creed of individual rights.

But even if we ignore for the moment the causes of popular attitudes toward basic individual liberties, the consequences of such attitudes for the functioning of the political system need not be those suggested by McClosky. It is important to realize that his sample is based on a mass-society model of politics that compares only political elites and an undifferentiated public. While McClosky institutes controls for education and high-status occupations, he does not attempt to determine if people who belong to secondary associations are as anti-civil libertarian as those who do not. On the basis of a variety of studies, including those of William Kornhauser, Philip Hastings, and James Coleman, we know that individuals who are well integrated into a network of group affiliations are not likely to support mass movements hostile to liberal values.[21] Philip Hastings noted in a study of Pittsfield, Massachusetts, that social isolation often leads individuals to be apathetic and uncommitted to established institutions.[22] Likewise, James Coleman has observed that when lower-status people are drawn into community affairs, they often show no respect for the constitutional rights of individuals who espouse unpopular or controversial points of view, but he pointed out that such behavior is merely a reflection of the fact that these individuals are often more isolated and less experienced with community forms of activities. [23] Because McClosky insists on comparing only the elites with the masses, we cannot determine if his data would reconfirm the findings of Kornhauser et al. This issue is an important one because it is possible that polyarchal democrats have greatly exaggerated the threat to civil liberties posed by citizen involvement in politics. If people who belong to groups are more civil libertarian in their outlook than those who do not, there is no reason to fear public participation so long as citizens participate in a group-oriented fashion.

But even if by chance citizens who oppose civil liberties happen to participate in politics, they may still prove to be ineffectual in undermining the individual rights of others. The larger and more heterogeneous the political system, the more unlikely it is that a majority of citizens could ever become organized enough to be able to restrain the activities of groups who subscribe to unpopular beliefs. As James Madison noted many years ago:

Extend the sphere and you take in a greater variety of parties and interests; you make it less probable that a majority of the whole will have common motive to invade the rights of other citizens; or if such a common motive exists, it will be more difficult for all who feel it to discover their own strength and to act in unison with each other. [24]

Similarly, when the policy-making arena is large, we are apt to see those citizens who are hostile to civil liberties becoming fragmented into many diverse issue publics with unrelated, if not opposing, concerns. While McClosky may have statistically identified a large number of individuals who would curtail basic rights, in practice this portion of the population may never be able to act in a concerted fashion to achieve its objectives.

However, even if people who are less than sympathetic with expanding individual rights ever do become organized and the groups they belong to fail to moderate their anti-civil libertarian attitudes, they still may not undermine public respect for individual liberties. While McClosky seems to imply that all forms of participation may lead to a serious erosion of our basic freedoms, it is possible that only unrestrained and unchecked forms of participation constitute a threat to liberal values. As mentioned earlier, pluralists recognize that not all persons may choose to respect the rules of the political game, including the right of individuals to espouse unpopular beliefs. But like James Madison before them, pluralists wish to control the consequences, rather than the causes, of factions.[25] It is better to control and check the manner in which anti-civil libertarians participate than to discourage them from participating in politics altogether. As long as there are restraints on the wishes of any one element in society, the dangers of public involvement in politics are likely to be minimal. When political elites and interest groups share responsibility for making decisions, it is difficult for any one element in society to override and curtail the liberties of other groups who advocate opposing goals. The political competition built into a pluralistic form of democracy is a means of insuring that citizen participation never gives way to popular misuse of power.

Polyarchy's View of Elites

While polyarchy's conception of the public seems excessively negative, its view of political elites appears overly optimistic. First of all, it is possible to take issue with the polyarchist's argument that elites display a greater commitment to democratic modes of conduct than do members of the general public. As noted above, McClosky detects more support for civil liberties among political leaders than among ordinary citizens, but his findings refer primarily to liberal—rather than to democratic—values, e.g., respect for due process or protection of free speech. Since these are values that elites themselves are more likely to exercise, it is not surprising that elites should believe more firmly in them. However, there is no indication in McClosky's study that political leaders value democratic norms, such as popular participation, more highly than do members of the public at large.

It should also be noted that political elites may not be as civil libertarian as McClosky makes them out to be. By relying only on attitudinal data, McClosky cannot adequately judge the potential threat to civil liberties posed by either leaders or the masses. If we look only at the attitudinal evidence that McClosky presents, elites do appear to be somewhat more supportive of civil liberties than do ordinary citizens. But upon consideration of the degree of influence that both parties exercise, the situation appears very different. If we weight the percentage of each party who appear hostile to civil liberties by the amount of influence they actually wield, then elites may pose as great a threat to the constitutional creed as do the masses. Public officials tend to be less authoritarian than ordinary citizens, but those who do have reservations about certain individual rights actually possess the power to curtail the enjoyment of civil liberties by their very position in society.

Finally, if we leave aside the above theoretical point and reexamine the actual evidence that McClosky presents, we find that a substantial number of political elites appear uncommitted to the protection of civil liberties. While his figures for the masses are disappointing, his data on political elites can be described only as less than encouraging. McClosky notes that over 42.5 percent of the general public is willing to flout the rules of the game and take the law into their own hands if they believe the situation warrants it, but at the same time he finds that over one-fourth, or 26.1 percent, of political elites have expressed similar views. Thirty percent of the masses state that they would disregard general rules of honesty and integrity on certain occasions, but over 12 percent of the elites echo similar sentiments. [26] However, one does not have to rely on McClosky's figures alone to know that political officials are often willing to abuse civil liberties. While McClosky argues that elites are the major carriers of the creed, episodes like the McCarthy era and Watergate indicate that political elites may also attempt to subvert the principles of that creed. Since the end of World War II the greatest threats to civil liberties have not been the outcome of mass movements but, on the contrary, have resulted from political leaders' abusing their legitimate authority.

The incidents of elite misconduct cited above serve to demonstrate the need for a pluralistic, rather than a polyarchal, form of democracy. Political elites as well as the mass public may at times constitute a genuine threat to important liberal values. [27] Although a large percentage of leaders may genuinely desire to protect individual liberties, McClosky's data also point to numerous political elites who appear uncommitted to the protection of civil rights. Under a pluralistic form of democracy a sharing of political power between public officials and a diverse number of private groups serves to prevent the potential misuse of authority by either party. A rich group life not only protects citizens against the misappropriation of government power by political elites but also helps filter out public requests that might jeopardize important civil liberties. In contrast, under a polyarchal form of democracy, we must place our faith solely in the good intentions of our political leaders.

Besides arguing that political officials are more likely to protect civil rights, some polyarchists have insisted that a unified set of elites is necessary in order to develop effective, long-range plans for solving our social problems. Theodore Lowi among others has often stressed the importance of consolidating public authority so that government elites will have not only the ability to develop rational, comprehensive plans but also the power to act in a decisive, expeditious manner.* However, for both theoretical and empirical reasons it is possible to argue that centralized decision making will achieve neither of these objectives. First of all, the idea of long-range synoptic planning has come in for widespread criticism. As Edward Banfield has noted, students of urban politics have lost much of their confidence in the feasibility, as well as the desirability, of master planning.[28] In retrospect, despite the best of intentions, many so-called master plans often failed to account for the diverse array of needs of a complex, heterogeneous society. The rather poor record of this type of synoptic planning suggests that polyarchists have place too much faith in the expertise of political elites.

---

*It should be stressed that Lowi's attack on pluralism is twofold. Besides arguing that more centralized planning is necessary in order to overcome pluralism's fragmentation of the decision-making arena, Lowi also insists that the law should be more strictly enforced and that less discretion should be granted to administrative agencies. He contends that pluralism's bargaining style of decision making results in bad planning and that its discretionary style of decision making leads to the breakdown of justice. While the discussion that follows outlines some of the difficulties with his views on decision making, I shall look in greater detail at Lowi's call for juridical democracy and limited agency discretion in chapters 9 and 10.

While polyarchists contend that a few experts have the capacity to rationally reorder their environment, it is possible to argue, as do Herbert Simon and Charles Lindblom, that individuals are characterized by bounded, rather than limitless, rationality. [29] In a study of organizational decision making, Simon notes that there are repeated examples of persons who are unable to anticipate—let alone plan for—all the consequences of their actions. [30] As Simon and Lindblom suggest, political elites have informed yet partial views of the problems they must deal with, just as voters have informed yet limited knowledge of the issues before them. Consequently pluralists insist, in contrast to polyarchists, that the expertise of political elites is inadequate for viable social planning and that popular participation in government decision making is essential if the needs of those affected by public policy are to be successfully met. When political officials are not directly affected by the policies they propose, they are not always able to fully understand the impact of their decisions; but by multiplying the number of decision makers, we may overcome the shortcomings of any one individual policy maker. Although a few political elites might overlook certain problems inherent in a new policy, a variety of groups debating a specific course of action are less likely to ignore any difficulties that might afflict a new program. If each affected interest can articulate and defend its own position on a specific issue, the pluralistic interplay of groups will insure that all pertinent information and values are exposed and fully debated.

Finally, it is possible to object to the assumption implicit in many elitist theories of democracy that people's needs can be objectively determined. As Hanna Pitkin has noted, most representative theories of democracy, including polyarchy, maintain that public officials can discern what the objective interests of their constituents actually are. [31] It is not necessary for the public to participate directly in the shaping of policy because their elected officials can represent their true interests for them. However, as Charles Lindblom has convincingly argued, individuals often do not achieve a clear conception of the objectives they hope to realize until they are forced to articulate them. [32] A person's preferences for one set of values over another usually grow out of and reflect the concrete decisions that he is forced to make. Consequently, when government officials try to act in the best interests of their constituents without consulting them, they run the risk of trampling on the public's subjectively determined needs.

Herbert Gans's sensitive study of the Italian community in Boston provides an excellent illustration of the types of misunderstandings that arise when decisions are made in this kind of manner. Gans describes how city planners decided to redevelop a ghetto because they believed that the Italian community had to be unhappy with its run-down neighborhoods. However, the outward appearance of the neighborhood may have been shabby by suburban standards, but the residents were nostalgically attached to the homes in which they had grown up. Because the city's planners had merely assumed in an a priori fashion that the residents would be happy to trade their old homes for new ones, they inadvertently overlooked the neighborhood's concern with other values. In this way the alleged ghetto came to be torn down for purposes of redevelopment even though the people who resided there would have preferred to leave the neighborhood as it was. [33]

Whenever power is placed exclusively in the hands of political or technical elites, the problem that troubled Gans's "urban villagers" is likely to reappear in other situations. People's needs are not static in nature; they change and grow depending on the situations that are confronted. While individuals may want better housing in the abstract, they may not want it at the cost of breaking up their old neighborhood. The relative importance people attach to different values, as found in the above situation, is not likely to become apparent until individuals are faced with making concrete decisions. People's preferences for different sets of values are likely to become crystallized only when they can participate in the formulation of those specific policies which directly affect them. However, when competing political officials have the sole responsibility for deciding policy, we must trust their alleged expertise to determine the "objective" needs of their constituents.

The Notion of Accountability

Having considered polyarchy's negative evaluation of the public and its positive assessment of political elites, we now need to examine in more detail the final piece of this theory of democracy: the notion of electoral accountability. Even though many polyarchists like Schumpeter and Sartori believe that the public is apathetic and ignorant about politics, they insist that the electorate should have the right to hold its officials responsible for their actions. The question we need to ask is whether the conditions that satisfy an accountability theory of democracy are actually present in American politics. Two prerequisites for electoral accountability have already been established: the voters must perceive policy differences between the candidates, and they must vote for one set of elites over another on the basis of the stands the two candidates take. There are, however, two additional yet related conditions that must be satisfied for a polyarchal model of democracy to be effective: political incumbents must encounter serious competition at election time, and opposing candidates for the same office must differ attitudinally on the issues. Unless candidates face serious challenges on the policy positions they have taken, there is no reason why they should be responsible to anyone. If elected representatives know that they are automatically going to be returned to office, there will be little incentive for them to consider the wishes of the electorate.

An examination of the evidence indicates that these two conditions are not always found in American politics. For instance, in a study of city governments Kenneth Prewitt has noted that a significant number of public officials are in effect drafted for office. Once elected, city commissioners are rarely retired from public life by the action of the voters. Over a ten-year period in his sample of cities four out of five incumbent councilmen were successful in their bid for reelection. It seemed that men entered and left public office according to their own self-defined schedules and not at the whim of the electorate. This lack of competition, Prewitt observed, seriously undercut the doctrine of electoral accountability. Since most councilmen never had to worry about major electoral competition, there was no reason for them to be sensitive to the needs of their constituents. In fact, most councilmen came to view their position as an outlet for discharging their social responsibilities rather than a vehicle for representing the public's needs. [34]

The data on Congress are more mixed but still not conducive to a polyarchal theory of democracy. John L. Sullivan and Robert E. O'Connor found in a study of the 1966 congressional races that there were significant attitudinal differences between the contenders for each House seat. They likewise discovered that the differences were not confined to the election campaign alone; the winning candidates usually voted as their pre-election positions indicated they would. However, despite the fact that most congressional candidates differed on their policy stands, few challengers ever managed to unseat incumbents. In fact, when Sullivan and O'Connor attempted to determine how many congressional races were competitive as well as offered a policy choice, they found that only 73 out of 435 seats met both these requirements.[35] In a similar vein, David H. Leuthold has discovered that during the years 1924 to 1956, 90 percent of the congressmen who sought reelection were returned by the voters.[36] And more recently, R. W. Apple has noted that in 1968, 98 percent of all incumbents running for the House were reelected, while in 1970 and 1972 the figure was 96 percent. Most of the changes that occurred in the House had taken place in districts where there was no incumbent. It thus appeared that once a person was elected to Congress, he rarely had to worry about being retired by the voters.[37]

Sullivan and O'Connor have also argued that attitudinal differences between congressional candidates may provide little or no incentive for representatives to be sensitive to the needs of their constituents. They note there is evidence that the issues that divide the public are not necessarily the same issues on which congressional candidates disagree. While there are significant differences between the candidates on various policy matters, the candidates do not necessarily argue over problems that the electorate itself finds highly salient.[38] The ever recurring elections thus provide few incentives for congressmen to be sensitive to the wishes of their districts since the debate between contesting candidates may have little relevance for the public at large.

For confirming evidence of this point we need only look at Warren Miller's and Donald Stokes's study of public opinion and congressional voting patterns. If congressional elections led representatives to be sensitive to the needs of their constituents, Miller and Stokes did not detect it. Except for the issue of race relations, they found little or no relationship between the votes of specific congressmen and the attitudes of the public within their districts. And even on the race issue the correlation between constituent opinion and representative roll-call votes was just 0.6, which in turn explained only 36 percent of the fluctuation in a congressman's voting pattern. [39] Moreover, there is evidence that congressmen themselves do not necessarily visualize their role as one of representing the views of their constituents. Donald Matthews has found that senators who aspire to be insiders are often more sensitive to the needs of their colleagues and to the protocol or folkways of the upper chamber than they are to the wishes of voters back home. [40] And more recently, Richard Fenno has argued that members of the House pursue a variety of roles, some of which (e.g., achieving influence within the House) deemphasize the importance of being responsive to constituent opinion. [41]

If congressional races do not necessarily provide meaningful opportunities for voters to hold their representatives accountable for their actions, the same can be said of presidential elections. For instance, as noted earlier, Page and Brody found that in 1968 Richard Nixon and Hubert Humphrey did not offer any meaningful choice to the American public on the issue of Viet Nam. [42] Instead of being able to hold one set of elites accountable for their actions, the public was faced with the unattractive position of choosing between two candidates who espoused foreign policy programs that were basically indistinguishable from one another. It should also be noted that voters have no way of holding their president accountable during his second term of office. If by law second-term incumbents are barred from running for reelection, presidents no longer face the prospect of electoral competition and thus have no real incentive to be responsive to the wishes of the constituents who elected them. Unless a person is able to run for reelection, electoral accountability breaks down.

The above studies of elections on the local, congressional, and presidential levels thus raise serious questions about the possibility of polyarchal democracy in America. It appears that on different levels of government the American political system does not meet the conditions that need to be satisfied for an accountability theory of democracy to work: on numerous occasions political elites do not encounter serious opposition, nor do they always face opponents who disagree with them on the issues.

It could be argued, however, that this form of criticism is basically unfair. A polyarchist could agree that there is presently very little meaningful competition between political elites, but he might argue that the situation can be corrected. After all, the advocates of the "responsible party doctrine" have always believed that our party system can be altered to provide for meaningful, issue-related competition between electoral contestants. However, as indicated before, it is difficult to believe that this situation is ever likely to occur. Even if we had two responsible parties, there is no guarantee that they would take a stand on the diverse number of issues that interest different segments of the public. While two programmatic parties might vigorously contest one another on a few key policies, there is no reason why they would be likely to take definite and contrasting stands on the numerous and often particularistic issues that concern the average citizen. The policy areas that political elites consider important are not necessarily the same ones that interest members of the public.

Even if political parties did formulate positions on a great variety of issues, the theoretical problems with an accountability theory of democracy would still remain. As soon as two political parties take contrasting stands on two or more issues, there is no theoretical way of insuring that the electorate can hold a party responsible for all of its actions. There is no logical relationship that necessarily links different political issues together. A person could favor public welfare legislation yet either approve or disapprove of U.S. policy towards Israel. Similarly, an individual could favor federal aid for education yet be opposed to federally sponsored health insurance. Thus if a political party takes a stand on two logically unrelated issues and a person does not agree with both of those positions, he is unable to hold that party accountable for all of its actions. Given the lack of logical connection among different policy areas, there is no way that competition between political elites can provide the individual with a clear-cut choice on all issues.

In fact, Robert Dahl has shown that if the public must choose between two candidates who differ on three issues, it is possible that a resounding majority of the voters might elect a candidate all of whose policies are the first choice of only a minority of the electorate. Suppose, as Dahl has demonstrated, that voters must choose between two candidates on the basis of three issues (see table 1).[43] Imagine that we are looking at the preferences of three distinct groups in society who make up 75 percent of the voters.

Table 1

	Candidate A prefers alternative	Supported by	Candidate B prefers alternative	Supported by
Foreign policy	u	25% of voters	v	75% of voters
Farm policy	w	25% of voters	x	75% of voters
Fiscal policy	y	25% of voters	z	75% of voters

Suppose that the first group of people regards foreign affairs as most important and consequently rank orders the different policies according to the following scheme: u, x, z, w, y. Even though they do not care for his farm and fiscal programs, these people will nonetheless vote for candidate A because they like his stand on foreign affairs. If the second group considers farm policy as most important and orders its preferences w, z, v, u, y, they will also choose candidate A even though they do not favor his position on foreign and fiscal affairs. Finally, if the preferences of the third group are arranged in an analogous fashion, we can see how candidate A might win 75 percent of the vote even though 75 percent of the voters opposed one or more of his positions on the issues.[44]

Polyarchy Reexamined

Thus while polyarchists believe that competition between elites insures public accountability, there are a variety of empirical and theoretical reasons for thinking otherwise. The polyarchal model of electoral competition is theoretically too blunt an instrument to provide meaningful accountability. In any election in which there are only two possible options, it is theoretically impossible for the candidates to offer a meaningful and clear-cut choice on a diverse number of issues. But even if electoral contests could insure that officials would act in a responsible fashion, there is no reason why the public's role in politics must be confined to that of choosing among competing elites. The public appears concerned and competent enough to have earned the right to participate in the actual formulation of policy. When the citizenry reacts in an uninformed or un-civil libertarian fashion, it is often in response to the muddled campaign appeals of political elites or to attacks on individual rights by prominent government officials. In contrast to the claim of polyarchal democrats that we need elite rule to protect the political system from the inadequacies of the public, it is necessary to realize that leaders themselves have often been responsible for the unenlightened behavior of the public in the first place. Instead of concentrating authority in the hands of a few elites, it seems far more desirable to parcel power out among a diverse array of groups. The more power is diffused and shared by many parties, the harder it becomes for any one element in society, whether it be elites or the public, to curtail the civil liberties of others. Similarly, when a multiplicity of parties is involved in formulating policy, insightful and well thought out plans are more likely to emerge than when a privileged few have sole responsibility for shaping government programs. In their desire to reduce democracy to the notion of electoral accountability, polyarchal democrats have failed to appreciate the beneficial effects of citizen involvement in the decision-making process.

NOTES

1. Joseph A. Schumpeter, *Capitalism, Socialism and Democracy*, p. 262.

2. Giovanni Sartori, *Democratic Theory*, pp. 96-124.

3. Herbert McClosky, "Consensus and Ideology in American Politics," pp. 361-82.

4. Theodore Lowi, *The End of Liberalism*.

5. Harold Lasswell, Daniel Lerner, and C. Easton Rothwell, *The Comparative Study of Elites*, p. 7.

6. See, among others, Paul Lazarsfeld, Bernard Berelson, and Hazel Gaudet, *The People's Choice*; Bernard Berelson, Paul Lazarsfeld, and

William McPhee, *Voting;* Angus Campbell, Gerald Gurin, and Warren Miller, *The Voter Decides;* Angus Campbell, Philip Converse, Warren Miller, and Donald Stokes, *The American Voter;* and Angus Campbell, Philip Converse, Warren Miller, and Donald Stokes, *Elections and the Political Order.*

7. Campbell et al., *The American Voter,* pp. 168-87.

8. Ibid., pp. 188-215.

9. Anthony Downs, *An Economic Theory of Democracy,* pp. 96-114.

10. John O. Field and Ronald E. Anderson, "Ideology in the Public's Conceptualization of the 1964 Election," pp. 380-93.

11. Benjamin Page and Richard Brody, "Policy Voting and the Electoral Process: The Viet Nam War Issue," pp. 979-96.

12. Norman Nie, Sidney Verba, and John Petrocik, *The Changing American Voter,* p. 318.

13. Ibid., p. 319.

14. Gerald M. Pomper, *Elections in America,* pp. 94-95.

15. David E. RePass, "Issue Salience and Party Choice," pp. 389-400.

16. Recent studies by Philip Converse, Norman Luttbeg, Joel Aberbach, and Jack Walker likewise seem to confirm Pomper's and RePass's argument that the political system is made up of numerous issue publics. However, Converse has argued that once we drop below the most educated 10 percent of the American populace, the various issue publics lack well-integrated or well-constrained belief systems. But Norman Luttbeg, Joel Aberbach, and Jack Walker have suggested otherwise. In a study of two Oregon communities, Luttbeg found that while the content of people's belief systems varies from one individual to another, the coherence and organization of their beliefs is comparable to that of elites. And more recently, Aberbach and Walker have discovered a very narrow, yet highly sophisticated, belief system on the race issue among the black population of Detroit. The members of this issue public are not among the most educated 10 percent of the American population, but they apparently have a well-informed and well-constrained belief system on matters related to race relations. See Philip E. Converse, "The Nature of Belief Systems in Mass Publics"; Norman Luttbeg, "The Structure of Beliefs among Leaders and the Public," pp. 398-409; Joel Aberbach and Jack Walker, "The Meaning of Black Power: A Comparison of White and Black Interpretations of a Political Slogan," pp. 367-88.

17. Sidney Verba and Norman Nie, *Participation in America,* p. 106.

18. McClosky, "Consensus and Ideology in American Politics," pp. 361-82.

19. Ibid., p. 376.

20. Richard Hamilton, *Class and Politics in the United States*, p. 448.

21. William Kornhauser, *The Politics of Mass Society*, pp. 60-70; James Coleman, *Community Conflict*; Philip Hastings, "The Nonvoter in 1952: A Study of Pittsfield, Massachusetts," pp. 301-12; Philip Hastings, "The Voter and Nonvoter," pp. 302-07.

22. Hastings, "The Nonvoter in 1952," pp. 301-12.

23. Coleman, *Community Conflict*, pp. 21-22.

24. James Madison, "Federalist 10," p. 83.

25. Ibid., pp. 77-84.

26. McClosky, "Consensus and Ideology in American Politics," p. 367.

27. See Kornhauser, *Politics of Mass Society*, pp. 21-39, for an elaboration of this point.

28. Edward C. Banfield and James Q. Wilson, *City Politics*, pp. 188-92.

29. Herbert A. Simon and James G. March, *Organizations;* Charles Lindblom, *The Intelligence of Democracy.*

30. Simon and March, *Organizations*, pp. 137-69.

31. Hanna F. Pitkin, *The Concept of Representation*, pp. 190-207.

32. Lindblom, *Intelligence of Democracy*, p. 206.

33. Herbert J. Gans, *The Urban Villagers.*

34. Kenneth Prewitt, "Political Ambitions, Volunteerism, and Electoral Accountability," pp. 5-18.

35. John L. Sullivan and Robert E. O'Connor, "Electoral Choice and Popular Control of Public Policy: The Case of the 1966 House Elections," pp. 1256-68.

36. David Leuthold, *Electioneering in a Democracy*, p. 127.

37. R. W. Apple, Jr., "The GOP Fears November Will Be No Grand Old Picnic."

38. Sullivan and O'Connor, "Electoral Choice and Popular Control of Public Policy," p. 1258. See also Steve Brown and Richard Taylor, "Objectivity and Subjectivity in Concept Formation: Problems of Perspective, Partition, and Frames of Reference."

39. Warren E. Miller and Donald E. Stokes, "Constituency Influence in Congress."

40. Donald R. Matthews, *U.S. Senators and Their World*, pp. 92-118, 218-42.

41. Richard F. Fenno, *Congressmen in Committee*, pp. 1-15.

42. Page and Brody, "Policy Voting and the Electoral Process," pp. 979-96.

43. Robert Dahl, *A Preface to Democratic Theory*, p. 128.

44. Ibid.

Chapter
4

Pluralism Vs. Populism:
Defining Who the People Are

To assert that the "people" should play an important role in the formulation of policy leaves many questions unanswered. If we want to build a theory of democracy around the idea of citizen participation, we must define who constitutes the relevant public, and we also must specify what form popular participation should take.

In place of a unified, homogeneous public with relatively constant preferences, pluralists see a wealth of different associations with varying interests and contrasting policy preferences. Pluralists contend that society is composed of myriad groups of people, many of whom might be called issue publics, that is, groups of individuals who are concerned about only a limited range of issues. The degree to which these interest publics are organized and active in the political arena may vary from one group to the next. An interest public may be a loosely knit group of people who are troubled about a particular problem in their local neighborhood, or it may be a well-organized and powerful interest, like the United Auto Workers, which actively seeks to improve the material well-being of its members. Alternatively, an interest public may be what S. E. Finer calls a "promotional group," an organization like Common Cause, which seeks to realize general and ideological goals above and beyond the concrete, material interests of its members. [1]

Because of this very diversity of the American populace, pluralists maintain that group bargaining is the most feasible method for the average citizen to influence the shape of government policy. Besides fostering the development of rational plans on a macro-level, the give-and-take of a pluralistic style of decision making results in policies that maximize welfare on a micro-level. When individuals have the opportunity to bargain with one another on specific policies, they can compromise their position on issues that do not interest them in return for specific benefits that they value highly. In the resulting exchange relationship, individuals may be able to hammer out compromises best satisfying the needs of all concerned.

While pluralists favor group bargaining as the most desirable method of formulating government programs, populist democrats like Michael Harrington have often argued that the interplay of groups works to the benefit of special interests rather than the citizenry at large.* They have insisted that the public consists not of interest groups but of the sentiments of the majority who make up society. Because of these fundamental differences in outlook between populism and pluralism, it is imperative that we examine the tenets of the populist model in more detail. It is necessary to raise certain questions about a number of the empirical, normative,

---

*While historically a great number of people have called themselves populists, today it is difficult to find many proponents of populist government. Some writers, such as Jack Newfield and Jeff Greenfield, authors of *A Populist Manifesto*, are really not concerned about substantive questions of democratic theory. Instead, like many other so-called populists, they are more interested in discussing specific policy proposals, such as tax relief, which they think will bring about a more socially just society. But these kinds of issues, which certainly need to be debated, should more properly be discussed in a book that analyzes public policy or one that deals with questions of social justice. A book on democratic theory—as opposed to a study of social justice—must focus on procedural questions concerning how policy should be decided and not just on substantive questions concerning what programs ought to be implemented. We need to know how the adoption of certain patterns of policy making, or inputs, will affect the outputs of that political system. In this regard Michael Harrington's book *Toward a Democratic Left* is a useful contribution to both the democratic and the social-justice components of populist government. It should be noted, however, that Harrington is a socialist as well as a populist. He wishes not only to increase the power of the majority but also to transform our capitalist economic system into a socialist one. Because it is beyond the scope of this study we shall not attempt a direct evaluation of his normative position as a

and theoretical assumptions that populism makes concerning the nature of the public and how it should participate.

Although populists have often chosen to emphasize very different concerns, certain key assumptions that characterize the doctrine today can be identified. First, populists insist that the public be given the opportunity to participate actively in the determination of government policy. In their view, democratic participation requires that the majority of the public, and not simply one portion of it, have the final say in the determination of government programs. Secondly, populists believe that participation should take the form of referendum voting. They reject the give-and-take of interest-group bargaining, arguing that if the majority of citizens can vote on specific policy issues, they will be able to thwart the efforts of more limited groups to dictate policy to the larger community. Thirdly, populists generally seek to remove all external checks on the ability of the majority to legislate its will.[2] While it is conceivable for a populist to argue that the power of the public should be limited to certain areas in order to prevent the majority from encroaching on individual liberties, most populists have called for unlimited majoritarian rule. If the principles of popular sovereignty and political equality are to prevail, the majority itself

---

socialist. Moreover, Harrington himself insists that *Toward a Democratic Left* can be analyzed solely on its political prescriptions. "It is not at all necessary," he notes in that book, "to agree with the socialist philosophy which I outlined in *The Accidental Century* in order to favor these ideas here" (p. 17). Nevertheless there are undoubtedly die-hard Marxists who will refuse to accept Harrington's statement that it is possible to debate the desirability of different forms of democratic government independent of economics. Such Marxists are likely to argue that institutional arrangements, alternative forms of decision making, or even politics, for that matter, have no independent influence on the way society allocates its resources. Serious socialists such as Harrington refuse to embrace this kind of economic determinism. While abstaining from directly analyzing Harrington's normative economic views, I shall attempt to assess whether his political prescriptions are likely to result in substantial socioeconomic reforms. As we shall see in this chapter and more specifically at the end of chapter 6, the evidence indicates that majoritarian, or populist, rule and significant political and economic change do not always go hand in hand. In this sense political institutions may be a major influence shaping our economic institutions.

must be the sole judge of the scope of its political power. Hence populists maintain that the only limits on the public's ability to act should be the result of its own actions. And last, populists stress the affirmative role that a powerful state can play in initiating new programs and policies. Populists like Harrington want not only to liberate the public from the pernicious influence of interests groups but also to develop the government into an instrument that can respond vigorously and effectively to the wishes of the larger community. As Harrington dramatically puts it, if one argues that this nation "is so heterogeneous that it must operate by deals between a myriad of factions then American history is tragic, for it does not permit the people to make the sweeping innovations upon which the survival—which is to say the deepening—of democracy depends."[3] In the populist creed today, the strengthening of government power is seen as complementing, rather than detracting from, popular participation.

Empirical Objections to Populism

The argument that majoritarian rule should supplant pluralistic bargaining among groups assumes empirically that the public has some clear ordering of values it wishes to realize. It is possible for the interplay of groups to frustrate the wishes of the general citizenry only if there is a clearly identifiable majoritarian position on most issues. However, the notion that the electorate has a well-defined set of priorities is at times highly dubious. On an abstract level of political values it might be possible to identify the existence of a general consensus, but on the level of concrete policy it is often extremely difficult to discover a majoritarian position. As Roger Hilsman has argued in *To Move a Nation*, on most issues there is not one public, but many publics:

Within the general public there is a division of labor—one "attentive public" for agricultural policy, another for Latin American affairs, and perhaps still another for policy towards Asia. Informed and interested groups follow each policy area, but the "general" public [or the majority] becomes involved in a particular policy only rarely.[4]

While Hilsman cited very little data to support his argument, there are a variety of empirical studies substantiating his point. For instance, Gabriel Almond and Sidney Verba find that very few people are interested in a great range of issues. [5] The public consists not of a unified majority but of various individuals who become agitated over a limited range of issues at different points in time. People seem to participate in politics in a cyclical fashion; as soon as an issue appears that troubles them, they become politically active, only to revert back to a role of inactivity once their particular concerns are resolved. Similarly, both David RePass and Philip Converse, whose work was discussed in the previous chapter, note that the political community is fragmented into many diverse and heterogeneous groups interested only in specific policy areas. [6] RePass observes that in 1964 over 86 percent of the population could be classified as members of one of twenty-eight different issue publics. [7] Thus while populists often talk of the necessity of breaking down the influence of special interest groups and maximizing the power of the majority, we can see that on many occasions it is difficult to identify—let alone implement—the majority sentiment on an issue. In place of a conscious majority, we often find a variety of issue publics interested in the outcome of different policy debates.

In light of the above findings, it is interesting to ask what significance should be attached to the results of public referendums. On the basis of our previous discussion, it appears that referendums may not always reflect majoritarian sentiment in the way that populists often assume they do. If members of the public at large are constantly asked to approve or reject proposals that they are not immediately concerned with, we might expect two patterns of behavior to occur. On the one hand, many people may decide to refrain from voting altogether; while on the other hand, people who do vote may select policies for purely whimsical or idiosyncratic reasons.

Although the evidence on referendum voting is often fragmentary, it nonetheless seems to confirm the above propositions. For instance, Duane Lockard argues in his study of state and local politics that the majority of people do not participate in referendums. "Any notion that the referendum turns over to the whole populace, or even to a majority of the adults, the power to legislate is grossly in error," he asserts. "Usually the number of voters participating is a minority of the registered voters, and of those who potentially are eligible voters."[8] Likewise those people who do vote usually come disproportionately from the upper levels of society. A good example of the skewed nature of many referendums can be found in a New London, Connecticut, election in which the residents of the city were asked to vote on a measure instituting nonpartisan elections. In the working-class wards of the city roughly 8 percent of the registered voters went to the polls; in the upper-class wards the turnout was close to 15 percent. But even more interestingly, while working-class districts opposed the measure by 66 percent, it carried by 53 percent of the votes cast. The limited turnout enabled a rather small group of citizens to cast the decisive vote.[9] Ironically enough, although populists often see referendums as an opportunity for the larger public to decide issues, in this case a small minority was able to dictate the final outcome.

However, when referendums are held at the same time as gubernatorial or presidential elections, the turnout of voters is substantially higher. If people come to the polling booth to vote for political officials, they are also likely to vote on referendum issues. Yet even under these favorable conditions a substantial number of people who vote for individual candidates abstain when it comes time to vote on policy questions. In a study of referendum voting in the state of California in the years 1948 to 1954, V. O. Key found that "in about four out of ten elections less than three-quarters of the voters at the polls voted on issues on the ballot."[10] However, in a more recent study of California referendums, John E. Mueller suggests that the rate of voter abstention may be declining over time.[11] Mueller finds a drop in average abstentions of about one percentage point every three years since the time of Key's study. Mueller does not offer any definitive explanation as to why this decline has occurred but he suggests that it can be attributed to a variety of causes, such as higher rates of literacy, wealth, etc. Yet despite this upward trend in the number of people who vote on issues, Mueller notes that the abstention rate on particular items is highly volatile. Voter turnout seems to fluctuate immensely depending on whether there is at least one highly controversial item among the various proposals voters are asked to decide. In the 1965 election, for example, abstentions were two to three times higher than they were a year earlier, when Californians were asked to vote on a very controversial fair housing law. [12]

If, as suggested earlier, the population is split up into a series of issue publics, we should not be surprised at the volatile and generally low rates of voter participation. When voters are asked to decide issues that fall outside of their main concerns, many of them may not vote. However, all uninterested voters do not necessarily stay at home on election day or abstain from voting on certain items. As the authors of *The American Voter* have pointed out, many people may go to the polls because they feel it is their duty to do so even though they are not necessarily concerned about the issues under consideration. But if individuals who go to the polls are really indifferent to the outcome of the election, they may vote for extremely whimsical or idiosyncratic reasons. Similarly, if the majority of citizens are concerned about a particular issue on the ballot, they may vote on other referendum items, which are peripheral to their main concerns, for purely arbitrary reasons.

This arbitrariness can take a variety of forms. For instance, Lockard has argued that if voters are either unconcerned or uncertain about the impact of a particular policy change, they may tend to veto complex legislation. He quoted one advertisement used in a Salt Lake City campaign on home rule: "Confused! Many Are. Play Safe—When in Doubt, Vote No!" [13] Similarly, James Coleman and Robert Crain have noted that the confusion and latent antagonism in the minds of many voters is in large part responsible for the defeat of fluoride legislation. [14] Despite overwhelming evidence that the fluoridation of water is beneficial, many citizens find the issue so baffling that they play safe and vote no.

However, Mueller argues that public indifference will not necessarily result in the rejection of referendum proposals. He believes that voters will act in a consistently informed fashion on hotly debated issues, but finds that voter behavior is highly idiosyncratic and even arbitrary in nature on noncontroversial items. More specifically, when people are asked to vote on many noncontroversial problems that do not directly concern them, they seem to fluctuate between moods of acceptance and moods of rejection:

"It appears that there are good years and bad years for noncontroversial propositions."[15] In some years, such as 1952 and 1960, the voters seem to be in an acceptance mood and approve most of the propositions, while in others, like 1958, they tend to reject most of the noncontroversial items on the ballot. Unfortunately, Mueller notes, it is difficult to determine why political moods arise or why they shift over time. Regression analysis reveals no strong relationships between voter moods of acceptance or rejection and other variables, such as percentage of voter turnout or number of propositions on the ballot.

Interestingly enough, Mueller argues that voting behavior fluctuates both from election to election and from item to item depending on the location of a particular proposition on the ballot. Thus the placement of a measure not only determines whether voters will abstain or not but also influences how they will cast their ballots. In Mueller's words, "on items of low visibility, voters seem to have a tendency to avoid over a long stretch a pattern of behavior which is obviously uniform."[16] That is to say, people are often reluctant to vote uniformly for or against all the propositions on the ballot. One reason state legislatures insist on placing state bond issues at the top of the ballot is that they believe many voters start out voting affirmatively, then switch their votes as the number of propositions increases. An analysis of the data lends support to this belief. Mueller finds that a small, yet significant, number of voters (7 percent) begin voting positively but then vote negatively on items placed lower down on the ballot.[17] However, there appear to be an equal number who follow the opposite course of action, casting negative votes on the initial items but voting positively on succeeding propositions. The outcome of a particular issue may thus be dependent on where it happens to be placed. The results of a referendum could be entirely different if the items on the ballot had appeared in a different order.

There is thus considerable evidence that many voters base their referendum votes on factors completely unrelated to the actual issues at hand. A strong element of arbitrariness is injected into referendum balloting by those who play safe and vote no on issues they do not understand, or vote in accordance with cyclical moods of affirmation or rejection, or vote yes or no depending on the location of the issues on the ballot. In this situation, it is difficult to accept the populist argument that referendums will reflect the true interests of the public at large. While populists often talk as if there were a popular or majoritarian sentiment on most issues, we can see that in many cases such sentiment simply does not exist. Since most people are concerned only with a narrow range of interests, we can understand why they may not participate actively in referendum elections. But if they do participate, we can likewise understand why their behavior may be dictated by such factors as the position of the item on the ballot. If the political system relied extensively on referendums to decide the many issues that it faces, referendums might end up playing a role in society just the opposite of that envisioned by most populists. Instead of identifying an already existing majoritarian position, referendums might artificially create a majority stand out of a large number of whimsical votes. Depending on the prevailing mood of the people or the organization of the ballot, today's majority position could very easily become tomorrow's minority position.

The difficulty in attempting to maximize the power of the majority is that in many cases it simply does not exist. Thus efforts to force a majority stand out of a diverse and heterogeneous set of publics are likely to lead to the problems that Lockard and Mueller have described. While the referendum will mechanically generate a majority opinion on an issue, that opinion may not correspond to any well-defined set of beliefs in the larger population.

The Paradox of Voting Problem

Although referendums often ask people to decide questions they are not interested in, there will always be some issues that will elicit overwhelming public concern and the majority will be interested in the outcome. But we must remember that for populism to work this is not enough: there must also be a majority that share similar standards for resolving the issue in question. If this latter condition is not satisfied, referendums may paradoxically result in collective decisions that do not reflect the individual preferences of the public. While individuals may have consistently ordered preferences, majority rule may result in decisions that are inconsistent with the ordered preferences of the voting public. This phenomenon, which is known as the *Arrow problem* or the *paradox of voting*, can be seen in the following example. [18]

Let us suppose that a national referendum was to be held in the late 1960s on the Viet Nam War. Without too much difficulty we could easily imagine that the population might be roughly divided into three groups of people who favored different courses of action: (A) immediately withdrawing from Viet Nam, (B) maintaining the conventional level of fighting and seeking a negotiated settlement, and (C) dramatically stepping up the fighting to win a complete victory. The preferences of the public would be ordered as in table 2.

Table 2

Doves	*Moderates*	*Hawks*
A immediate withdrawal	B maintain status quo	C step up fighting
B maintain the status quo	C step up fighting	A immediate withdrawal
C step up fighting	A immediate withdrawal	B maintain the status quo

The first group of citizens prefers that the United States withdraw immediately. As an alternative to this policy they desire that the American government maintain the status quo rather than step up the level of warfare. However, the moderates favor maintaining the status quo in the hopes of securing a negotiated settlement. If that course of action fails, they want the government to go all out in an effort to win the war. Immediate withdrawal would thus be seen as the least desirable course of action to follow. The last segment of the population favors an intensification of the war effort in order to secure a complete victory. In case the government is not willing to pursue that option, they support immediate withdrawal, arguing that if the government is not serious about winning, it has no business prolonging American presence in a foreign country. So people in this last category favor stepping up the fighting first, withdrawing second, and maintaining the status quo last.

If we held our referendum on the war, paired the alternative courses of action, and counted the votes, we would discover that a majority of citizens would favor immediate withdrawal over maintaining the status quo, or A over B, and that a majority would favor maintenance of the status quo over stepped up fighting, or B over C. Now if a society prefers policy A over policy B, and policy B over policy C, we would think that to be consistent it must also prefer policy A over policy C. But when we look at our example, such is not the case, for the public favors stepped up fighting over immediate withdrawal, or policy C over policy A. The political system has thus produced an inconsistent or irrational social ordering since A is preferred to B, and B is preferred to C, but C is preferred to A. Given the logic of majoritarian voting, it is possible for people with perfectly consistent individual preferences to arrive at a collective decision that is inconsistent with their own ranking of the alternatives. The transitive, or consistent, individual preferences have been transformed by a majority vote into an intransitive, or inconsistent, social decision. Regardless of which policy is finally adopted, a majority of citizens would prefer an alternative other than the one selected.

When the conditions of the Arrow paradox exist, voting procedures can become highly arbitrary in nature. The alternative that is finally adopted may be determined merely by the order in which the electorate votes on the various policy options. For example, suppose the public voted on each proposition one at a time until a decision was finally reached. Every individual would vote against the Viet Nam option under discussion if he favored another course of action; however, once a proposal had been rejected the electorate could no longer continue to consider it as a real possibility. If, as in our Viet Nam case, there are only three alternative policies to choose from, then there are only six different ways the policies can be voted on, namely ABC, ACB, BAC, BCA, CAB, and CBA. If we hold our elections and eliminate the various possibilities, we find that the following pattern develops. [19]

CASE ONE: Proposition A is voted down because two-thirds of the public favors another course of action. Proposition B wins the referendum since with option A (immediate withdrawal) eliminated, two-thirds of the population favors B to C (stepped up fighting).

CASE TWO: Proposition A is again put before the public and defeated, then followed by proposition C, which is also defeated. Policy B (maintain the status quo) wins.

CASE THREE: Proposition B is now the first proposal presented to the public and is defeated. Option A is then voted on and rejected, leaving proposition C, which wins.

CASE FOUR: By the same electoral mechanism, proposition C wins the referendum.

CASE FIVE: Beginning with proposition C, policy A wins.

CASE SIX: Proposition A wins.

From the above discussion we can see that the alternative favored by the majority of citizens is determined merely by the manner in which the different options are presented. When alternative A (immediate withdrawal) is voted on first, option B (maintain the status quo) wins the election; when proposition B is voted on first, alternative C (stepped up fighting) wins; and when option C is voted on first, proposition A (immediate withdrawal) becomes the first choice. Paradoxical as it may seem, a populist form of democracy can lead to highly irrational forms of decision making; public referendums may be decided merely by the order in which different propositions are presented.

In order to escape this paradox of voting, one of two possibilities must occur. First, individual rank orderings of policy options must exhibit the characteristic that Duncan Black has labeled "single peakedness."[20] That is, all individuals must use the same dimensions or criteria for evaluating a set of policy alternatives. The reason public decisions often do not reflect the rank ordering of different individuals is that people frequently use a variety of standards for assessing the merits or deficiencies of a possible course of action. When individuals try to harmonize their preferences in a referendum vote, the majority position that is generated is likely to reflect the inconsistent standards held by the voting public in a disaggregate form. However, if people can locate their standards for evaluating public policies on a single continuum so that their preference for any alternative declines the further it

diverges in either direction from their first choice, no voting paradox results. Whenever individuals with single peaked preferences
vote on varied alternatives, the alternative preferred by the median
voter always prevails, and the problem of socially intransitive
decisions is avoided.

However, it should be pointed out that the position of the median voter does not necessarily reflect the will of the majority. We
thus face the anomalous situation that if people's preferences are
not single peaked, the collective decision of the referendum will
be irrational in the sense that it will not reflect the individual rank
ordering of different policies. But if people's values are single
peaked, the resulting collective decision will certainly be rational
(that is, transitively ordered), but it may not reflect the wishes of
the majority. For referendums to yield a majoritarian as well as a
nonparadoxical outcome, the public must share single peaked
beliefs and a majority must favor the median position. We can thus
see that on many occasions, contrary to what populists believe,
referendum voting is not an effective means for making known
majority preferences.

However, as should be obvious from the above discussion, the
indeterminacy problem in majoritarian voting is primarily one of
logic. While the paradox of voting is a theoretical possibility that
may occur in any referendum, the actual empirical distribution of
attitudes in society will determine the frequency of its appearance.
Unfortunately, there is very little empirical research on how often
the Arrow problem actually occurs since very few polls attempt to
determine people's rank ordering of different policy options. Richard Niemi has attempted to describe the conditions under which the
Arrow paradox is most likely to occur, and for a variety of reasons
he thinks it may not be that prevalent. [21] But a careful examination
of Niemi's discussion reveals that his argument is not necessarily
supportive of a populist view of politics. Niemi argues that one
reason the paradox occurs very infrequently is that the political
system operates to standardize the options open to the public. For
instance, the Democrats and Republicans either echo one another's
proposals, or, if they offer a choice, they usually limit it to two
options, which makes it impossible for the paradox to appear in
the first place. Similarly, if there are referendums on issues like

Viet Nam, people are allowed to vote only on one course of action. A diversity of opinions is thus never allowed to find expression.

Besides mechanically limiting the options people can vote on, the political system also attempts to standardize values through its various socialization processes. In fact, Niemi thinks the socialization process is most successful in developing a similar outlook among elite groups such as politicians or businessmen.[22] By and large the people recruited into these categories come from relatively homogeneous groups and so are likely to share many of the same beliefs about the political system. Since elites can often define the terms of debate surrounding an issue, they can simplify or standardize the political choices open to the public and thus prevent the Arrow problem from ever arising.

Niemi may be correct in arguing that the above factors help to limit the occurrence of the voting paradox, but his argument raises some troublesome problems for a populist theory of democracy. Niemi suggests that the indeterminacy problem occurs sporadically—not because voters have a well-defined and shared belief system—but because at best they often follow the lead of political elites in favoring certain policies and at worst they are mechanically limited in the number of options from which they can choose. In either case, sentiment on a particular issue may be more problematic than that pictured by the populist. The wishes of the alleged majority that emerge in a referendum may reflect more the options from which the public can choose than the underlying sentiments of large segments of the population. As Niemi himself concedes:

Our findings suggest that intransitivities are most likely to occur in unstructured situations, where there are no common guidelines for judging the alternatives, or in situations involving multiple dimensions. For example, intransitivities might be found relatively often when new issues must be resolved. Similarly, the paradox probably occurs more often in *ad hoc* groups, which are less likely to be influenced by the socialization, selection, and discussion factors which contribute to greater uniformity of judgmental criteria. Such groups might be newly formed ones, groups which meet infrequently and irregularly, or groups which purposely bring together many diverse elements. In elections, the paradox may occur most frequently when parties are absent or when the parties vary along two or more major dimensions.[23]

We can see from Niemi's analysis that populism may face a dual dilemma. If the political system ever decided to increase its reliance on referendums, it would run the risk of having a diverse, hetero-geneous set of people decide policy in an unstructured situation. As Niemi notes, the more diverse the portion of the population formu-lating policy, the more difficult it is for socialization and recruit-ment procedures to generate a uniform outlook and thus the more likely it is for the voting paradox to arise. However, if the political system attempted to direct public opinion into narrower channels or to limit the policy options placed before the public, the resulting majoritarian sentiment would be open to suspicion. As argued before, a referendum can always mechanically generate a majority position on an issue, but that position may not correspond to any well-defined set of beliefs in the larger population.

Many of these problems can easily be avoided if public policy is made in a pluralistic fashion through bargaining and negotiation. As we have seen, if the electorate is split up into at least three dif-ferent groups with different rank orderings of various policy op-tions, the problem of indeterminacy will always be present. Unless a populist can empirically show that the public at large actually shares similar values, there is no way he can avoid this difficulty. However, in a pluralistic form of democracy the Arrow problem presents no problem at all. William Baumol and James Coleman, among others, have shown that it is only when various policy options are decided by elections that the issue of indeterminacy occurs.[24] If the members of the political system agree to weight, as well as to count, people's votes, the logical problem of arriving at a transitively ordered collective decision no longer exists. When we account for the intensity as well as the order in which various individuals favor different policy options, it is always possible to reach a determinate, transitively ordered collective decision. If the political system can arrange exchanges between groups who feel intensely about a particular policy and groups who are only mildly concerned with that same policy, it can aggregate individual pref-erences in such a fashion that the Arrow paradox disappears. Whether the groups in society will actually be responsive to the intensities with which different interests value their preferences is a separate and empirical, rather than logical, question. But if the political system is open and responsive to a diverse array of groups, as public pluralists believe it can be, then a pluralistic form of decision making represents a way of circumventing the paradox of voting.

Normative Objections to Populism

While so far this chapter has stressed the empirical problems likely to plague a populist theory of democracy, it is necessary to point out that pluralism's objections to populism are not confined to empirical considerations alone. Even if it could be demonstrated that there was a genuine majority position on most issues, a pluralist would still have reservations about allowing an unrestrained majority to prevail on every issue. To debate who the people are is as much a normative as an empirical issue. To emphasize this point we shall now assume that the two empirical issues discussed above no longer exist. We shall accept the populist argument that a majority of the public is interested in a particular issue and shares similar values for resolving it. In assuming away the above empirical issues, we are left with two separate, yet related, normative questions. First, we need to decide if the wishes of the majority should always prevail over those of minorities; and secondly, we need to ask how the majority should go about establishing its priorities, whether it should rely on referendums or on some other means like bargaining.

Populists have been inclined to argue that the majority should dictate public policy and that it should do so through the mechanism of referendum voting. In contrast, pluralists not only have wanted to restrain the ability of the majority to dictate policy; they also have suggested that political bargaining rather than referendum voting is the preferable way of arriving at public decisions. The reasons for these sharp differences are many, but in large part they reflect the fact that populists and pluralists attach very different weights to certain key values. On the one hand, as a matter of first principle, populists have stressed the need to maximize the values of political equality and popular sovereignty.[25] All men should be treated equally, they have implied; each man's influence should be the same as any other's. Thus to decide policy issues all the political system needs to do is count the public's preferences and implement those policies which are favored by a majority of the population. While some critics have suggested that such a system of unrestrained majoritarian rule might lead to abuses, populists have tended to minimize the possibility of such an occurrence, arguing that if the political system guarantees the equality of all, then the public will exercise its power in a judicious and responsible fashion.

On the other hand, pluralists not only question the accuracy of populism's view of the public, but also have reservations about the values that populists wish to maximize. As argued earlier, pluralism is a form of liberal democracy that seeks to enhance the opportunities for people to participate in politics at the same time that it protects the basic liberties of the individual. While pluralism certainly wants to insure that the public has some influence over government policy, it does not want to sacrifice other principles, such as equity or individual freedom, in the process. Robert Dahl has argued that political equality and popular sovereignty should not be maximized at the expense of other important values:

For most of us . . . the costs of pursuing any one or two goals at the expense of others are thought to be excessive. Most of us are marginalists. Generally we experience diminishing marginal utility the more we attain any one goal; or in the language of contemporary psychology, goal attainment reduces the drive value of the stimulus. Political equality and popular sovereignty are not absolute goals; we must ask ourselves how much leisure, privacy, consensus, stability, income, security, progress, status, and probably many other goals we are prepared to forego for an additional increment of political equality. [26]

In weighing the advantages and disadvantages of maximizing political equality and popular sovereignty, two conditions would warrant limiting the power of the majority: (1) if majority rule ever threatened to infringe on the rights of minorities, or (2) if an apathetic majority ever adopted a policy that was intensely opposed by a substantial minority.

The Problem of Minority Rights

Traditionally the main reason pluralists have been wary of maximizing majority rule and political equality is the fear that the larger public may abuse the rights of minorities. While the public should have an important voice in politics, this role should not be achieved at the cost of important individual rights, such as free speech or free assembly or the right of all people to receive equal treatment in employment or housing regardless of their racial background.

In addition, apart from the question of individual rights, pluralists believe that the principle of political egalitarianism should govern the allocation of social resources. That is to say, if certain segments of society are outvoted by a majority on one particular issue, they should at least be given the opportunity to influence policy on another issue or on the same issue at a later point in time. Each of the diverse interests that make up society should have its own turn to play an important role in the political process; if an identifiable majority exists and wants to set policy, it should not have the power to permanently exclude other groups from receiving some minimal benefits. However, if one posits political equality and popular sovereignty as the key values to maximize, then one must logically abide by the majoritarian decision in each and every case. Unless the majority willingly agrees to refrain from achieving its wishes on every occasion, it must override the claims of groups that have previously failed to gain a favorable hearing of their views.

Populist views on majority prerogatives and minority rights have been less than uniform. Some populists may be willing to prevent the majority from passing restrictive legislation in the area of civil liberties, but others believe that the only limitations on majority rule should be self-imposed. Austin Ranney and Willmore Kendall have argued that if we try to realize both majority rule and inviolate rights, majority rule is likely to be transformed into minority rule. [27] Unless the public has the sovereign power to decide all issues of importance, and unless the preferences of each man are counted equally, the wishes of the larger public may be superseded by the wishes of various minority groups, thereby violating the spirit of democratic government.

This is not to say, however, that most populists completely ignore the importance of protecting the right to free speech or free assembly. It is essential for a populist to defend a great variety of individual liberties in order to protect the integrity of majority rule. If individuals do not have the opportunity to challenge public officials or contest specific pieces of legislation, their ability to develop a new majoritarian position on a particular issue could be frustrated. The protection of certain fundamental rights is necessary for achieving majority decisions. However, although populists must theoretically defend many basic rights, their defense of civil liberties is limited in two respects. First of all, the civil liberties that a populist must defend in order to guarantee majorities the freedom to form and reform are basically the traditional rights of free speech and assembly. There is no logical reason why a populist who is theoretically committed to these essential liberties must likewise defend the more recently acquired right of minority groups to eat, sleep, and live where they please. The logic of majority rule requires a populist to defend a limited, rather than exhaustive, list of civil liberties. Secondly, while majoritarian democrats like Ranney and Kendall adopt what might be called "liberal principles," they consider them as means rather than ends. Even if majority rule may not be able to operate without them, these freedoms are not viewed as essential liberties. Although the rights of free speech and assembly are necessary to preserve majoritarian democracy, an existing majority always retains the prerogative of terminating majority rule altogether if it exercises the proper procedures in seeking its own demise.

Besides disagreeing over the normative importance of certain key rights, pluralists and populists also differ in their empirical estimate of the public's willingness to respect individual liberties. As mentioned earlier, much of the available evidence does not inspire confidence in the ability of the majority to use its power responsibly. We know from the research of Herbert McClosky that a sizable percentage of the American populace appears willing to deny people the right to advocate unpopular views. [28] However, although the attitudinal evidence suggests that the public is not likely to respect the rights of unpopular minority groups, the actual behavior of the American populace may be less threatening to civil liberties. But our argument has been contingent on the fact that society is organized along pluralistic, rather than populist, lines.

As William Kornhauser has argued, individuals are most likely to respect liberal values when they are well integrated into a network of group relationships, since interest groups serve as filtering devices to screen out the periodic anti-civil libertarian demands of their members.[29] For example, during the 1964 and 1968 presidential elections labor unions played an important role in convincing their members not to support the candidacy of George Wallace. Like many other groups, unions provide alternative sources of information to their members about the dangers of pursuing certain courses of action, and through a more general process of socialization they moderate the feelings of any members who pose a threat to the institutions and liberties of the larger society. However, even when a group does not perform this moderating function, as is the case with an association like the Ku Klux Klan, the existence of other groups in society serves as a restraining influence on anti-civil libertarian behavior. Under a pluralistic system groups can check one another and thereby soften the impact of anti-civil libertarian views, but under a populist system there are no similar restraints if the majority votes in favor of suppressing individual rights.

The record of referendums in California bears out the contention that a populist form of democracy would not be conducive to the protection of civil liberties. These referendums, which most closely approximate the kind of majoritarian rule that populists envision, failed to confirm the argument that the majority will exercise its power in a responsible fashion. As the late Senator Richard Neuberger commented:

In recent years California, the state where initiative and referendum are used most frequently, has voted down bills to create a state housing authority, to redistrict the legislature on the basis of present-day population, to repeal a consumer's sales tax, and to adopt a state FEPC [Fair Employment Practices Committee] forbidding racial discrimination in employment. These setbacks, all by overwhelming margins, have given pause to liberals and welfare workers.[30]

Moreover, in 1964 California voters went to the polls and repealed a fair housing law that would have banned racial discrimination in the sale or purchase of homes. This referendum, which has been studied extensively by Raymond Wolfinger and Fred Greenstein, was one of the few issues on the 1964 ballot that seemed to interest a majority of citizens. [31] As Mueller notes, only 4 percent of the voters abstained on this issue while 25 to 30 percent abstained on other propositions that happened to be on the ballot. Moreover, as Wolfinger and Greenstein have observed, pre-election surveys indicated that people were aware of the implications of the fair housing proposition despite the fact that it was worded in a very vague and confusing manner. While there was no problem in this case of empirically identifying a genuine majority sentiment on the issue in question, the normative problem of majority power and minority rights was very much in evidence. Even though the legislature, which had passed the fair housing law the year before, was willing to guarantee minority members the right to purchase a house, the majority of citizens were not so inclined. The repeal of the fair housing proposition passed by a better than two-to-one margin. Despite populist insistence that the majority will not empirically misuse its power, we can see that on many occasions this has not been the case. In the past when the majority has had the opportunity to decide issues involving civil liberties, it has often voted to curtail, rather than to expand, the scope of individual rights.

The Problem of Intensity

Another danger in always permitting a numerical majority to prevail is that an apathetic majority may overrule minorities who feel very strongly about a particular policy. But because most populists believe that political equality and popular sovereignty are cardinal values, they insist that all issues should be decided on a one-man one-vote principle. Regardless of how intensely people may feel about a particular issue, populists believe that it is essential to equalize the influence of all citizens.

While political equality and popular sovereignty are important values, pluralists like Dahl argue that in seeking to achieve these principles, we should not sacrifice too many other values that we deem important. In particular, if there are extreme variations in the intensities with which people value different political alternatives, it may be desirable to weight, as well as to count, the preferences of individual voters. The principle of one-man one-vote may be an adequate form of representation when people feel equally intensely about an issue, but the same standard may be inequitable and too costly in terms of alternative values foregone when applied to situations in which individuals' concerns about a particular policy vary considerably. In such a case it may be more fair for the political system to decide in favor of those government policies which are most preferred rather than those programs which are preferred by most.

Ironically enough, while on a normative level populists have minimized the importance of weighting votes, on a practical or empirical level they have often argued that the problem of intensity presents no insurmountable difficulties. Even though theoretically they oppose weighting some people's opinions more heavily than others, they often defend a populistic referendum because in practice it achieves exactly this end. In arguing this point, populists make a twofold argument. On the one hand, they maintain that the public takes account of the intensity of people's concerns before going to the polls. In other words, even though referendums cannot weight people's votes, the individual may let the pattern of public sentiment on a particular issue influence the manner in which he discharges his electoral responsibility. Thus the weighting of preferences takes place even though the voting process per se counts each person's vote equally. While this argument undoubtedly has some merit, it needs to be carefully qualified. To attempt to judge the intensity of different people's preferences requires a concerted amount of effort on the part of the public. Without any meaningful incentives, it is difficult to imagine that the majority would ever try to account for the intensity of other people's beliefs. Moreover, given the communication problems that would be involved in a large political system if every voter tried to assess the depth of other people's preferences, it can be argued that the process is not likely to occur. In fact, Willmore Kendall and George Carey have argued that we can expect people to account for the intensity of other people's beliefs only in small, homogeneous communities.[32] The more homogeneous the community, the easier it becomes for each individual to assume that the wishes of others are similar to his own. However, in a large political system the public is more likely to be unable to gauge the intensity of other people's beliefs as well as indifferent to doing so.

If the problem of intensity is not resolved directly by the voters themselves, then populists often suggest that the issue can be handled indirectly through variations in election turnouts. As we have already seen, not all citizens go to the polls, and of those who do, not all vote on every proposition on the ballot. Although populists admit that referendums theoretically cannot account for intensity of feeling, they argue that in practice this issue presents no real problem since fluctuations in voter turnout reflect the depth of concern with which individuals regard different propositions. There is a considerable degree of evidence to support this argument, but it must also be remembered that citizens often go to the polls even though they are not interested in the issues at hand. Many people cast their ballots because they feel it is their duty as good citizens to participate in all elections and as a result they vote on propositions in which they are only minimally interested. Moreover, the fate of various referendum items is often related more to their position on the ballot than to the intensity of public sentiment for or against the propositions themselves. Thus while it is undoubtedly true that many apathetic people abstain from voting, referendums are still a far from perfect mechanism for recognizing and accommodating intensely, as opposed to nominally, held beliefs.

How Should the Public Express Its Sentiments?

For a variety of reasons we can see that it may be desirable to impose some restraints on the exercise of majority rule. However, even if we are willing to concede that on some occasions the wishes of the public at large should prevail over those of particular interests, we still need to ask if populistic referendums are the most preferable mechanism for deciding issues. Because one insists that the will of the majority should always govern, it does not necessarily follow that the majority should always express its sentiments through public referendums. As pluralists in particular want to argue, political bargaining, compromise, and logrolling may maximize public welfare while referendum voting may generate a set of policies that will achieve only minimal utility. The drawbacks of referendum voting are directly related to the intensity problem discussed earlier. The intensity with which people favor certain policies is to a large extent a reflection of the utility or welfare they would derive from the enactment of these programs. Referendums are generally poor mechanisms for identifying and accommodating intensities of feeling and hence they often tend to be poor decision-making procedures for maximizing public welfare in an aggregate sense. If an apathetic majority prevailed over an intense minority in a public referendum, the final policies that were adopted might restrict, rather than maximize, the total amount of utility in society. Although a certain course of action might greatly hinder the well-being of a minority group, an alternative policy might provide only minimal satisfaction for the majority of people in society. Therefore if policies were decided by referendum vote the final outcome would result in a reduction of the aggregate welfare of all.

To illustrate this point, let us look at table 3 and assume there are three sets of voters who must decide two separate issues. [33] Let us also assume that there are extreme variations in the utility that various citizens would derive from the adoption of certain policies.

Table 3

	Voter X	Voter Y	Voter Z
Issue I			
Policy A	1	51	60
Policy B	99	49	40
Issue 2			
Policy C	51	52	45
Policy D	49	48	55

If decisions had to be made strictly by referendums and there were legal proscriptions against vote trading or bargaining, policy A and policy C would be chosen. Voters Y and Z prefer policy A to B; voters X and Y prefer policy C to D. However, while voters Y and Z both receive some minimal satisfaction from Policy A, voter

Z incurs a high loss in utility. On policy C, however, voters X and Y both receive some minimal increase in their welfare while voter Z suffers an equally mild loss in utility. If the utilities of all three sets of voters are summed, we find that there would be a net reduction in the total amount of welfare in society. However, if the same decision is made in a pluralistic fashion and the various parties can bargain and trade with one another, the above situation need not occur. Voter X can agree to vote for policy D on issue 2 if voter Z will agree to vote for policy B on issue 1. Both voters X and Z can thus make a net increase in their welfare even though voter Y will suffer a net decrease in his utility on both issues. Because the gains to both voters X and Z are so much greater than the losses to voter Y, there is also a net increase in the collective welfare of the community.

From the above example we can see that whenever a political system relies on referendums to formulate public policy, there is always the possibility that the policies adopted may decrease, rather than increase, the aggregate well-being of society as a whole. This is especially likely to be the case when there is extreme variation in the intensities with which various segments of society prefer alternative courses of action. By and large referendum voting is preferable to political bargaining only if the utilities people attach to particular options are roughly the same.

While political bargaining may increase public welfare, there are two conditions under which it may cease to work effectively. If groups bargain over policy and sincerely state their preferences, the ensuing exchanges will produce the results described above. However, if they overstate or disguise their true preferences, the exchange relationship may fail to maximize public welfare. Our example assumes that the stated preferences are sincere, rather than disguised, preferences. Secondly, the benefits of political bargaining work only if other groups do not incur extensive external costs from the exchanges agreed to by our three parties.[34] A bargaining situation that may increase the aggregate welfare of the parties involved may entail enough offsetting external costs to erase the gains of any political exchange. Obviously, under such circumstances the agreements struck by various groups would not result in optimal decisions. However, this situation is most likely to occur in a political system in which many potential groups fail to become organized or lack access to the policy-making process. If a public form of pluralism can insure that most potential groups are not shut out of the political system, it can minimize, if not contain, the external costs that might result from extensive political bargaining.

Populist Participation: Substantive or Symbolic?

While so far we have looked in great detail at both the empirical and normative problems that are likely to plague a populist theory of democracy, it is also imperative that we critically examine the theoretical suppositions of populist government in order to determine if they are entirely consistent with one another. One of the fundamental assumptions that populists like Harrington have made is that the intensification of public participation and strengthening of government power are entirely compatible objectives. In the opinion of many populists, unless the government has the power to implement the wishes of the public, the effectiveness of participation will be undercut. But it must be pointed out that this relationship between government power and popular participation is a necessary—but by no means sufficient—condition for public involvement to be genuinely meaningful. While the government will need sufficient authority to implement the wishes of the majority, populists must be careful that the state does not misuse its power in interpreting the so-called will of the people. As soon as the problem is defined in these terms it can be seen that a conflict might easily arise between what the public wants and what government officials actually do. When referendums are held on extremely complex problems, they may be stated in such an abstract fashion that they will provide little or no meaningful guidance to the administrator who must actually implement what the majority decides. For example, the public may want the state to enact tough anti-pollution laws, but they may not be willing to accept a slowdown in the rate of economic growth in exchange for clear air. It is difficult to see how the electorate can convey these diverse sentiments in any concrete and specific fashion through the rather unrefined mechanism of a referendum.

The danger thus exists that under a populist form of democracy, government bureaucrats will begin to wield more and more discretionary power in the formulation of policy. While the state will have the power to implement the wishes of the majority, it may increasingly have to rely on its own interpretation of what the public really wants. In the process the very quality of popular participation may become more symbolic than substantive in nature, since instead of actually deciding policy the public may find itself merely authorizing the government to deal with a problem that it considers highly important. As the scope and complexity of the government's activities become enlarged, it stands to reason that the linkage between the public's original wishes and the operations of the state will become more tenuous. While on a theoretical level the majority of citizens may be sanctioning the state to act on a particular issue, the managers of the government may wield the real substance of power by formulating the measures to implement the alleged wishes of the electorate.

NOTES

1. S. E. Finer, "Groups and Political Participation," pp. 58-79.

2. Austin Ranney and Willmore Kendall, *Democracy and the American Party System*, pp. 35-37.

3. Michael Harrington, *Toward a Democratic Left*, p. 266.

4. Roger Hilsman, *To Move a Nation*, p. 542.

5. Gabriel Almond and Sidney Verba, *The Civic Culture*, pp. 337-75.

6. David E. RePass, "Issue Salience and Party Choice," pp. 389-400; Philip E. Converse, "The Nature of Belief Systems in Mass Publics."

7. RePass, "Issue Salience," pp. 392-98.

8. Duane Lockard, *The Politics of State and Local Government*, p. 253.

9. Ibid., p. 237.

10. V. O. Key, *Politics, Parties, and Pressure Groups*, p. 630.

11. John E. Mueller, "Voting on the Propositions," pp. 1197-1212.

12. Ibid., p. 1212.

13. Lockard, *Politics of State and Local Government*, p. 251.

14. James Coleman, *Community Conflict*; Robert L. Crain, Elihu Katz, and Donald Rosenthal, *The Politics of Community Conflict*.

15. Mueller, "Voting on the Propositions," p. 1198.

16. Ibid., p. 1208.

17. Ibid.

18. Kenneth Arrow, *Social Choice and Individual Values.*

19. Robert Paul Wolff, *In Defense of Anarchism,* p. 63.

20. Duncan Black, *The Theory of Committees and Elections,* pp. 39-40.

21. Richard Niemi, "Majority Decision Making with Partial Unidimensionality," pp. 488-97.

22. Ibid., 494.

23. Ibid.

24. William Baumol, *Economic Theory and Operations Research,* pp. 270-74; James Coleman, "The Possibility of a Social Welfare Function," pp. 1105-23.

25. Ranney and Kendall, *Democracy and the American Party System,* pp. 20-35. See Also Robert Dahl, *A Preface to Democratic Theory,* pp. 45, 50.

26. Dahl, *Preface to Democratic Theory,* p. 51.

27. Ranney and Kendall, *Democracy and the American Party System,* p. 24.

28. Herbert McClosky, "Consensus and Ideology in American Politics," pp. 361-82.

29. William Kornhauser, *The Politics of Mass Society,* pp. 60-70.

30. Richard Neuberger, "Government by the People," p. 490.

31. Raymond Wolfinger and Fred Greenstein, "The Repeal of Fair Housing Legislation in California," pp. 753-69.

32. Willmore Kendall and George Carey, "The 'Intensity Problem' and Democratic Theory," pp. 5-24.

33. The example is adapted from Richard Musgrave and Peggy Musgrave, *Public Finance in Theory and Practice,* p. 95.

34. See William H. Riker and Steve J. Brams, "The Paradox of Vote Trading," pp. 1235-47, for a fuller treatment of this issue.

Chapter

5

Pluralism and the Problem of Group Membership

Pluralists disagree with the populist belief that the public consists of a relatively homogeneous majority with similar interests and concerns, arguing instead that the electorate is fragmented into numerous and diverse issue publics whose interest in politics is often quite limited in scope. However, detractors of pluralism, such as Richard Hamilton and Robert Paul Wolff, claim it is ironic that a doctrine that defines the public in terms of issue publics neglects two facts: many people do not belong to any groups at all, and marginal groups often have difficulty making themselves heard in the determination of public policy.[1] Many important segments of society—for example, the poor or consumers—often lack the financial resources and organizational skills to protect their interests effectively vis-a-vis opposing groups in the political system. While pluralists insist that the citizenry is divided into various issue groups, critics maintain that these interest publics can never become mobilized enough to play a prominent role in formulating policy.

The argument that pluralism ignores the wishes of numerous interests in society raises what are analytically three separate questions. First of all, to determine if most groups are represented in a pluralistic system of decision making, we need to ask if members of issue publics are likely to join either temporary, ad hoc movements or organized groups to achieve their objectives. While some critics accept the fact that society is divided into numerous issue publics, they argue that very few individuals will translate their potential interests into active political behavior. Mancur Olson, for instance, has claimed that it is not rational for individuals to join organizations even though the associations are pursuing objectives they would like to see realized. [2]

Secondly, we need to determine whether the members of issue publics that do join groups represent a cross-section of the population at large. Richard Hamilton has argued that minority-related associations and associations seeking to institute consumer or environmental reforms are likely to experience difficulty in recruiting stable and loyal memberships. Unlike many other types of organizations, consumer or public interest groups are concerned with securing public goods rather than private benefits, and as a consequence, the number of incentives they can use to recruit prospective members is extremely limited. Poverty organizations face equally severe recruitment problems in that they must attempt to attract people who have limited skills in working with organizations and limited expectations that such activities will bring meaningful political change.

Finally, even if individuals are willing to join minority action or consumer associations, we need to ask if they will be able to wield any substantial power in the formulation of public policy. Even if potential groups become activated, the problem of gaining access to important centers of decision making still remains. To meet these criticisms, a pluralist must show how the distinct problems of organizational membership and organizational access can be resolved. In this chapter and the one that follows, I will examine each of the above points in turn.

Potential Groups and Active Members

To defend a pluralistic theory of politics, we need to show that citizens will join or support groups if they feel their interests are threatened. To argue that power should be shared by political elites and the various issue publics in society assumes that these segments of the population can become active in politics when issues of concern to them are being debated. The reason for using the word "can" is that potential groups do not always have to become mobilized in order to wield influence. As Truman has pointed out, the possibility that an issue public will clamor for change may encourage political elites or opposing groups to accommodate the wishes of unorganized citizens despite their lack of overt activity.[3] However, for interest-group politics to be effective over the long run, we also need to demonstrate that potential groups actually become mobilized, rather than merely threaten to do so.

If we look at events in recent American politics, we find repeated examples of issue publics joining temporary, ad hoc associations, or what James Q. Wilson has called "movements," in order to press for political change.[4] Perhaps the most dramatic instances are the civil rights movement and the antiwar movement of the 1960s, which recruited a small yet highly committed number of citizens to support their respective causes. Similarly, there seems to be evidence that the Drug Amendment Act of 1962, the Auto Safety Act, and the various clean air and water bills of the last decade passed Congress because of lobbying by temporary and amorphous issue publics who felt strongly about these issues.[5] In a discussion of these legislative acts, Wilson has noted that each bill "represented not the triumph of an organization, but rather the successful mobilization of a new, usually temporary, political constituency."[6] Members of issue publics do not necessarily become mobilized overnight. In many cases there will have to be a dramatic crisis— such as the thalidomide disaster of the 1960s or a new investigation by Ralph Nader—to galvanize people into pushing for social change. On other occasions mobilization may require "no crisis but only the successful appeal, often through adroit use of the mass media, by a policy entrepreneur," to the relevant issue public.[7] Policy entrepreneurs who can capture the headlines can not only provide issue publics with necessary information, but also goad them into action; e.g., Martin Luther King had a flair for dramatizing the cause of equal rights that stimulated many previously acquiescent black people to actively seek the repeal of segregation laws in the South.

But showing that there are numerous examples of people joining or supporting temporary political associations or movements seeking change still leaves open the question of whether members of issue publics will also be willing to join full-time, permanent groups. For a pluralistic system of politics to function properly, organized groups, as well as more amorphous movements, should have a prominent voice in the policy-making process. The evidence on both the present degree of individual participation and the possibility of increased participation in ongoing group activities is somewhat inconclusive, but at least it provides us with some standards for evaluating the merits or defects of a pluralistic approach to democracy. It also indicates that people's propensity to join groups has changed over time. In 1953, a National Opinion Research Center study of membership in voluntary associations found slightly more than half the population (52 percent) belonged to at least one organization. Similar research in subsequent years showed membership in one or more organizations to fluctuate: 1954 Gallup poll, 55 percent; 1955 NORC, 46 percent; 1960 NORC, 57 percent; 1963 study by Gabriel Almond and Sidney Verba, 57 percent. And a 1972 study by Sidney Verba and Norman Nie found that 62 percent of the public was affiliated with at least one organized group, that 39 percent belonged to more than one organization, and that roughly 40 percent claimed to play an active, rather than nominal, role in their association. [8]

Whether these figures are large or small depends on one's perspective. If one is a participatory democrat and believes that everyone should participate in some form of association or community, then admittedly these statistics will appear inadequate. However, if one compares the number of people who are group members with the number of people who vote in presidential elections, the percentages are roughly comparable. To argue that low membership rates in organized groups undermines a pluralistic theory of democracy raises the issue of how many people need to abstain or support established organizations before pluralism is either undermined or reinforced. We must keep in mind that pluralism has never shared participatory democracy's belief in the beneficial results of highly intensive forms of participation. Because people have diverse and restricted interests, their desire to immerse themselves totally in political and social affairs is likely to be limited. Pluralists believe that if the actual opportunities for individuals to influence the community are enhanced, then participation is apt to increase dramatically. But even though added incentives are likely to stimulate more people to take part in group affairs, many individuals will no doubt always want to restrict both the degree and the scope of their political and social participation.

The above data also indicate that in the last twenty years there has been a sizable increase in the number of people affiliated with organized groups. While the NORC studies of the early 1950s found that from 46 to 52 percent of the public were members of secondary associations, the more recent studies indicate that an additional 10 to 16 percent have become joiners. Why this trend is developing is difficult to say, but it appears that individual membership in organizations is related to a host of environmental variables. Research by Almond and Verba and by Kornhauser indicated that participation in group activities increases as the degree of education and the socioeconomic status of the individual rise.[9] Hence more individuals are likely to join groups as they acquire more education and improve their economic standing. Similarly, structural or political variables seem to explain why people elect to join organizations. The comparative literature on interest groups suggests that individual membership in organizations is directly related to the degree of modernization of a society. Gabriel Almond and Bingham Powell have argued that whereas in the past a few kinship organizations could satisfy most people's demands, a modernized society requires innumerably more organizations to cater to its vastly more numerous and complex needs.[10] By the very nature of a modernized community, the increasing differentiation of tasks fragments society into a large number of groups needed to provide important services for the survival of the political community.[11] In addition to increasing the need for new groups, modernization also makes it easier for groups to become organized. As people become more mobile and the problem of communication declines, it becomes easier for individuals who share common concerns to join organizations seeking political or social change. Finally, the specific actions of the government have spawned the creation of numerous new groups. As David Apter has remarked, the growth of the social welfare state in the last couple of decades has stimulated the development of many new organizations. Or as

H. R. Mahood has observed, the growth of government intervention in the field of labor relations and business regulation has resulted in the proliferation of whole new organizations.[12] While
interest-group activity often stimulates government action in the
first place, government-sponsored programs often reciprocally
stimulate the growth of groups to contest, monitor, or support
government action.

In short, the extent to which a nation becomes a nation of joiners
may depend on a variety of factors, including the level of income
and education of its citizens, the degree of modernity or complexity
of its political system, and the scope of its government programs
for dealing with important social and economic issues. The higher
a nation scores on each of the above factors, the more likely its
citizens will engage in some form of interest-group activity. Given
the fact that over time our political and economic institutions are
becoming increasingly differentiated and complex and our citizens
are becoming better educated, it seems likely that more people
will join secondary associations in the future.

The Problem of Marginal and Public Interest Groups

While there are a variety of reasons for believing that organizational membership will grow in the future, we need to ask if rising
membership levels will also characterize public interest groups and
marginal, or poverty, associations. Although group activity might
increase, it might very well work to the disadvantage of certain
key elements in society. Thus instead of asking whether we are a
nation of joiners, we need to ask whether we are a nation that will
join reform or so-called promotional interest groups. If only certain
kinds of organizations are likely to be successful in attracting members, then the interplay of interest groups in a pluralistic form of
democracy may work to the detriment of numerous people in the
political system.

Mancur Olson suggests in an extremely insightful and provocative book, *The Logic of Collective Action,* that poverty groups or
public interest associations will have considerable difficulty in
attracting a sufficient number of supporters.[13] He insists that only
certain kinds of interest groups are likely to develop effective or-

ganizations: those with limited membership and those which have either the resources to provide selective inducements to their rank and file or the authority to apply legal sanctions against their natural membership.[14] Like many other economists, Olson posits a traditional utilitarian picture of man as a rational, self-interested individual who seeks to minimize the costs while maximizing the benefits associated with his every course of action. Unless a group can provide positive benefits to the individual or invoke negative sanctions against him, the rational, self-interested person will have no incentive to support an association actively even though he may fully agree with its objectives. Borrowing from the terminology of public finance, Olson notes that groups provide their members with "public goods." That is, once a good is created, there is no way of excluding others from obtaining its benefits. While an individual may share with many other people a common interest in acquiring a certain collective benefit, he does not share with them a desire to pay the cost for providing the good. The rational person knows that if the group secures the desired objective, he will receive its benefits regardless of whether he bears any of the cost necessary to realize the objective in the first place. Since the individual is likely to enjoy the benefits of group action whether he contributes or not, he has no incentive to support or join the organization. In addition, the individual may find it irrational to support a group activity if he discerns no perceptible effect of his activities on either the burden or benefit accruing to the other members of the association.

Olson admits that these difficulties are less severe in small groups. The smaller the organization, the easier it becomes for the individual to gauge the impact of his actions on the success or failure of the group's activities. Also, the smaller the organization, the greater the likelihood that the individual "will find that his personal gain from having the collective good exceeds the total cost of providing some amount of the collective good."[15] Therefore in small groups we are apt to find members actively advancing the cause of the organization since each individual is likely to receive a substantial portion of the public good merely because there are so few members with whom he has to share the desired benefits. Ample incentives thus exist for the rank and file to support the cause of the group enthusiastically. But even in small organizations,

Olson argues, the amount of the public good secured by the group may be suboptimal. The optimal amount of a collective good for an individual to obtain occurs when "the rate of gain to the group, multiplied by the fraction of the group gain the individual gets equals the rate of increase of the total cost of the collective good."[16] However, according to Olson's assumptions, the individual's decision to join a group and provide a portion of its public good is determined by the relationship between the marginal costs and benefits associated with his actions. There is no incentive for a person to independently provide any of the collective good once the amount that would be purchased by the individual receiving the largest fraction of group value is available. When the size of the group increases, the willingness of the individual to support the organization's objectives declines even more, for as the group becomes larger, the fraction of benefits that accrues to each member simultaneously becomes smaller.

There are, however, two factors that can offset this tendency of individuals to abstain from supporting organizations whose goals they may happen to agree with. First, Olson points out that an interest group can employ legal sanctions or coercion to force a person to support its activities.[17] Labor unions, for example, often rely on compulsory membership as a means of forcing potential constituents to further the common objectives that most working people supposedly seek to realize. Secondly, Olson argues that an interest group may try to elicit popular support for its activities by providing selective inducements to its constituents that are not necessarily related to the organization's central objectives.[18] For instance, a labor union might offer special privileges to its members—such as cut-rate air fares abroad—as a way of cementing an individual's commitment to the organization. While the central objectives of an interest group may be classified as public goods, the selective inducements that it offers to its members are personal, non-collective goods. Unless an organization provides some individualized benefits to its members, there will be no incentive for people to support an association whose central benefits they would enjoy whether they were members not.

The implications of Olson's argument do not seem to augur well for the success of either public interest groups or poverty associations. He insists that to mobilize a latent or potential group, individuals need to be either legally coerced or provided with non-collective benefits. Since it is obvious that poverty associations or consumer groups cannot legally force anyone to join their organizations, their only possibility of attracting supporters—at least according to Olson's assumptions—is to offer selective inducements to their potential members. However, marginal groups often have negligible resources for providing such kinds of benefits. Their ability to rely on side payments or selective inducements to win supporters may thus be contingent on some form of outside assistance.

Before developing this line of inquiry, we need to ask if Olson's theory of interest groups adequately explains group behavior. The availability of selective inducements may not be the only factor determining how successful reform interests will be in recruiting supporters. Olson is probably correct in arguing that organizations like labor unions have an easier time recruiting new members when they can offer positive benefits or impose negative sanctions on their potential supporters. But as Brian Barry has perceptively pointed out, such an analysis does not account for the significantly different levels of union membership in various countries at different points in time.[19] It is well known that there is a higher level of support for union activity in England than in the United States, but certainly we cannot explain why unions are more successful in attracting followers in England merely by analyzing how many selective inducements they have at their disposal. Similarly, the notion of selective inducements does not seem very successful in explaining why mass unionism in England developed when it did and why it declined precipitously in the late 1920s.[20] On the contrary, to account fully for the success or failure of groups to attract members, we need to include other variables in our analysis. For instance, the reason people might be more willing to join unions in England is that they perceive the prospects for collective action to be better. In contrast, when they experience failure, as occurred during the General Strike of the 1920s, they may decide to abstain from further union activity. In either case, the overall prospects of group action—rather than the portion of the public good or the amount of selective inducements received by the individual—may account for the success or failure of groups to recruit new members.[21]

As a further means of confirming this hypothesis, we might ask why some cities seem to have more group activity than others or why certain marginal groups seem especially active in some regions but not in others. As we have seen, Olson has no way to account for these differences except to refer to the legal sanctions or selective inducements various organizations might offer to their members. However, if we look at the literature on urban politics, an alternative explanation appears. Edward Banfield finds that the structure of city politics, rather than the inducements of groups, accounts for the degree of interest-group activity. Banfield argues that interest groups are active in a city like Chicago because the decision-making process there is extremely fragmented and open. [22] As the prospects of influencing the political process increase, so does a group's ability to attract new members. Another way we might illustrate this same point is to ask why a marginal group like the John Birch Society was more active in southern California in the early 1960s than in other parts of the country. There is no apparent reason for believing that the selective inducements the John Birch Society offered its members were necessarily higher in this area than elsewhere. Indeed, a study of the radical right by Raymond Wolfinger et al. maintained that individuals were encouraged to join extremely conservative organizations in a region like southern California because their activities were likely to succeed. [23] Since California has never had a strong party system, conservative groups have been able to wield significant influence in the political arena, which has meant that such groups have been able to attract even greater support.

If the insights of Barry, Banfield, and Wolfinger are correct, we need to modify Olson's model of group behavior. Regardless of the selective inducements or legal sanctions available to the group, an organization may have no trouble attracting supporters if its chances of political success appear reasonable. An individual may be willing to join an interest group that has some prospects of success even though he would be able to share in the benefits it secured without having to join the organization in the first place. Similarly, if the prospects for collective action are a factor affecting the recruitment efforts of groups, we must realize that our earlier distinction between the problem of organizational membership and

that of organizational access is purely an analytic one. The degree
to which an organization can wield political influence may determine in part the degree to which it can recruit an active membership. When we discuss in greater detail how the political process
can be made more receptive to the demands of reform interests, we
need to keep in mind that any such actions may likewise strengthen
the internal organization of the reform groups in question. The
more effectively a public interest group can make its voice heard
in the councils of government, the greater is the possibility that it
will recruit more supporters, which in turn will increase its effectiveness.

Besides overlooking the fact that the success of an organization
may affect both the number and enthusiasm of its supporters,
Olson has also failed to realize that his theory of group behavior
rests on an extremely narrow view of human motivation. Olson
has carefully constructed his argument around a view of man as a
rational, self-interested individual.[24] In contrast, I have pictured
man as a more social animal with distinctly limited interests as
well as limited rationality and limited knowledge of his own actions. While so far I have refrained from explicitly discussing
whether an individual's specific interests and knowledge are used
for purely personal or for more inclusive ends, there seems to be
ample evidence to indicate that people often join groups for what
they consider to be altruistic ends. Olson would no doubt insist
that his assumptions of individual self-interest and rationality are
responsible for the predictive power of his theory, but these assumptions seem to limit his ability to explain the behavior of groups
like Common Cause or Nader's Raiders.

From examining studies of voting behavior as well as from
observing the commitment of people in so-called public interest
groups, we can argue that political behavior is not solely motivated
by self-interest. As mentioned earlier, *The American Voter* found
that a significant number of individuals exercise their right to vote
because they feel that it is their public duty to do so. For similar
reasons many people might join public interest groups because
they feel they ought to take an active part in political affairs. Olson
himself concedes this very point, but he tries to minimize its importance by arguing that even if individuals were altruistic, rather

than self-interested, they would still not support certain kinds of groups out of purely utilitarian calculations. As Olson puts it, "even if the member of a large group were to neglect his own interest entirely, he still would not rationally contribute toward the provision of a collective good or public good since his own contribution would not be perceptible."[25] However, Barry has pointed out that this argument seems fallacious: "If each contribution is literally 'imperceptible,' how can all the contributions together add up to anything?"[26] If the efforts of ten thousand members of Common Cause add up to something, then the contribution of each member must on the average equal one ten-thousandth of the total effort. Furthermore, if all Olson means in the preceding context is that people would not be rational in supporting an organization that has no prospects of being effective, we can certainly agree with him. As hopefully I have shown, individuals are more likely to join an interest group when its prospects for success are enhanced. Regardless of the shifts or alterations in his argument, Olson does not seem very willing to accept the fact that many people are currently supporting organizations like Common Cause for what appear to be altruistic reasons. While it is possible that the consumer-environmental movement may be short-lived, at present many individuals do seem willing to work for groups that seek to realize public, rather than narrowly defined private, interests.

However, even if we insist that a sense of individual duty or altruism may complement or even substitute for the factors Olson focuses on, we must recognize that marginal groups may still have a difficult time recruiting members. The problem of organizational recruitment will probably affect poverty groups more severely than it will more middle-class reform groups. In order to support an organization out of a sense of duty, an individual must be willing to incur certain costs. Whether one contributes his evenings to the activities of the group or merely offers a monetary donation, any kind of organizational membership imposes burdens on the individual. As might be expected, these burdens are likely to weigh more heavily, the lower down on the socioeconomic scale we go. Consumer or environmental groups that recruit members primarily from the relatively affluent layers of the upper middle class are likely to be more successful than poverty or marginal groups in attracting a committed following. Only when people have sufficient resources at their disposal are they able to afford the cost of acting in an altruistic fashion. When organizations of the poor seek to win support for their activities from lower economic neighborhoods, they are likely to find that very few individuals can afford the luxury of public service. Moreover, as Kenneth Clark and other observers of the ghetto have noted, people who live in slums often suffer from feelings of inadequacy and self-hatred. Their ability to widen their horizons and to support group programs that will eventually benefit them is thus likely to be limited. As the cost of engaging in collective action increases, it should be expected that fewer people will elect to spend their time supporting group activities. Regardless of their motives, individuals in marginal groups may find that the cost of supporting organized efforts to secure reforms from the bottom up is prohibitively high.

The obvious problem we must face is how to provide the poor with sufficient incentive so that they can engage in interest-group activity. Left to their own resources, marginal groups are not likely to organize themselves effectively for political action. A laissez-faire version of pluralism, which believes the poor are yet another potential group that will become organized when conditions warrant it, fails to recognize the complexity of the problem. Only when some form of outside assistance is provided to marginal groups will the poor be able to afford the cost of lobbying for collective goods.

Thus a public form of pluralism, which advocates government assistance to poverty organizations, may be essential if marginal groups are ever to become mobilized. Once poverty or Community Action programs are established and funded by government agencies, the poor will be able to afford the luxury of pursuing objectives that will collectively benefit the residents of ghetto areas. While at present there are very few poor people who can altruistically donate their time and energy to group activities, a government-sponsored program of organizing people from the bottom up will significantly reduce the costs such individuals must incur in pursuit of political change. In addition, the resources various government agencies would dispense under a federally financed poverty program could be used by poverty associations as selective inducements to recruit even more supporters. As we all know, old-time political machines often relied on a variety of patronage jobs in order to develop an effective instrument for achieving political objectives. If a sufficient amount of funds can be funneled to poverty groups, there is no reason why such associations cannot provide similar benefits. When adequate resources are available to poverty associations, they too can rely on personal, non-collective rewards as a means of strengthening their internal organizations. Finally, a public form of pluralism may also help to lessen the psychological tendencies of self-hatred that often characterize individuals who live in situations of deprivation.[27] If the federal government assists members of the poor to mobilize themselves, it may help eliminate the psychological, as well as the political and economic, causes of poverty. Unless individuals have the opportunity to wield power, they will always feel powerless. When the poor have assistance in organizing themselves, they are likely to acquire both the confidence and the skills prerequisite for successful political action; but when they must fend for themselves, their psychological and economic dependence may prevent them from collectively pursuing objectives that individually they would no doubt support.

NOTES

1. Robert Paul Wolff, Barrington Moore, Jr. and Herbert Marcuse, *A Critique of Pure Tolerance*, pp. 3-53; Richard Hamilton, *Class and Politics in the United States*, pp. 35-46.

2. Mancur Olson, Jr., *The Logic of Collective Action*.

3. David Truman, *The Governmental Process*, p. 114.

4. James Q. Wilson, *Political Organizations*, p. 7.

5. Ibid., p. 335.

6. Ibid.

7. Ibid.

8. The 1953, 1955, and 1960 studies by the National Opinion Research Center and the 1954 Gallup poll are analyzed in more detail in Hamilton, *Class and Politics in the United States*, pp. 37, 67. See also Gabriel Almond and Sidney Verba, *The Civic Culture*, p. 247; and Sidney Verba and Norman Nie, *Participation in America*, pp. 41-42.

9. Almond and Verba, *Civic Culture*, pp. 186-207; William Kornhauser, *The Politics of Mass Society*, p. 68.

10. Gabriel Almond and Bingham Powell, *Comparative Politics*, pp. 255-98. See also David Apter and Harry Eckstein, *Comparative Politics*, p. 389.

11. Almond and Powell, *Comparative Politics*, pp. 299-333.

12. Apter and Eckstein, *Comparative Politics*, p. 389; H. R. Mahood, ed., *Pressure Groups in American Politics*.

13. Olson, *Logic of Collective Action*.

14. Ibid., pp. 53-76.

15. Ibid., pp. 48-50, 53-76.

16. Ibid., p. 24.

17. Ibid., pp. 66-75.

18. Ibid., pp. 132-33.

19. Brian M. Barry, *Sociologists, Economists and Democracy*, p. 29.

20. Ibid., p. 29.

21. Ibid.

22. Edward C. Banfield, *Political Influence*, pp. 235-306.

23. Raymond E. Wolfinger, Barbara K. Wolfinger, Kenneth Prewitt, and Sheila Rosenhach, "America's Radical Right: Politics and Ideology," pp. 262-93.

24. Olson, *Logic of Collective Action*, p. 64.

25. Ibid.

26. Barry, *Sociologists, Economists and Democracy*, p. 32.

27. Kenneth B. Clark, *Dark Ghetto*, pp. 63-80.

Chapter

6

Pluralism and the
Problem of Group Access

As we have seen in the preceding chapter, individuals like Richard Hamilton have attacked a pluralistic form of democracy because they believe that many persons presently belong to no groups at all. Other commentators, such as Elmer Eric Schattschneider, Peter Bachrach, and Morton Baratz, criticize pluralism for ignoring the fact that many interest groups have difficulty gaining access to important centers of decision making. [1] These critics tend to write off pluralism as an inequitable form of democratic government because they believe it provides relatively few opportunities for the less affluent and less well-educated to defend their interests. The point at issue here is that even if the various issue publics in society do become organized, they are not likely to wield any appreciable degree of influence. "The flaw in the pluralistic heaven," Schattschneider argues, "is that the heavenly chorus sings with a strong upper-class accent." [2] Although he does not cite actual evidence, Schattschneider insists that "probably about 90 percent of the people cannot get into the pressure system." [3] Similarly, Bachrach and Baratz criticize pluralism for overlooking the "important area of what we have called nondecision making, that is, the practice of limiting the scope of actual decision-making to 'safe' issues by manipulating the dominant community values, myths, and political institutions and procedures." They maintain that the "mobilization of bias" in any community, that is, the organization and direction of society's values, often works to the disadvantage of marginal or promotional groups who wish to place their demands on the public agenda.[4] Finally, Robert Paul Wolff insists that even if marginal interests gain access to the bargaining arena, the rules of group competition are likely to frustrate any demands for social change.[5] Wolff believes that the disparities in resources between well-entrenched, established groups and so-called reform groups are so great that the prospects for meaningful bargaining and compromise are slim indeed.

Whether such criticism of pluralism is warranted is the question that will be examined in this chapter. As we shall soon see, it is possible to argue that many of the critics have not been very careful in specifying why they think pluralism has inherently conservative tendencies. First of all, a number of commentators have not specifically stated whether the alleged "conservative bias" of pluralism is primarily a theoretical or practical problem.[6] If one argues that certain key groups are systematically discriminated against under a pluralistic form of democracy, one needs to specify whether the problems are inherent in the theory of pluralism or in the practice of American politics. It is certainly plausible to argue, as do Bachrach and Baratz, that the dominant values in society may limit the range of issues that a political system is willing to consider. But this fact of political life may and probably will hamper the efforts of any theory of democracy—whether it be populism, polyarchy, or pluralism—to respond adequately to demands for reforms that go against prevailing norms. While what Bachrach and Baratz call the mobilization of bias may work to the disadvantage of marginal groups in a pluralistic form of democracy, it may also prevent majorities from voting on "unsafe issues" in populist referendums. Or it may even prevent Lowi's reform-oriented elites from entertaining legislative proposals that threaten to upset well-engrained patterns of behavior. The problem of overcoming cultural norms that reflect and reinforce disparities in power among different elements in society is not a difficulty unique to any one form of democracy, let alone pluralism.

Given the unwillingness of pluralism's detractors to sort out the normative, as opposed to empirical, claims of pluralism, it is all the more essential for us to differentiate carefully between these various kinds of assumptions. As simple as the point may seem, many commentators either ignore it altogether or concede its existence while ignoring its importance in discussing the merits or drawbacks of pluralism. To evaluate pluralism fairly, we must analyze how the doctrine prescriptively responds to the demands of groups that are not necessarily in the mainstream of American politics. This chapter will show that normatively both laissez-faire and public pluralists do not favor restricting any interests, let alone marginal interests, from placing their demands on the public agenda. (As pointed out in chapter 2, only corporate pluralism advocates limiting the number of groups that may participate in the decision-making arena). In addition, I will argue—the claims of critics like Wolff notwithstanding—that the criteria that both laissez-faire and public pluralists believe should govern the settlement of policy issues do not necessarily penalize or favor the demands of any group, including poverty or consumer action groups.

Secondly, this chapter will examine in more detail why pluralists believe that the political system is flexible enough to accommodate the wishes of reform-oriented interest groups. In particular, it will be necessary to determine whether the considerations that laissez-faire and public pluralists believe should determine who prevails in a dispute—such as the intensity of a group's demands—do in fact govern the settlement of issues. If there is some discrepancy between the operations of the political system and the norms pluralism advocates, I will try to show how a public form of pluralism can tilt the partisan give-and-take among groups to the advantage of interests that presently have little or no power. If marginal elements lack access to important centers of power, there is certainly no compelling reason why the resources of those particular groups cannot be altered through federal sponsorship and supervision of interest-group interaction. Finally, instead of simply defending pluralism against the charge that it necessarily excludes marginal groups like the poor, this chapter will make the counterargument that pluralism may in fact be the only feasible method for such groups to acquire influence over public policy. I will argue that the discrepancies in resources between consumer-environmental groups and large business organizations are likely to be minimized when the two parties can bargain directly with legislative and bureaucratic institutions instead of having to win mass support in public referendums.

The Normative Component of Pluralistic Democracy

Before examining in more detail why some pluralists argue empirically that the political system is open and responsive to the needs of most groups in society, we need to analyze how a pluralist prescriptively believes the political system should react to the demands of previously unorganized or inactive groups. If we may rephrase Schattschneider's comments, there may be nothing wrong in the "pluralistic heaven"; the problems may arise in the more prosaic, empirical earth below. As a way of illustrating this point, it should be noted that pluralism—like any other theory of democracy—must take a normative stand on what are analytically two separate issues. Roger Cobb and Charles Elder have conveniently called the first problem one of *agenda setting;* and for purposes of symmetry we may call the second problem one of *agenda resolution.*[7] By agenda setting, I mean that any theory of democracy must decide how and for what reasons it wishes to let various groups place demands on the political system. Polyarchal democrats like Herbert McClosky and Gabriel Almond have argued that in the interest of stability the government should attempt to restrict the number of demands that the public can place on the political system.[8] Laissez-faire and public pluralists, as we shall soon see, argue otherwise. Besides taking a stand on the issue of agenda setting, a theory of democracy must also articulate a set of principles for resolving disputes over alternative policies. This is the problem that I have chosen to call agenda resolution. Once a proposal is on the public agenda, we need to ask what criteria will be used in either rejecting or accepting its suggestions for some kind of policy alteration.

If we look first at the problem of agenda setting, we can argue that neither laissez-faire nor public pluralism can be accused of normatively justifying the exclusion of any group from the political process. Both laissez-faire and public pluralists believe that the effectiveness of public policy can be greatly enhanced by multiplying, rather than limiting, the number of decision makers. As pointed out in chapter 2, the best made plans often go awry because no one set of policy makers can anticipate—let alone prepare for— all the contingencies that might surround the alteration of an existing policy. [9] Therefore both laissez-faire and public pluralists advocate opening up the process of agenda setting, since by increasing the number of actors who have some say in the formulation of public decisions, the defects in a policy that might be overlooked by one set of decision makers can be pointed out by alternative participants.

In addition, laissez-faire and public pluralists insist that all groups must have some say in the policy-making process if they are to arrive at an accurate assessment of their own needs. As noted in chapter 3, while theories of representative democracy such as polyarchy often assume that political officials can act in the best interests of their constituents without consulting them, pluralism believes there is a subjective side to people's welfare that necessitates public participation in the political process. [10] People's demands cannot always be objectively known in an a priori fashion as individuals often come to a realization of what they wish to accomplish only in the process of negotiating and bargaining with opposing interests. Thus the public agenda cannot be arbitrarily determined by a set of political elites even if they have the most praiseworthy intentions of furthering the welfare of their constituents. In dealing with the problem of agenda setting, the models of pluralism we have been looking at seek to expand, rather than restrict, the opportunities for any group to gain a hearing of its demands. In order both to increase the rationality of public planning and to accurately define the needs of the different interests in society, laissez-faire and public pluralists normatively advocate the creation of a form of decision making in which all groups can easily air their objections to existing policy.

If we now turn to the question of agenda resolution, we can likewise argue that neither of the above two forms of pluralism necessarily benefits nor works to the disadvantage of any particular group in society. Contrary to what critics like Wolff imply, pluralism does not normatively believe that the wealth an interest group can command, nor the amount of raw political power it can mobilize, nor even the number of voters it can attract should be the determining factor in resolving a dispute. While Wolff insists that pluralists advocate a vector-sum theory of decision making, in which decisions are the result of the organized pressure brought to bear on public officials, the situation in reality is far more complex. [11] As indicated earlier, pluralists believe a variety of factors— including the intensity of feeling of a particular group—should determine how an issue is resolved. [12] For example, while chemical companies or oil refineries may be able to mobilize more resources than environmental groups, a pluralist would not necessarily argue that pollution laws should be tailored to business needs. Depending on the intensity of feeling of consumer or environmental interests, government officials should reject the demands of the more powerful business community. Similarly, if blacks feel intensely about integrating certain businesses from which they have previously been excluded, a pluralist would argue that a prima facie case exists for changing present policy. However, in an alternative situation, in which whites feel very intensely about a proposed modification in community living patterns and blacks are indifferent, a pluralist might agree that radical change need not be instituted. The pluralist criterion of group intensity is a standard for resolving agenda disputes that may or may not benefit the interests of environmental or community action groups. The key issue is how seriously the contending parties feel about the particular matter in question. If groups like the Sierra Club or Common Cause or SCLC are intensely interested in preserving or altering certain business or government practices, then the two forms of pluralism we have been discussing would be highly receptive to their demands.

However, if a pluralist encountered a situation in which a variety of parties felt equally intensely about the outcome of a particular policy, he would argue that other criteria—for example, the protection of liberal rights or the egalitarian notion of guaranteeing some minimal benefits to all parties—should be employed to resolve group differences. By minimal benefits to all parties, I mean the standard Lindblom has described: no group should ever be completely shut out of the decision-making process. [13] Both laissez-faire and public pluralists would argue that each group should have "its turn" to influence the shape of public policy. Regardless of how intensely any one specific interest may feel about a particular issue, a pluralist would argue that no group should be given veto power if other groups are similarly concerned about the outcome of the same issue; public policies should guarantee at least some minimal values to interests seeking redress of their grievances. In contrast to a populist form of democracy in which referendums render decisions of a zero-sum nature, laissez-faire and public pluralism seek to resolve disputes between equally intense groups in a nonexclusive manner.

The adequacy of using egalitarian norms to resolve policy disputes, however, may be limited to certain kinds of issues. It is possible to argue that one could settle a disagreement between equally intense groups in an egalitarian fashion only if the dispute involves what Theodore Lowi has called a "distributive" policy, i.e., a policy that is "characterized by the ease with which [it] can be disaggregated and dispensed unit by small unit, each unit more or less in isolation from the other units."[14] In any disagreement over a distributive issue, it is possible for the contending parties never to come directly into conflict with one another in resolving their dispute.[15] For instance, the question of what kind of transportation services a municipality should provide its citizens could be classified as a distributive issue. If two different groups felt intensely about whether public or private transport should be emphasized, each interest could alternate in an egalitarian fashion in deciding how and where the city allocated its resources for transit improvement. In one fiscal year, the city might buy more buses while in another year it might allocate its funds to improve off-street parking for privately operated cars. No one group would dominate the way in which the community utilized its resources; every group would be guaranteed the right to receive some minimal benefits.

However, if two different parties disagree intensely over what is basically a redistributive issue, then the inadequacy of using egalitarian norms to settle disputes becomes readily apparent. For instance, if an issue involved the demand of minority groups to settle in previously all-white areas, a community could not alternately desegregate and then resegregate the same neighborhood. It is impossible to argue that each group should have its chance to determine public policy on the issue in question if the issue itself cannot be disaggregated. By their very nature redistributive policies necessitate substantial compromises from one party or another.[16] But when neither the intensity of a group's demands nor the norm of egalitarianism provides sufficient grounds for resolving all possible political disputes, what other criteria can a laissez-faire or public pluralist espouse? If the problem involves a question of minority rights, a pluralist can be expected to defend the essential liberal freedoms of all groups. Even if both blacks and whites feel equally intensely about a redistributive issue like segregated housing, a pluralist would insist that the protection of certain basic liberties should dictate that the issue be resolved to the benefit of the minority group. However, when issues like civil rights elicit intense reaction from opposing parties, a pluralist would argue that some compensatory rewards should be granted to the party forced to make substantial compromises. While two groups may feel equally intensely about the same issue, they may have different reasons for feeling strongly about the matter, which creates the possibility of developing a compromise settlement that is not completely unpalatable to the losing group. Whites may resist integration of their communities because they may feel that it will lead to the physical deterioration of their neighborhoods; but if a community upholds the right of minorities to live where they please, it can offer to increase the degree of city services to the neighborhood being integrated, or it can offer tax concessions to those property owners who have resisted a change in the status quo. Through a process of logrolling, distributive benefits can be granted to those interests which are forced to make substantial concessions on a redistributive issue. Thus if groups disagree intensely on a redistributive issue that involves civil rights or liberties, it is essential that liberal values be upheld; but by providing some distributive rewards to those groups which are required to compromise their position on the issue in question, the political system can try in an egalitarian fashion to guarantee some minimal benefits to all interests.

On the basis of the above discussion, we can see that the criteria a laissez-faire or public pluralist would normatively use both to define the public agenda and to resolve matters of dispute would not necessarily work to the detriment of any specific group in society. By alternately permitting different parties to decide distributive issues or by granting some minimal level of benefits to groups that lose on redistributive issues, these models of pluralism would attempt to prevent any set of interests from being permanently excluded from the political process.

The Empirical Component of Pluralistic Democracy

While both laissez-faire and public pluralists agree in a normative sense that no set of interests should be denied the opportunity to influence the content of public policy, they disagree empirically on how open or closed the political system presently is to the demands of so-called public interest groups or other marginal elements in society. Even though both models of pluralism espouse criteria for agenda setting and agenda resolution that do not discriminate against the demands of reform interests, they differ as to how often various groups actually have an opportunity to shape public policy. As pointed out in chapter 2, laissez-faire pluralists—like Dahl, Cobb and Elder, Kaufman and Sayre, and Banfield—believe that the political system is basically open and receptive to the demands of a wide array of groups. [17] Dahl, in particular, has described the process of agenda building as a flexible one, "in which there is a high probability that an active and legitimate group in the population can make itself heard effectively at some crucial stage in the process of decision [making]." [18] Sayre and Kaufman have echoed a similar theme in their study of New York, arguing that public decisions are usually made in an open and fragmented fashion:

No part of the city's large and varied population is alienated from participation in the system. The channels of access to the points of decision are numerous, and most of them are open to any group alert to the opportunities offered and persistent in pursuit of its objectives. [19]

However, we noted in chapter 2 that a public pluralist would strike a slightly more pessimistic tone. Even though it is possible to agree in part with many of the observations laissez-faire pluralists have made of urban politics, it should be pointed out that the pattern of pluralistic bargaining on both local and national levels often works hardships on marginal or reform interests.[20] While a great variety of groups do enjoy considerable influence in shaping the content of government policy, the mere appearance of group participation often conceals the unequal distribution of power among various interests.

In order to assess the contention of laissez-faire pluralists that the political system is open, it is necessary to examine how they approach the problem. Since each of the authors cited above relies on very different explanations to account for the flexibility of the decision-making process, we must examine the arguments of each in turn. The next section will deal separately with the laissez-faire pluralists, while later sections will deal with the public pluralist critique of their arguments.

Characteristics of Groups

Interestingly enough, while laissez-faire pluralists like Dahl, Cobb and Elder, and Sayre and Kaufman see a high potential for interest-group success, each relies on a different explanation to account for this phenomenon.[21] Dahl focuses on the characteristics of groups—in particular, the resources various groups have at their disposal—to support his belief that the political system is an open one. In contrast to critics like Wolff, who contend that the discrepancies in power among groups are so great that the prospect of meaningful social change is dim, Dahl argues that the political system contains plenty of slack to accommodate a diverse array of demands for change.[22] Although he accepts the charge made by many of pluralism's critics that the resources available to different groups vary immensely, he tends to minimize its political importance by pointing out that inequalities in resources are usually noncumulative in nature.[23] Dahl insists there is no single asset such as wealth or skill that will enable its possessor to dominate the formulation of public policy. Even though some groups may have more financial assets than others, they also may have considerably less social standing or expertise. In terms of the empirical issue of who wields political power, the important question for Dahl is not whether resources are inequitably distributed but whether they are inequitably distributed in a dispersed or concentrated fashion. If a variety of groups possess a surplus of at least one kind of political asset, as is the case in New Haven, the system may be highly receptive to a great variety of demands. When a group employs its resources in an effort to dominate the political system, opposing interests can tap alternative forms of resources in order to thwart such an attempt.

Besides attacking pluralism's critics for not distinguishing between cumulative, as opposed to dispersed, inequalities in assets, Dahl also points out that the size of a group's resources merely indicates the potential, and not the actual, political power that it wields.[24] While many interests may have more potential power than others to affect the direction of public policy, their actual power to shape political decisions may lag behind groups with far fewer resources. In large part this phenomenon occurs for two very different reasons. First, as Dahl convincingly argues, people with very few resources can often exercise more power than those with considerably more assets if they are skillful in investing the resources they do possess. The effectiveness with which a group uses its assets is certainly as important as the number of assets it can marshal. In addition to the skill with which people employ their resources, Dahl insists that a group's willingness to use all or very little of its resources determines in large part who prevails in most disputes. Although certain groups may possess more assets than others, some interests may be willing to spend a larger percentage of their resources to achieve their objectives. In particular, Dahl claims that groups which feel very intensely about a specific issue may be able to exercise considerable power if they are willing to pay a high enough price.[25] In *Who Governs?* he notes that a few hundred enraged members of an Italian working-class neighborhood were able to prevent a group of wealthy businessmen from building a low-cost housing project in the community. While the businessmen, who had close ties with the incumbent mayor, seemed to possess more potential power, the neighborhood, which spent more of its resources to persuade the city council to reject the plans of the developers, wielded more actual power.[26]

The considerations that laissez-faire and public pluralists believe should determine who prevails on a disputed issue—particularly the intensity of a group's demands—may thus on numerous occasions actually decide issues of policy. If a group feels more intensely about a matter than a contending party, it may, as Dahl's example illustrates, be able to use resources more thoroughly to block the requests of a potentially more powerful adversary. Once we recognize that potential power is not the same as actual power, we can argue that the normative and empirical aspects of a laissez-faire theory of pluralism complement one another. When decisions are made in a bargaining fashion, those groups which feel most intensely about a particular issue can translate all of their potential assets into actual political influence. The size or the number of assets a group possesses may be less important than the manner in which it employs them.

The Nature of Group Demands

While Dahl focuses on the characteristics of groups to account for the alleged openness of the political system, Cobb and Elder show how the manner in which a group defines its objectives may be a crucial factor in affecting its success or failure. By drawing heavily on the work of Schattschneider, they argue that the success of an interest may depend less on its own resources than on the influence of the allies it can enlist. [27] Even if resources are noncumulatively distributed, and even if some groups are more willing than others to expend their assets, they may not succeed in placing their demands on the public agenda unless their requests are supported by other elements in society. Thus the manner in which a group articulates its objectives may have a significant bearing on its ability to disarm its opponents and attract potential supporters. For an interest to achieve its objectives, it must try to associate its policies with the symbols of legitimacy in the larger political system, while conversely demonstrating that the wishes of its adversaries fall outside the boundaries of the key values espoused by the political community. [28] Cobb and Elder point out that when a group's demands are seen as legitimate in terms of the symbols prevailing in the political system, the ability of the group to form alliances with other strategically placed elements in society is facilitated, while the flexibility of its opponents is diminished. [29] Depending on how an interest identifies its goals, it may either galvanize its adversaries into open opposition or confuse and divide its opponents while strengthening its own ties with like-minded groups.

For example, if a group finds itself unable to place its demands on the public agenda, it should try to reformulate its objectives in order to widen the arena of conflict and draw more participants into the dispute. Conversely, if an interest finds the political system amenable to its suggestions, it should try to confine any challenge to its power by monopolizing the symbols of legitimacy. While the weaker group wishes to widen the nature of the dispute in the hopes of attracting more allies, the dominant group wants to narrow the definition of the political issue to limit the entry of new parties. If a well-established group can no longer succeed in defining the issues facing the polity, it may be confronted by an array of opposing interests that it can no longer defeat. The leverage an interest group can exercise in society may in large part be dependent on its skill in defining and redefining its objectives as political circumstances change.

Although Cobb and Elder do not explicitly deal with the issue, their work implicitly represents a rejoinder to the neo-elitist critique of pluralism by Bachrach and Baratz.[30] The latter attack pluralistic theories of power for defining the determinants of interest-group success too narrowly. In particular, they severely criticize pluralists like Dahl for focusing on actual decision making and on the resources interests employ to secure their ends while ignoring other characteristics—or, as they prefer to call it, "other faces of power"—that determine the success or failure of groups. As noted earlier, Bachrach and Baratz insist that the mobilization of bias within a community is a second face of power that greatly influences the way in which a society allocates its values.[31]

However, while Bachrach and Baratz repeatedly use the phrase mobilization of bias, they often seem to employ a variety of definitions to explain the term. On the one hand, they argue that mobilization of bias refers to "a set of predominant values, beliefs, and rituals, and institutional procedures ('rules of the game') that operate systematically and consistently to the benefit of certain persons and groups at the expense of others."[32] They seem to be arguing that the general cultural values of a society will undermine the acceptability of some demands while enhancing and legitimizing others; they imply that any group trying to implement changes that go against the grain of these well-entrenched values is not likely to enjoy much political success. As pointed out earlier, mobilization of bias in this sense suggests that the possibility of achieving any radical social change will be minimal indeed. Regardless of what form of democracy society embraces, the political system is bound to be hostile to unconventional ideas that threaten to undo well-established patterns of behavior.

But Bachrach and Baratz often seem to use the phrase mobilization of bias in a much more limited sense to refer to a group's ability to monopolize community symbols in such a way as to exclude the demands of potential opponents. They note that a form of nondecision making occurs when a group "invokes an existing bias of the political system—a norm, precedent, rule or procedure—to squelch a threatening demand or incipient issue."[33] In this sense Bachrach's and Baratz's argument, like that of Cobb and Elder, can be seen as a reformulation of Schattschneider's observation that the group that defines the nature of the debate will usually emerge victorious. If a group succeeds in monopolistically defining the stakes involved in a dispute, it may be able to drive a wedge between its adversaries while consolidating its own ties with other strategically placed interests. The important question is whether this tactic can be used only to the advantage of conservatively oriented groups.

While Bachrach and Baratz seem to argue that status quo groups will try to use the symbols of the larger society to prevent marginal interests from placing their demands on the public agenda, Cobb and Elder suggest that this tactic may not always succeed. Unlike Bachrach and Baratz, Cobb and Elder contend that there is plenty of slack in the political system to accommodate a diverse array of demands if groups only learn how to dramatize their requests properly.[34] If marginal interests challenge established political norms, they are likely to fail; but if they attempt to couch their demands in terms of more conventional political symbolism, they may be able to achieve a considerable degree of success. For example, in their study of the grape strike, Cobb and Elder note that once Cesar Chavez tried to identify the cause of migrant workers with the goals of organized labor as well as with the civil rights movement, he began to receive considerable moral and financial support from such diverse groups as the AFL-CIO, the Catholic church, and the liberal wing of the Democratic party. By carefully articulating his objectives and expanding the nature of his goals, Chavez was able to enlist the efforts of more established reform interests, which provided the margin of influence his union needed to negotiate successfully with the grape growers. While the symbols of the larger political system may be used by status quo groups to prevent social change, they may—as Cobb and Elder have shown— also be used by marginal interests to institute reform.

The Influence of Government Structure

If laissez-faire pluralists like Dahl stress the noncumulative nature of resources while others like Cobb and Elder focus on the manner in which groups articulate their goals, still others—like Sayre and Kaufman and, to a lesser extent, Banfield—emphasize the structure of government decision making to account for the behavior of the political system. [35] In their study of New York City, Sayre and Kaufman argue that the decentralized nature of the city's decision-making process explains its receptivity to a diverse array of demands. They insist that since there are so many stages at which key decisions are made, no groups can easily be shut out of the political process. If an interest is denied access at one center of decision making, it has numerous other points at which it may try to place its demands on the public agenda. [36] Regardless of how many resources a group possesses, it is likely to be more active in the political process if it perceives numerous opportunities to influence the formulation of public policy. Banfield makes a similar argument in his classic study of Chicago to account for the widespread participation by interest groups in the affairs of Cook County. [37] Banfield notes that despite the attempts of the city machine to centralize power, there are numerous points at which various interests can intervene in the political process. Thus the price a group must pay to publicize its wishes is anything but prohibitive. Because a decentralized style of decision making reduces the costs an interest must incur to participate in the policy-making process, a group is always likely to find some forum to dramatize its requests even though it possesses minimal political or economic resources.

Conversely, as Sayre and Kaufman point out, when the formal authority of a political system is decentralized, it becomes prohibitively costly for any one group to try to shut out the demands of competing interests. In the case of New York City, Sayre and Kaufman observe that at every stage of the policy-making process a variety of "core" and "satellite" groups seem to share responsibility for making public decisions. Depending on the particular issue at hand, different core or government groups bargain and negotiate with a wide assortment of satellite, or private interest groups. In place of one centrally directed political system, there are a whole series of decision-making points at which various core and satellite interests share in the formulation of specific and limited policy issues. [38]

Sayre and Kaufman also argue that a decentralized pattern of decision making tends to facilitate a style of resolving disputes that guarantees at least some minimal benefits to all interests. They note that when power is fragmented, it is often easier for groups to veto proposals than to initiate change. [39] To enact a modification in existing policy, a group must try to form coalitions of similar interests in order to overcome its opponents, or it must be willing to grant some concessions and side payments to those groups which will be affected by the change. The more decentralized the structure of decision making, the greater the chances that the group that wants to satisfy its demands will be willing to grant compensatory benefits to aggrieved interests. As Sayre and Kaufman point out, every decision of importance in New York must be the product of mutual accommodation. Even though interest groups can put together coalitions strong enough to override the wishes of their opposition, the fragmentation of governmental authority provides the losing interest with enough residual power to extract some minimal compensation from the victorious party.

The Limitations of Laissez-faire Pluralism

Laissez-faire pluralists thus insist that whether one focuses on (1) the resources of groups, (2) the symbols they employ to justify their requests, or (3) the actual structure of government decision making, there seems to be sufficient reason for believing that a variety of interests have both the opportunity and the inclination to exercise influence over the shape of public policy.

However, even though laissez-faire pluralists cite numerous examples to substantiate their claim that the political system is receptive to many diverse demands, their findings are open to criticism. First of all, it is necessary to keep in mind that pluralists like Dahl or Sayre and Kaufman have primarily shown that no single elite influences all public decisions. But to demonstrate that multiple parties have some power to influence crucial policy issues is not the same as to prove that marginal groups like the poor or so-called public interest groups can likewise play an important role in the political arena. If one can find several examples of numerous groups participating in the formulation of public decisions, one can easily argue the negative case that the political system is not a closed entity catering only to the needs of a particular few. But to argue in a positive vein that marginal interests do in fact wield influence is a slightly more difficult task. If we wish to maintain that the polity is receptive to the needs of many groups, we need to recognize that there are varying degrees of openness and receptivity. A system that is open to the demands of labor unions and business organizations may not be equally open to the demands of the poor or consumers who wish to complain about the behavior of more established interests. Except for Cobb and Elder, most of the pluralists we have looked at have cited very few examples of groups like poverty or consumer-related associations that actually exercise any degree of influence.

In order to account for the discrepancies between the conclusions of the laissez-faire pluralists and their actual findings, we need to examine their studies in more detail. In many cases, by using the tools of analysis developed by the laissez-faire pluralists, we can show why marginal groups may have trouble gaining access to the political arena. For instance, Dahl argues that because resources are noncumulatively distributed, every major interest is likely to have some bargaining power. Likewise he points out that because potential power is not the same as actual power, groups that feel intensely enough about an issue can often override the wishes of adversaries who are potentially much more influential. While Dahl's observations about how people use their political resources may be correct, it is possible that they are correct only up to a certain point. If we are talking about unions, for example, we can certainly agree that the sheer number of workers was an effective form of political power that labor employed at the polls to curb the actions of the business community. If, in contrast, we attempt to enumerate the noncumulative resources available to the poor, we have a harder time identifying some countervailing assets they can use to defend their interests. The poor possess neither social standing, nor numerous financial assets, nor great numbers of people. It is true that the ability to disrupt the rest of society is in some sense a form of political power. But it is a type of power that I suspect most laissez-faire pluralists would consider unacceptable as a means of securing one's goals. Riots in most cases reflect a breakdown in the bargaining process rather than an alternative form of interest-group give-and-take. In addition, the ability to disrupt society is a form of power that may have only short-run consequences. Even if the poor can dramatize their needs through periodic riots, they may not be able to secure what Murray Edelman has called "tangible benefits" until they acquire more conventional and dependable political resources.[40] By themselves riots are too diffuse a means for any group to obtain benefits from the rest of society.

Similarly, Dahl may be correct in implying that groups which feel very intensely about a specific issue and commit most of their potential resources to it may wield a considerable amount of actual power. Naturally, if the discrepancies in resources between groups are not immense, the party most willing to use its assets is likely to be victorious. However, when marginal groups, which possess only minimal resources to begin with, expend most of their resources to secure their objectives, they still may not be able to exercise a significant degree of political power. Regardless of how totally a group may commit itself to securing its objectives, it may fail to overcome the advantages of its potentially more powerful adversaries if it has very few assets to draw on in the first place.

We can illustrate yet additional shortcomings in the laissez-faire model by analyzing how the structure of government decision making affects the distribution of political power. Sayre and Kaufman argue that because the political system is fragmented into many separate policy-making centers, no group is ever permanently alienated from the political process. Since no one core group dominates all points of decision making and since interests denied access at one point can choose to go elsewhere, a variety of groups can make their voices heard. While Sayre and Kaufman's analysis merits our serious attention, it is possible that they greatly overstate their case. Whether we confine ourselves to New York, or take a more inclusive look at national politics, there is ample evidence that numerous, as well as fragmented, centers of decision making often tend to shield powerful established interests from the demands of competing groups. For instance, as Marilyn Gittell notes, the school bureaucracy in New York achieved a striking degree of success in insulating itself from the pressures of the mayor's office, the various neighborhoods, civic educational groups, and the then poorly organized teachers' union. [41] By demanding that educational issues be taken out of politics, by eliminating the mayor's right to appoint the new superintendent of schools, and by securing a "lump sum" appropriation from the Board of Estimates, school administrators were able to screen out all demands for educational reform that did not conform to their liking. Gittell's findings do not appear to be an isolated case. Gittell suggests, and even Sayre and Kaufman concede at one point in their book, that other policy areas in New York might be equally closed off from outside pressure. [42] In the various studies of corporate pluralism cited in chapter 2, we find additional examples on the state and national levels of groups successfully fragmenting the policy-making process in order to insulate themselves from external competition.

Although Sayre and Kaufman may be correct in pointing out that no single group makes all the decisions in New York, they overlook the fact that the fragmentation of the decision-making process greatly enhances the ability of core and satellite groups in each separate policy area to disregard the wishes of a great number of interests. The argument that multiple centers of decision making facilitate interest-group participation rests on the assumption that the various decision-making points overlap on certain key policy issues. If, as Gittell shows, the reality of policy making violates this assumption, then it may be easy for key groups to frustrate the wishes of numerous other interests in society. First, when the policy that various groups seek to change is formulated at only one highly specialized and contained decision-making center, there are no incentives for groups denied access at that location to go elsewhere. Secondly, when policies are formulated at separate decision-making points, established interests have the advantage in defining the parameters of any possible disagreement. As we saw in chapter 2, when the decision-making process becomes increasingly specialized, the dominant interest in a field like education or transportation can refuse to consider certain demands that ostensibly fall outside the narrow boundaries of professional education or transit policy.

While Cobb and Elder believe that any group can learn to employ the symbols of the larger political system to advance its own objectives, it is apparent that the structure of government selectively benefits some interests while working to the disadvantage of others. By its very nature a fragmented style of decision making hinders reform groups from enlarging the number of participants in any specific policy domain and upsetting the existing distribution of power. As issues become narrowed and depoliticized, the power of specialists to decide policy grows progressively greater. Thus instead of opening up the political system, a decentralized form of policy making facilitates the growth of numerous, semiclosed decision-making centers.

Public Pluralism: The Revision of Laissez-Faire Pluralism

If, for the various reasons cited above, the existing political system is not as open as laissez-faire pluralists would have us believe, we need to ask how we can remove some of the obstacles that hinder group participation in the political arena. On the one hand, some groups like poverty or consumer-environmental associations seem to possess inadequate resources to bargain with their adversaries, while on the other hand, the decentralized, fragmented style of much public decision-making tends to maximize the assets at the disposal of more established interests. The various reform programs which I have called public pluralism represent one attempt to open the political system to groups that have previously been denied access. Many of the obstacles to group participation can be minimized by fostering competition and bargaining among units of government. Instead of assuming, as do Sayre and Kaufman, that decentralized centers of policy making will interact with one another, the federal government can consciously try to expand the decision-making arena by building duplication and overlap into the jurisdiction of various governmental bodies. When the responsibilities of public officials crisscross one another, groups denied access at one government forum will have meaningful opportunities to seek redress of grievances from alternative decision-making centers. Only such a system of policy making, which actively seeks to build checks and balances into the deliberative process, will afford marginal or consumer groups a reasonable chance of competing with more powerful adversaries. As James Madison noted years ago, the larger the political arena and the more numerous the points at which groups can make themselves heard, the harder it becomes for any one element in society to monopolize the decision-making process.

Secondly, and even more importantly, the federal government must also offer direct assistance to marginal or reform interests that possess only minimal resources of their own. There are a variety of institutional measures that can be undertaken to 'mprove the bargaining position of reform-oriented associations that presently enjoy little or no power. For instance, the federal government has recently established a Consumer Product Safety Commission to test products that consumer groups feel are defective. Such an agency can significantly reduce the expenses imposed on consumers for investigating questionable practices of business organizations. Similarly, Congress could seek to institute changes in the legal code so that private organizations like Ralph Nader's could more easily bring class action suits against firms they suspect of engaging in dubious practices. Likewise, the federal government can try to help poverty associations and public interest groups gain entry into the political arena by continuing to stipulate that there be participation by a cross-section of the larger population in the planning and implementation of all federal programs. By altering the legal rules that regulate the interaction among different kinds of interest publics, government officials could go a long way toward reducing the discrepancies in resources that various groups now enjoy.

Finally, the federal government can also act as a direct advocate for potential groups like the poor through the continued support of organizations such as Vista and OEO. If the government provides low-income citizens with the resources to become organized and the legal right to participate in the planning and implementation of federal policies, it can make sure that the bargaining process is more representative of the diverse interests in society.

A logical question to ask, however, is whether such a policy is ever likely to succeed. As pointed out earlier, there is a long tradition of federal assistance to associations such as labor unions and farm groups, which at one time or another have been excluded from the decision-making process. Commentators like Grant McConnell and Theodore Lowi, who have closely studied public efforts to increase the influence of the above groups, believe that such government activities have been quite effective in achieving their objectives. Indeed, in *Private Power and American Democracy*, McConnell asserts that the federal government has been and can be a powerful advocate for potential groups if it decides to throw its financial and legal resources behind them. Nevertheless, despite impressive evidence that the government has enjoyed considerable success in increasing the political clout of many groups, a number of critics continue to doubt whether public efforts to mobilize indigents will result in any significant social change.

This is not to say that all observers believe programs like OEO will be unable to enhance the power of the poor. Patrick Moynihan and, to a lesser extent, James Sundquist insist that agencies like OEO were almost too successful in helping the poor to mobilize and gain access to the decision-making table. [43] Ironically enough, while some critics believe that pluralism is too status quo oriented to bring about any degree of social reform, Moynihan argues just the opposite about a public form of pluralism. Reviewing the early Community Action Programs, or CAPs, he notes that in several cities intense factional battles broke out when the government attempted to organize the poor in self-help projects. In contrast to those who assert that OEO programs have been too conservative, Moynihan implies that they have been far too radical and disruptive in their attempt to redistribute power and resources to the poor. Quoting Arthur Schlesinger's observation that John Kennedy had "an acute and anguished sense of the fragility of the membranes of civilization, stretched so thin over a nation so disparate in its composition," he maintains that government efforts to mobilize the poor jeopardized the political health of the country by attempting to alter existing social relationships too drastically and too rapidly. [44]

Although Moynihan's pronouncements reflect a genuine concern for the stability of the political system, his assessment of OEO appears premature since his evidence is based on only a few cases that occurred in the formative years of OEO. He overlooks the fact that the politics of pluralism in providing access to a new interest may be very different from the politics of pluralism once a new group is firmly established in the political arena. As James Sundquist notes in his study *Making Federalism Work*, many cities often felt overwhelmed by the demands of OEO in its earliest years but much of their hostility to Community Action Programs soon dissipated, as the poor became incorporated into the decision-making arena as just another interest group. [45] In fact, as Moynihan even admits, many mayors had concluded by 1967 that if community action agencies did not exist, they would have to be invented, since OEO played an important liaison role in linking together the mayor's office and the often tense inner city. [46] Thus to properly assess public pluralism's ability to institute social and political change, we need to evaluate it both before and after new groups have gained access to the bargaining table.

While Moynihan argues that OEO has been too successful in enhancing the power of the poor, other critics like Lowi maintain that OEO's accomplishments have been more symbolic than substantive in nature. Lowi criticizes government efforts to organize the poor on the grounds that such programs result in the cooptation of community leaders in the ghetto. The problem according to Lowi is that the masses of poor will be the recipients of only minor policy changes because the leaders of Community Action Programs will use their position to enhance their own careers rather than to ameliorate the economic and political situation of their followers. He implies that the officials of poverty programs will tend to eschew radical proposals since the continued existence of their position in Community Action Programs is dependent on maintaining favorable ties with political higher-ups.

In spite of Lowi's cynicism about the willingness of poverty leaders to fight for improved conditions for the poor, it is debatable how many leaders in the poverty program were coopted by their political adversaries. J. David Greenstone and Paul E. Peterson have found in one of the most detailed and exhaustive studies of Community Action Programs that leaders were often genuinely concerned with advancing the interests of their constituents. They note that

the elites can win mass support necessary for success only if the institutions they build serve some of the economic, political, or cultural needs which prove appealing to the black community. And significantly enough, in Detroit and New York, where participation was greatest, black leaders focused their attention on bringing additional institutions—Model Cities programs, schools, housing bureaucracies, and the welfare system—under greater client and community influence. [47]

Similarly, Ralph Kramer finds little evidence in his study of five CAPs in the San Francisco Bay area to indicate that poverty leaders sought to advance their own interests rather than those of their constituents. He notes that "although the belief was widespread in many Oakland advisory committees that their representatives to the OEDC (Oakland Economic Development Council) had 'sold out,' there were surprisingly few instances where cooptation was clearly evident." Kramer admits that "the target area representatives were 'different' from their membership in being among the more able, ambitious, and articulate persons in these groups" and that "their experience . . . [in CAP] often enhanced their organizational skills." But he goes on to argue that "whether they were selected on a rather casual basis, as in Oakland, or by means of a series of 'elections,' as in Santa Clara, the target area representatives . . . did not seem to separate themselves in any substantial way from their members." [48] Sar Levitan and Robert Taggart make the same point in their review of Johnson's poverty programs. They maintain that "community participation was not substantial in terms of election turnouts or influence on the boards of community-based organizations," yet they insist that "these organizations generally did represent their constituencies."[49]

If Lowi believes that Community Action Programs were designed to pacify the leaders of OEO—a charge that is not completely substantiated by the evidence—other critics maintain that government efforts to mobilize low-income individuals were designed to induce quiescence among the majority of the poor. Peter Marris and Martin Rein, as well as Frances Fox Piven and Richard Cloward, suggest that government efforts to organize indigents were intended to appease the poor rather than to institute significant reforms that would substantially improve their well-being. As a result, OEO's accomplishments were more symbolic than substantive in nature. By bringing the poor into the policy-making arena, the political system could socialize them into the necessity of making incremental changes and thus defuse any radical proposals for altering social relationships. [50]

This is not to suggest, however, that the poor were not able to squeeze some tangible benefits out of the polity. Piven and Cloward note that OEO was instrumental in securing more welfare benefits for thousands of people in the black ghetto. By providing the poor with the financial assets they needed to organize themselves, the federal government enabled ghetto residents to bargain and negotiate with local welfare boards over the decisions they perceived to be detrimental to their interests. Similarly, Piven and Cloward would no doubt agree with Sundquist's findings that Community Action Programs were often highly successful in forcing state employment agencies to launch outreach programs to identify potentially employable people in the ghetto. [51] Prior to the establishment of the poverty program, most state agencies had played a passive role, merely passing on information from business firms to unemployed persons who happened to visit their offices. When Community Action groups were established, pressure was placed on employment bureaus to play a more positive role in reducing the ranks of the unemployed poor. As the federal government began to finance the operations of thousands of Community Action centers across the nation, the poor acquired an advocate agency that would bargain on their behalf with other government bureaus.

The important question, however, is whether these reforms significantly advanced or retarded other efforts to bring about

major political and economic changes. Piven and Cloward maintain that these policies were merely minor tactical concessions the
government agreed to in order to shore up the political order and
undermine the need for more far-reaching social change. In their
provocative book *Regulating the Poor* they argue that in politically
unstable times the government expands its welfare activities in
order to mollify the demands of restive citizens in large urban
ghettos. [52] The poverty program of the late 1960s played its part in
stabilizing the political system by speeding up the expansion of the
welfare rolls and inducing quiescence among the poor. Likewise, by
stressing the participation of indigents in the decision-making
process, OEO provided low-income citizens with a symbolic stake
in the political system, which undoubtedly had a moderating effect
on their demands for further economic and social reform. According to Piven and Cloward, the inclusion of marginal groups in the
bargaining process is an effective strategy through which the political system consciously or unconsciously maintains the existing
distribution of power. Granting access to the bargaining table
serves as a means of forestalling, rather than furthering, a significant reallocation of society's scarce resources.

While Piven and Cloward are extremely critical of government
efforts to organize the poor, it is questionable whether the record
of OEO completely substantiates all of their conclusions. We must
recognize that in an organization as large as OEO, which had
thousands of community action agencies, there were numerous
successes as well as failures. We must also keep in mind that until
recently, most of the studies of OEO focused on Community Action Programs in their first year or two of operation, when they
inevitably experienced the troublesome birth pangs of any newly
established organization. Despite the mixed nature of much of the
data, there is considerable evidence to indicate that in many communities OEO significantly advanced the interests of lower-income
individuals. After reviewing the relevant literature on the topic,
Levitan and Taggart conclude that

the products of the Great Society's community-based programs are significant. A variety of clearly useful services were provided: child care, pre-
school education, vocational training, health care, narcotics treatment,

and on and on. The innovations and institutional changes resulting from community participation and control were of lasting significance. CAP and Model Cities were the precursors of the contemporary movement for greater governmental responsiveness, more direct forms of citizen involvement in local public affairs, and the decentralization of municipal government. [53]

They also point out that CAPs and Model Cities had high "target efficiencies."[54] Services were focused on the poor and near poor or were restricted to poverty neighborhoods. In contrast to the critics, they insist, "if employment services, schools, or other established agencies had initiated similar operations, it is doubtful that minorities and the poor would have fared as well."[55] Levitan and Taggart also argue that OEO had other benefits such as identifying and developing leaders, like Kenneth Gibson, the black mayor of Newark, who are now active in minority communities. Moreover, Levitan and Taggart stress the fact that "community action must be credited with increasing the responsiveness of delivery agents to client needs." While they concede that "there may be less than 'maximum feasible participation' in decision making," they point out that the poor "have a much greater voice than in the past."[56]

Not surprisingly, however, assessments of OEO vary from city to city as well as from author to author. Walter Grove and Herbert Costner maintain that OEO's efforts to build an association of the poor have been a failure in Seattle;[57] while in contrast, Bachrach and Baratz conclude that "federal programs and federal funds have been the main means, directly or indirectly, by which the black poor have gained a foothold" in Baltimore.[58] Greenstone and Peterson argue that in the cities of New York and Detroit "some power redistribution occurred as low-income and minority groups gained representation on city and neighborhood poverty councils and managed to influence the operations of various governmental bureaus."[59] Likewise, Kramer concludes that the five California CAPs that he analyzed "demonstrated some ability to bring about minor adjustments and modifications in environmental conditions."[60] He finds that OEO displayed the highest degree of effectiveness in Santa Clara County, where the local Community Action Program "became another center of power . . . largely representative of the interests of Mexican-Americans and some of the poor."[61] The Santa Clara poverty groups engaged in mild forms of social action and were particularly successful in influencing major policies in public housing. Among other things they "persuaded the San Jose City Council to adopt a rent subsidy program . . . and also influenced the County Board of Supervisors to establish a public housing authority."[62]

In yet another study of CAPs in fifty cities, Barss, Rietzel, and Associates conclude that "changes directly credited to CAP have tended to be auxiliary in nature," but they add that "these changes may be meaningful first steps towards a basic reordering of these institutions to provide more substantial satisfaction to the needs of the poor."[63] Kenneth Clark and Jeannette Hopkins likewise find a mixed picture of success and failure in their study of ten CAPs, concluding that three programs are definite failures, three others are still in an unclear state of evolution, and four appear to be relatively effective.[64] Finally, an internal analysis of CAPs by OEO substantiates Sundquist's early findings that poverty groups have significantly changed the employment practices of state and local governments and of private employers and have also made many government services more accessible to the poor.[65]

However, the nagging issue still remains as to whether the above successes of OEO are purely symbolic in content. We can certainly argue that numerous Community Action Programs initiated a variety of important structural reforms that have materially benefitted lower-class citizens. The alterations OEO secured in such diverse fields as welfare, housing, and government employment practices are substantial reforms in the sense that they not only have improved the well-being of the poor in the short run but also have increased the long-range opportunities for lower-income individuals to climb out of the ranks of the poor. Why, then, do critics such as Piven and Cloward insist that such benefits are merely symbolic reforms that do not actually enhance the overall conditions of the poor?

Perhaps one reason is that the manner in which they have formulated their point precludes any meaningful test of their thesis. Piven's and Cloward's argument is seductive in that it can explain every government response in simple, unequivocal terms regardless of the scope of the government's activities or the intentions of its planners. Nowhere, it should be stressed, do Piven and Cloward explicitly state the standards for determining when a program such as OEO has achieved a purely symbolic, as opposed to meaningful, reform. To use Karl Popper's terminology, they have formulated a hypothesis about the government's poverty program that seems difficult to falsify. [66] If there is a criterion implicit in Piven's and Cloward's argument for gauging to what extent a poverty program is symbolic, it is perhaps whether or not such public efforts have had a pacifying effect on the poor. Piven and Cloward suggest that the federal government mobilized the poor and undertook temporary ameliorative action in order to induce quiescence among a restive population. But if the presence or absence of vocal dissent is the standard they wish to use, it is not a very good indicator of whether or not a particular program is symbolic. The evidence indicating that the turmoil surrounding CAPs eventually died down may reflect the fact that in many communities the poor had finally become vested as another participant in the bargaining process with a claim to a certain share of the community's resources. As noted earlier, the actions of a group seeking to become incorporated into the polity may be very different from the actions of a group that has already secured a role within the political system. The absence of strife in the late 1960s—which Piven and Cloward believe is a sign of the government's success in temporarily buying off the poor—may instead reflect the success that indigents and minority members achieved in acquiring membership in various local communities.

Secondly, Piven and Cloward often seem guilty of failing to distinguish between the pace at which CAPs have sought to bring about social change and the goals which they have attempted to realize. Greenstone and Peterson, Levitan and Taggart, and Kramer note that many poverty associations have tried to greatly expand opportunities afforded their constituents in the areas of employment, housing, and education. Greenstone and Peterson stress the fact that in the cities of Detroit and New York, black leaders have focused their attention on bringing numerous public services, such as housing and schools, under greater client and community influence. If programs like OEO were designed to coopt the poor, they seem to have had little success in dissuading low-income individuals from seeking significant changes in the services they receive. Admittedly, Community Action Programs have often sought to achieve these objectives in an incremental fashion, but we must not confuse the pace at which they have tried to facilitate change with the content of the goals they wish to achieve.

Even in those cases in which the poor have secured only the formal right to be consulted by public officials, we must refrain from glibly concluding that the victory of Community Action Programs is meaningless. All too often Piven and Cloward fail to see that even symbolic victories may have long-range, beneficial consequences for the poor. As noted earlier, Bachrach and Baratz suggest that the political symbols of a community may in part determine which grievances of the population become the subject of public debate and which are ignored or neglected. It is possible that even in cases where CAPs did not result in immediate or significant benefits for lower-income individuals, they were still effective in altering the bureaucratic view of the poor as passive subjects who need to be catered to in a paternalistic fashion. By the end of the 1960s, it certainly seemed apparent that OEO had helped change the mobilization of bias previously prevalent in many communities by sanctioning and legitimizing the right of the poor to have a say in the formulation and implementation of government services. Even when public officials were opposed to transferring power or resources to indigents, they increasingly had to operate in a political system that legally and culturally sanctioned more intensive citizen participation—including that of the poor—in a wide assortment of government activities. OEO had definitely helped move the issue of poverty from the status of a nondecision to that of a central issue facing American communities. While not all CAPs have immediately improved the well-being of the poor, they nonetheless have insured that the invisible poor of the 1950s, whom Michael Harrington dubbed "the other Americans," are now a very visible part of the political scene.

But even more importantly, we should recognize that Piven's and Cloward's assessment of OEO's success is colored by their normative belief concerning the proper share of the nation's resources that the poor ought to receive. While the issue of whether government assistance can help the poor gain a meaningful voice in policy deliberations is an empirical one, Piven's and Cloward's normative values are bound to influence their view of whether the poor are securing an adequate, and therefore nonsymbolic, share of society's benefits. Although we have no definite statement of their theory of social justice, it can be surmised that they favor an extensive redistribution of power and wealth among various segments of the population. Implicit in their writing is the belief that a more egalitarian society with few if any differentials in wealth is inherently more just. Piven and Cloward have a tendency to minimize the accomplishments of poverty programs that do not bring the political system substantially closer to this egalitarian ideal. However, if one believes that the poor are entitled to a decent, rather than exactly equal, share of society's resources, then one must be inclined to view OEO's achievements in a more favorable light. In too many cases OEO's critics have had such high normative expectations of what government efforts to mobilize the poor should accomplish that they have often needlessly deprecated the results of Community Action Programs.

Finally, Piven's and Cloward's attacks on OEO can be criticized on simple tactical and strategic grounds. Their work raises the important issue of whether low-income individuals would have fared better if there had been no government efforts to mobilize the poor. Inherent in their argument is the assumption that if minority members had been left to their own accord, they would have militantly fought for more significant changes in the present make-up of society. [67] But as pointed out in the previous chapter, without some outside assistance, low-income people are likely to experience difficulty in organizing and in gaining access to important centers of decision making. It is difficult to see how the poor without the help of Community Action Programs could ever become active members of a militant coalition that would seek radical changes. And even if they were able to become organized, it is also debatable whether any such coalition would have much success in influencing important policy decisions. As Moynihan has pointed out, severe attacks on existing groups or existing forms of decision making are bound to elicit intense and hostile reaction from those interests that feel threatened. In contrast, if the poor can be established as a legitimate group in the bargaining process, they can seek reforms in a fashion that will not threaten opposing interests and therefore not jeopardize their long-range chances of success. The initial problem, however, is to make sure that blacks and low-income citizens are duly represented in the pluralistic process of group bargaining.

Thus instead of debating whether low-income people will disrupt the political system or be coopted by it once they achieve access to the bargaining table, we must ask what conditions will facilitate the incorporation of the poor into the bargaining process as a legitimate interest group. One of the best studies to look at in accounting for the uneven impact of Community Action Programs is Greenstone's and Peterson's description of the poverty programs in New York, Detroit, Philadelphia, Los Angeles, and Chicago.[68] In a rather complicated analysis they insist that a variety of factors, including local elite attitudes toward OEO, were of crucial importance in determining the relative success of different poverty programs. Greenstone and Peterson maintain that the inclinations of political officials, and especially the attitude of the mayor, were a significant factor in deciding whether the poor actually wielded power in Community Action Programs. In New York and Detroit, the two cities in which CAP was judged most successful, Mayors Lindsay and Cavanagh were strong supporters of OEO efforts to mobilize the poor. In contrast, in Chicago, where Mayor Daley was determined to see that OEO did not stir up black neighborhoods, the municipal administration succeeded in imposing its will on the activities of the local poverty program. According to Greenstone and Peterson, unless the poor can establish a mutually supportive coalition with public officials at the top, they are not likely to become permanently vested as legitimate members of the decision-making process.[69]

However, as Greenstone and Peterson also argue, the lack of executive support need not always be fatal. Depending on the allies CAPs can enlist to help fight their battles or on the tactics they use, they may still be able to secure important concessions for their constituents. In addition, Greenstone and Peterson insist that the mechanism by which Community Action Programs relied to choose representatives of the poor had a significant impact on their subsequent behavior. Representatives of the poor who decided the policy of local OEO councils were chosen in one of three ways: (1) appointment by local city administrators, (2) selection by the poor in special elections, or (3) appointment by local neighborhood groups in poverty districts. As should be expected, representatives chosen by municipal officials were often reluctant to pursue policies that might antagonize the existing city administration. However, representatives of the poor who had won special elections often sought very particularistic goals for their neighborhoods and avoided more universal goals that might have benefited all poor or minority members. In elections that lacked well-organized groups, candidates tended to run on a "friends and neighbors" platform. Thus if any local poverty leaders were likely to be coopted or satisfied by the acquisition of limited and parochial objectives, they were the ones chosen through special elections. In contrast, Community Action representatives who were selected by neighborhood groups tended to seek more universalistic goals that affected whole categories of people. Greenstone and Peterson observe that Community Action personnel in New York, who were appointed by local groups, "tried to organize the local population on behalf of causes which might benefit all neighborhood residents."[70]

The reasons for the differences in behavior are difficult to specify, but Greenstone and Peterson suggest that when various groups in the ghetto could appoint members to poverty councils, the members often competed with one another for larger community support. "Competition for power within the community forced the competing leaderships to justify the appeal for community support by representing broad community interests."[71] Even though the constellation of forces supportive of or opposed to an active Community Action Program initially determined the manner in which representatives of the poor were selected, the selection process itself also seems to have had an independent impact on the success or failure of subsequent OEO activities. Thus if the supporters of OEO had drafted their legislation more carefully to stipulate how the representatives of the poor were to be chosen, Community Action Programs might have been even more successful in overcoming the intransigence of those city mayors opposed to increased participation by low-income citizens. As Greenstone and Peterson point out, had Mayor Daley been forced to allow community organizations to control the appointments to local poverty councils, he might not have been as successful in hindering their organizational activities.

While the above findings are based on a detailed study of Community Action Programs in only five cities, they are nonetheless significant in that they suggest that under the proper conditions the federal government can help marginal groups to gain access to important centers of decision making and to secure tangible benefits for themselves. This is not to say that public efforts to mobilize the poor will be easy. Altering the political system by institutionalizing the poor as another group in the decision-making process is bound to be a difficult and time-consuming task. But as was the case with many other groups (like the Farm Bureau and the CIO) that received government assistance, the poor appear to have made important strides in gaining access to the bargaining table as a legitimate interest group.

The Alternatives Reevaluated

On the basis of the above discussion we can argue that a pluralistic form of decision making need not work to the disadvantage of either marginal or consumer-environmental groups. By the government's undertaking certain institutional changes in the way present policies are made, it is possible that marginal interests may acquire a significant voice in the political system. But even if none of the above measures were instituted, there are other reasons for believing that a pluralistic sysem offers more opportunities for reform groups to secure their objectives than do alternative forms of democracy. Instead of simply defending pluralism against the charge that it necessarily excludes marginal interests like the poor, we can make the counterargument that pluralism may in fact be the most feasible method for marginal groups to acquire influence over public policy.

First of all, it should be pointed out that polyarchists are interested in restricting, rather than enlarging, public access to the decision-making process. Even among reform polyarchists like Lowi, there is a belief that elites, perhaps imbued with a sense of noblesse oblige, will maximize the resources that accrue to environmental or poverty elements, provided they are given a free hand in setting public policy. However, there are enormous pitfalls in allowing elites to enact reforms on behalf of their constituents without consulting them.[72] While polyarchists have sought to insulate government officials from outside pressure, participatory democrats have been very concerned with increasing public access to the decision-making process. But in order to maximize opportunities for public participation, they have called for the creation of small political units that make it considerably more difficult for environmental or poverty groups to gain a redress of their grievances. For by reducing the size of the polity, participatory democrats reduce the amount of resources a community can draw on to solve problems, such as pollution or poverty, that by their very nature require a massive commitment of effort and funds. Since this issue will be dealt with in more detail in chapter 8, the bulk of this section will be devoted to the third and final alternative, that of populism.

As mentioned earlier, populists like Harrington believe it is possible to organize a majoritarian form of democracy that will support substantial changes in the present economic and political system. However, while Harrington insists that a sizable portion of the population will support liberal programs, it remains to be seen whether such will be the case. As less and less people find themselves below the poverty line, we are likely to find diminished popular support for programs that are basically redistributive in nature. For similar reasons we are likely to find only limited popular sentiment for programs that radically alter existing racial balances. Consequently, if decisions are made in a populist fashion, we might expect minority groups to receive considerably fewer benefits than they would under a pluralistic form of interest-group bargaining. As a case in point, we can look once again at Wolfinger's and Greenstein's study of fair housing legislation in California.[73] In 1963 the California legislature passed a fair housing law, but the majority of citizens nullified this law in a public referendum. Although the legislature was willing to take into account the intensity of feeling of different segments of society and to strike compromises among various elements in the community, the larger population was not of a similar mind. Wolfinger and Greenstein state that in a legislative or administrative arena, where decisions are made in a bargaining fashion, considerations other than the mere quantitative distribution of attitudes are relevant, but in a referendum "compromise is impossible once the issue has been formally posed."[74]

Even if reform groups like the Sierra Club do not elicit popular resistance, they may still fail to achieve their objectives in populist referendums because of their minimal financial resources. When consumer or environmental interests and large business organizations must compete with one another in legislative and bureaucratic arenas, the discrepancy in resources between the two groups can be minimized. However, while any well-organized interest like the Sierra Club can match the lobbying efforts of oil companies, it may not have sufficient funds to inform the public about the necessity of voting in favor of referendum items that will advance environmental causes. An excellent example of this phenomenon can be found in the 1972 California referendum on financing mass transit from the highway trust fund. Through intensive lobbying, environmental interests were initially successful in convincing the legislature to underwrite mass transit with the revenues in the highway trust fund. However, in a statewide referendum, the powerful highway lobby prevailed. Because there was no crystallized majority sentiment on the issue, the public was susceptible to the media campaigns of the two contending parties. Since the highway lobby and the oil companies had more money to publicize their position than the environmentalists, their mass media appeal eventually won over a majority of the populace. What had initially been a victory for the environmental groups in the pluralistic give-and-take of the legislative arena turned into a defeat once the results of the state's populist referendum were tabulated. While lack of funds had not crippled a well-organized environmental interest in a legislative setting, it had proven fatal in a campaign to persuade the public at large.

Finally, even if it were possible to persuade a majority of citizens to support environmental propositions on referendums, their votes might prove to be highly ineffective in stopping pollution, while the demands of smaller and more tightly organized groups, like

Nader's Raiders, might produce greater results. The reason for this possible difference in impact is related to the way government programs are administered. As Edelman has convincingly argued in *The Symbolic Uses of Politics*, bureaucrats usually engage in mutual role taking vis-a-vis the various parties with which they constantly have to deal. [75] Officials are not likely to be sensitized to the demands of the public, since the groups they bargain with are a constant reality while the general public is much more remote. Thus if voters make diffuse demands on bureaucrats for tightening up pollution standards, they are likely to receive symbolic, rather than tangible, benefits. Similarly, as Raymond Bauer, Ithiel de Sola Pool, and Lewis Dexter have noted in their study of tariff policy, government officials often have difficulty knowing how to implement diffuse calls for reform. [76] When bureaucrats face amorphous appeals for lowering tariffs as opposed to specific demands for raising duties on certain hard-hit commodities, they are likely to accede to the latter. If consumer-oriented groups want to achieve specific, tangible gains, they need to bargain on a semipermanent basis with the relevant public officials. Until the consumer-environmental movement becomes a consistent participant in the concrete deliberations of the FTC and EPA, these agencies are likely to lack the information—as well as the incentives—to view problems from the viewpoint of the consumer. Regardless of how many people support referendums to protect consumer interests, their efforts are likely to be frustrated at the administrative level unless they pursue their objectives in a concrete, pluralistic fashion.

Thus pluralism's critics insist that "the pluralistic heaven . . . sings with a strong upper-class accent," but in reality it may contain a variety of melodies. Even though certain groups may face a difficult time gaining access to the bargaining table in a laissez-faire model of pluralism, they will have a greater opportunity to air their grievances under a system of public pluralism. With government assistance, any chorus can come to reflect the diverse accents prevalent in the larger society.

NOTES

1. Elmer Eric Schattschneider, *The Semi-Sovereign People*; Peter Bachrach and Morton S. Baratz, *Power and Poverty*; Peter Bachrach and

Morton S. Baratz, "Decisions and Nondecisions," pp. 641-51; Peter Bachrach and Morton S. Baratz, "Two Faces of Power," pp. 947-52.

2. Schattschneider, *Semi-Sovereign People*, p. 35.

3. Ibid.

4. Bachrach and Baratz, *Power and Poverty*, p. 18.

5. Robert Paul Wolff, Barrington Moore, Jr., and Herbert Marcuse, *A Critique of Pure Tolerance*, pp. 3-53.

6. Wolff in particular fails to make this distinction; see ibid., pp. 3-53. See also Donald Hanson, "What Is Living and What Is Dead in Liberalism," p. 25.

7. Roger W. Cobb and Charles Elder, *Participation in American Politics*, pp. 1-36.

8. Herbert McClosky, "Consensus and Ideology in American Politics," pp. 361-382; Gabriel Almond and Sidney Verba, *The Civic Culture*, pp. 337-74.

9. Charles Lindblom, *The Intelligence of Democracy*, pp. 165-81.

10. See Hanna F. Pitkin, *The Concept of Representation*, for an alternative view.

11. Wolff, Moore, and Marcuse, *Critique of Pure Tolerance*, p. 46.

12. Lindblom, *Intelligence of Democracy*, pp. 226-65; Robert Dahl, *A Preface to Democratic Theory*, pp. 34-62.

13. Lindblom, *Intelligence of Democracy*, pp. 246-65.

14. Theodore J. Lowi, "American Business, Public Policy, Case Studies, and Political Theory," p. 690.

15. Ibid., p. 690.

16. Ibid., p. 691.

17. Robert Dahl, *Who Governs?*; Cobb and Elder, *Participation in American Politics*; Wallace Sayre and Herbert Kaufman, *Governing New York City*; Edward C. Banfield, *Political Influence*.

18. Dahl, *Preface to Democratic Theory*, p. 145.

19. Sayre and Kaufman, *Governing New York City*, p. 720.

20. See Grant McConnell, *Private Power and American Democracy*; Theodore J. Lowi, *The End of Liberalism*; Martha Derthick, *The Influence of Federal Grants*.

21. In particular see Harry Eckstein, *Pressure Group Politics*, pp. 15-39.

22. Dahl, *Who Governs?*, p. 305.

23. Ibid., pp. 85-88.

24. Ibid., pp. 270-75.

25. Ibid., pp. 270-75.

26. Ibid., pp. 192-99.

27. Schattschneider, *Semi-Sovereign People*, pp. 1-40.

28. Cobb and Elder, *Participation in American Politics*, pp. 82-110.

29. Ibid., pp. 94-110.

30. Bachrach and Baratz, *Power and Poverty.*

31. Ibid., p. 43.

32. Ibid., p. 43.

33. Ibid., p. 45.

34. Cobb and Elder, *Participation in American Politics*, pp. 67-71.

35. Sayre and Kaufman, *Governing New York City;* Banfield, *Political Influence.*

36. Sayre and Kaufman, *Governing New York City*, p. 712.

37. Banfield, *Political Influence*, pp. 235-85.

38. Sayre and Kaufman, *Governing New York City*, pp. 710-14.

39. Ibid., p. 714.

40. Murray Edelman, *The Symbolic Uses of Politics.*

41. Marilyn Gittell, *Participants and Participation.*

42. Ibid., pp. 24-100; Sayre and Kaufman, *Governing New York City*, pp. 714-16.

43. Daniel P. Moynihan, *Maximum Feasible Misunderstanding*, p. 70; James L. Sundquist, *Making Federalism Work*, pp. 32-60.

44. Moynihan, *Maximum Feasible Misunderstanding*, p. 193.

45. Sundquist, *Making Federalism Work*, pp. 60-80.

46. Moynihan, *Maximum Feasible Misunderstanding*, pp. 156-57.

47. J. David Greenstone, and Paul E. Peterson, *Race and Authority in Urban Politics*, p. 309.

48. Ralph M. Kramer, *Participation of the Poor*, p. 208.

49. Sar A Levitan and Robert Taggart, *The Promise of Greatness*, p. 187.

50. Peter Marris and Martin Rein, *Dilemmas of Social Reform;* Frances Fox Piven and Richard Cloward, *Regulating the Poor.*

51. Sundquist, *Making Federalism Work*, pp. 49-54.

52. Piven and Cloward, *Regulating the Poor.*

53. Levitan and Taggart, *Promise of Greatness*, pp. 185-86.

54. Ibid., p. 173.

55. Ibid., p. 173.

56. Ibid., p. 186.

57. Walter Grove and Herbert Costner, "Organizing the Poor," p. 654.

58. Bachrach and Baratz, *Power and Poverty*, p. 69.

59. Greenstone and Peterson, *Race and Authority in Urban Politics*, p. 5.

60. R. M. Kramer, *Participation of the Poor*, p. 238.

61. Ibid., p. 107.

62. Ibid., p. 102.

63. Barss, Rietzel, and Associates, "Community Action and Institutional Changes," pp. 16-17.

64. Kenneth B. Clark and Jeannette Hopkins, *A Relevant War Against Poverty*, pp. 205-30.

65. Office of Economic Opportunity, Office of Operations, "Utilization Test Survey Data for 591 CAA's."

66. Karl Popper, *The Logic of Scientific Discovery*, pp. 78-92.

67. Greenstone and Peterson, *Race and Authority in Urban Politics*, pp. 304-15.

68. Ibid., pp. 304-15.

69. Ibid., pp. 229-60.

70. Ibid., p. 181.

71. Ibid., p. 183.

72. See chapter 3 above, pp. 52-53.

73. Raymond Wolfinger and Fred Greenstein, "The Repeal of Fair Housing Legislation in California," pp. 753-69.

74. Ibid., p. 768.

75. Edelman, *Symbolic Uses of Politics*, pp. 44-73.

76. Raymond A. Bauer, Ithiel de Sola Pool, and Lewis Anthony Dexter, *American Business and Public Policy*, pp. 320-30.

Chapter

7

Pluralism and the Problem of Elitist Groups

Another common criticism of pluralist theory is that groups are dominated by small elites, or *oligarchies*. Disagreeing with David Truman, who claims that groups serve to protect the interests of their members, many observers argue that private associations often enhance the well-being of their officials rather than the rank and file. Henry Kariel maintains there is an internal contradiction within pluralism, for "the voluntary organizations which the early theorists of pluralism relied upon to sustain the individual against a unified government have themselves become oligarchically governed hierarchies."[1] In a similar vein, Grant McConnell criticizes pluralists for disregarding the implications of Robert Michels's famous "iron law of oligarchy." If private associations are to play an important role in politics, we need to ask how they have governed themselves, and in McConnell's eyes, they have not governed themselves well at all.[2]

Because of the frequency of these attacks, it is essential to determine if such harsh criticism of the internal activities of interest groups is actually justified. Before rejecting a pluralistic style of decision making, we need to examine in a more critical fashion the claims of pluralism's detractors. In particular, the argument that an iron law of oligarchy exists raises questions that call for analytic clarification as well as normative and empirical verification. First, in order to assess the contention that interest groups are oligarchical in nature, it is imperative to define analytically what one means by the word *oligarchy*. When scholars like Kariel and McConnell argue that groups are elitist in nature, we need to know whether that means that officials misuse their power to advance their own interests or whether it merely signifies that power is unequally distributed within various organizations. Secondly, when critics maintain that the oligarchical tendency of groups creates an internal contradiction within pluralism, it is essential to stipulate in exactly what way the allegedly elitist nature of groups compromises pluralism or poses a threat to its central tenets. As a normative doctrine, pluralism is adamantly opposed to the leadership of a group abusing the rights of its members, but it does not necessarily see anything wrong with members of a group voluntarily playing a passive role. Thirdly, once we have determined in exactly what sense the oligarchical nature of groups violates pluralistic norms, we need to know whether the alleged iron law of oligarchy of Michels applies to all organizations or whether it applies merely to certain kinds of groups in particular. Finally, we need to ask how any elitist abuses of power that we may find might be curtailed. In particular, it is important to know if a pluralistic form of democracy can contain the misuse of power by group officials without violating its own principles. While Kariel maintains that a pluralistic system of politics is inherently incapable of controlling elite power, this chapter will suggest that his argument stems from a failure to realize that there are different types of pluralism.

Oligarchical Organizations: Variations on a Theme

Analytically it is possible to identify three different conceptions of oligarchical leadership.[3] First, the assertion that groups are run by small elites may mean only that power is differentially, rather than evenly, distributed within an organization. In this sense the charge that groups are run by oligarchies may be a rather mild statement. It indicates merely that whenever organizations develop, so will positions of leadership. This definition of oligarchy does not imply that the leaders of a group are necessarily unresponsive or insensitive to the wishes of the larger membership. On the contrary, an organization may at times concentrate power in the hands of its officials in order to pursue its objectives more effectively vis-a-vis other groups in society.

The word oligarchy is often used in a second sense to suggest that the power of officials is uncontrolled or unchecked. In this case, the presence of elites means not only that power is unevenly distributed but also that it is unrestrained by other elements within the group. In essence the members of the organization have no effective means for directing or blocking the activities of their leaders. But the fact that the leaders of a group may not be accountable to their constituents does not necessarily mean that they will misuse their power; group officials may still look after the interests of their members even though they are relatively immune from rank-and-file pressure.

Finally, a third way in which critics argue that groups are elitist in orientation is to suggest that the leaders use the resources of the group to advance their own interests rather than those of the rank and file. In this case a select few not only (1) wield more power than most members of the organization, but also (2) exercise power unencumbered by the wishes of the rank and file, and most importantly, (3) pursue objectives that often disproportionately benefit the leadership at the expense of the membership. This third conception of oligarchy assumes that the leaders will develop interests distinct from the goals of the larger organization and that they will deliberately choose to exploit the goodwill of the rank and file to further their own objectives.

Unfortunately, when critics like Kariel or McConnell argue that groups are elitist in nature, they often fail to distinguish clearly among these three different definitions of oligarchy. Kariel asserts that the organizations that the early pluralists relied upon to shield the public from arbitrary or capricious government action "have themselves become oligarchically governed hierarchies," yet nowhere does he systematically explicate what he means by this phrase.[4] As a result, his critique of pluralism is not always clearly stated or rigorously developed. At times he seems to be talking about unequal—as opposed to unchecked or misused—power, particularly when he deals with the kinds of large-scale bureaucracies that characterize modern industrial life. Kariel argues that the imperatives of technology have forced organizations to become more centralized and impersonal: "To operate harmoniously and continuously the fully rationalized system of mass production demands . . . a hierarchical apparatus of control which can encompass the continually proliferating parts of the system."[5] In this case the presence of oligarchical leadership results from "seemingly irresistible bureaucratic tendencies in the modern organization."[6] However, this first form of oligarchy is a rather benign form of elitism. To state that an organization is oligarchical in this sense is simply to indicate that the leaders wield disproportionately more power than those who occupy the lower rungs of the hierarchy.

On other occasions, Kariel uses the term oligarchy to signify power that is unchecked as well as unequal. In his description of labor unions, for example, he argues that "the power to make decisions has come to reside in well-protected, self-perpetuating incumbents whose prestige and skill—backed by an extensive staff of professional attorneys, economists, statisticians, writers, and administrators—is such that the rank and file, perhaps gratefully unconcerned, only rarely challenges their word."[7] In this case, the leadership has evolved into our second form of oligarchy, that is, an elite that enjoys a completely free hand in running the affairs of the organization. Kariel notes that elite predominance is facilitated by rank-and-file apathy but in many instances it is also reinforced by institutional arrangements that render mass participation virtually meaningless. In any case, the end result is the same: the membership is transformed into "little more than a massive organ of assent and affirmation."[8]

However, Kariel is somewhat ambiguous when it comes to assessing the consequences of this type of uncontrolled leadership, particularly when he deals with the case of labor unions. On the one hand, he suggests that union officials who are unaccountable to the rank and file inevitably utilize their authority to further their own personal ends; while on the other hand, he implies that these very same leaders often seek to promote the best interests of their constituents. At one point he argues that labor officials have selfish reasons for perpetuating their immunity from rank-and-file control since union leadership provides them with a unique avenue for personal advancement. "The union leader finds himself in a peculiar situation," Kariel asserts. "His stake in office is doubly great since, unlike his counterpart in the business corporation, the loss of his office is likely to be a serious matter for him . . . Unless he has cultivated nonunion business, he must remain attached."[9] Thus "what began as a movement to protect individual members from outsiders [has] generally ended as one to protect the leadership from insiders."[10] However, a short while later, in a slightly different context, Kariel goes on to suggest that labor leaders "are beginning to be exhilarated by the prospects of securing not only readily calculable economic benefits but of guaranteeing the worker self-realization in all phases of his life."[11] Here Kariel clearly implies that union officials do not seek to betray the rank and file for their own self-serving purposes but, on the contrary, seek to further the best interests of their constituents. In short, Kariel fails to make a clear-cut distinction between unchecked power (oligarchy two) and misused power (oligarchy three). While he speaks of oligarchies "interested in advancing their own welfare," nowhere does he systematically distinguish between this kind of elite, which abuses its position for self-seeking ends, and the type that exercises unchecked power but nonetheless acts to promote the well-being of its followers.[12]

Kariel's rather vague usage of the term oligarchy is shared by another prominent critic of pluralism, Grant McConnell. Like Kariel, McConnell rejects a pluralistic theory of democracy on the grounds that groups are elitist in nature, but as is the case with Kariel, he often jumps back and forth between very different conceptions of elitism. McConnell recognizes that power will be unevenly distributed within any large organization "since as a matter of technical necessity direct government by the membership is 'mechanically' impossible" (oligarchy one).[13] But he suggests that the real implication of the term oligarchy is that elites come to wield power for their own particular ends (oligarchy three). Because leaders "engage in different activities and come to enjoy a different status," they will pursue goals that diverge from those of the rank and file. "Leaders tend to identify their own interests with those of the organization and seek to preserve the foundations of their own position, thus laying the foundation for conflict of interests between leaders and led."[14] However, at other times McConnell suggests that oligarchy involves unchecked, rather than misused, power (oligarchy two). "Public governments have a long tradition of grappling with the problem of controlling and limiting power," McConnell argues. "With private associations, however, this tradition has not applied."[15] Here the issue is not whether leaders misuse their authority for private gain but whether there are any institutional restraints on the exercise of that authority. Moreover, the implication is that even though there may not be any meaningful checks and balances governing the internal politics of voluntary associations, such bodies have nonetheless addressed themselves to obtaining benefits for their rank and file.[16]

In his analysis of oligarchy, McConnell relies quite heavily on the work of Michels. "The weight of available evidence on private associations is overwhelmingly on the side of Michels' 'law' of oligarchy," he declares and argues that those who seek to defend an interest-group theory of democracy must come to grips with the implications of this "law."[17] However, it should be noted that Michels himself was often somewhat unclear as to what the phenomenon of oligarchy involved. In his study of the German Social Democratic Party, which has long been cited as the classic work on organizational elitism, Michels utilized the term oligarchy to describe several very different kinds of leadership. On the one hand, he argued that the SPD was oligarchical in nature simply because it was made up of leaders and led (oligarchy one): "organization implies the tendency to oligarchy," he asserted. "As a result of organization, every party or professional union becomes divided into a minority of directors and a majority of directed."[18] On the other hand, he often implied that the SPD was elitist in the sense that the rank and file was incapable of monitoring or checking the activities of its leaders (oligarchy two). Since the working class was made up of apathetic and uninformed individuals who were "incapable of looking after their own interests," the leaders of the SPD were able to run the party as they saw fit.[19] However, on other occasions Michels maintained that the SPD was oligarchical in the sense that its officials had developed goals distinctly different from those of the rank and file (oligarchy three). Many leaders "regarded their position . . . simply as a means for personal advancement" and were more interested in pursuing a conservative policy line that would not jeopardize their status as party officials than they were in fighting for increased benefits for the membership.[20] In arguing that the interests of the leaders of the SPD and their rank and file often diverged, Michels acted on the assumption that the workers were militant revolutionaries whose goals were being thwarted by conservative leadership. This view of the working class departed significantly from his earlier picture of the rank and file as basically inert and apathetic.

To account for this discrepancy, several scholars have argued that Michels often entertained yet another and even more contradictory view of the SPD leadership. In particular, Philip Cook and John May assert that Michels was critical of the SPD because it catered to the expressed wishes of its conservative membership rather than adhering to the Marxian path of militant revolution.[21] Cook insists that Michels wanted party officials to be more responsive to the "true" interests of workers, as defined by the Marxian revolutionary tradition, and less concerned about the actual conscious wishes of the rank and file. Since workers often achieved nothing more than trade union consciousness, it was only natural that leaders who were attuned to their wishes would pursue moderate and conciliatory policies. Ironically enough, Cook implies that Michels's displeasure with the SPD was less a result of the fact that it had developed a closed and self-serving elite than of the fact that it had created an elite responsive to the sentiments of its membership.[22]

The manner in which Kariel, McConnell, and even Michels often unconsciously jump back and forth between very different conceptions of organizational elites suggests the need for caution in glibly attacking the allegedly elitist tendencies of groups. While some groups have elected officials who systematically use the organization for their own benefit, many other so-called elitist groups have not. If we are not careful, however, we may inadvertently place possibly autocratic associations under the same rubric with highly centralized yet responsive interest groups. Even though the term oligarchy can and has been applied to the leadership of many different organizations, it is a word that often conceals more than it reveals.

The Alleged Conflict Within Pluralism

Once we realize that the word oligarchy has various meanings, it is essential to ask in what manner these different forms of elitism constitute a threat to pluralism. While critics like Kariel sometimes appear to suggest that the mere presence of any oligarchical tendencies within groups creates an internal dilemma for pluralism, the question we need to ask is whether the doctrine is prescriptively opposed to all forms of organizational elitism or merely to certain varieties. Obviously, pluralism is normatively opposed to group elites abusing the rights of their members for self-seeking purposes (oligarchy three). If secondary associations are to serve as a mechanism for protecting the interests of the individual, group officials must not be allowed to exploit their rank and file for private gain. However, there is nothing wrong with a set of officials wielding a considerable amount of power within an interest group (oligarchy one). While participatory democrats envision a communal group life in which there is intensive and equal participation by all in the affairs of the organization, pluralists have a much more limited conception of what participation should involve. Pluralists look upon organizations in utilitarian terms as vehicles through which the individual can satisfy certain of his basic personal and political needs. Groups not only can protect individual liberties from unjustified government interference; they also can serve as positive instruments for bringing about changes in existing legislation. But groups need not be *gemeinschaft* organizations in which people participate as an end in and of itself. If the members of a group either are satisfied with the activities of their organization or have competing commitments, it is only natural that they will be willing to grant a considerable degree of latitude to their officers.

While a pluralist would not be opposed to organizational elites in our first sense of the word, he would insist that restrants be placed on the power of group officials. However, pluralism seeks to check the action of group leaders in two different and often antagonistic ways. First of all, provisions must be made for the rank and file to influence the content of a group's policies. As an obvious example, the membership—rather than the officials of a union— should have the final say in deciding whether a union should go on strike, stay on the job, or accept a proposed settlement from management. However, it can also be argued that other groups in society should be able to externally pressure or limit the actions of an association's leadership. The rank and file of any particular group should not have a monopoly on those issues that happen to concern it; the demands of any one group must always be weighed by the demands of competing interests in society. By insisting that the leaders of every interest group be checked in a dual fashion, internally by the association's own membership as well as externally by other organizations, a pluralist recognizes that group officials will often have to play a crucial yet precarious role. The leaders of a group cannot become so committed to the wishes of their members that they refuse to seek out compromises or to bargain in good faith with other groups. Conversely, they must not be so amenable to the wishes of other interests in society that they ignore the needs of their own rank and file. If the officials of organized groups are not significantly influenced by their own membership, the danger of organizations developing oligarchies in either our second or third sense of the word is very real. But if organizational elites do not periodically attempt to influence as well as be influenced by their own membership, they may disrupt the give-and-take of a pluralistic form of bargaining. Rather than being a threat to pluralistic tenets, the presence of an independent set of officials (oligarchy one) may be essential to the smooth functioning of a pluralistic form of democracy.

The Empirical Problem of Oligarchy

While we can thus see that certain kinds of elitism are inimical to pluralism, we must recognize that other varieties are not. Unfortunately, critics of pluralism have often failed to make this distinction and, further, have made assertions about the existence of group elitism without providing substantiating evidence for their claims. In order to make a case against an interest-group theory of politics on the grounds of organizational elitism, pluralism's detractors need (1) to show that the diverse array of groups in society—from labor unions and business associations to public interest groups like Common Cause—are dominated by either our second or third form of oligarchy and (2) to argue convincingly that these kinds of elitism are inevitable and not merely transitional forms of leadership. However, the critics have failed to offer impressive empirical or theoretical reasons for believing that these two conditions are widespread. Many rely more on fragmentary incidents, scattered anecdotes, or appeals to personal knowledge than they do on systematic studies of interest-group behavior. McConnell, for instance, merely asserts that those who are familiar with Michels have "found disturbing corroboration [of the iron law of oligarchy] from their personal experience with many modern American associations."[23] And although he declares that virtually all private associations that "have been made the subject of careful study have to some degree substantiated that 'law,'" he fails to provide any documentation for this assertion.[24] Similarly, Kariel states that the policy-making process is dominated by a "plurality of entrenched oligarchies," but he offers very little empirical evidence to back up this contention.[25] We are merely told that oligarchies have come to prevail in all types of groups. "It would not seem to matter whether an organization is composed of businessmen, industrial workers, farmers, attorneys, or morticians," Kariel alleges, "provided only it is large in scale, complex in its interests, and heterogeneous in its membership. The rights of members to dissent, and to make their dissent effective, are not being habitually exercised."[26]

Kariel and McConnell are not alone in regarding Michels's law of oligarchy as a self-evident proposition. Although a vast body of literature has grown up around the topic of interest groups, very few studies explicitly address the task of testing the validity of this iron law. One of the few exceptions is a study by Seymour Martin Lipset, Martin Trow, and James Coleman of the International Typographical Union, in which they make a systematic attempt to deal with the question of the self-government of trade unions.[27] Generally, however, the major focus of the research on interest groups revolves around their role in the larger political system and their impact on the policy-making process.[28] In a good deal of the literature, Michels's pronouncements concerning the inevitability of oligarchical leadership are simply mentioned in passing or treated as axioms needing no further verification.

Nevertheless, even though many studies of voluntary associations do not systematically deal with the question of oligarchical leadership, it is possible to find data—albeit fragmentary in nature —that suggests the rise of unchecked or misused power is by no means a universal occurrence. The existing body of literature on interest groups provides a good deal of evidence that most organizational leaders do not abuse their positions for their own gain. The same data also indicate that many group officials are often quite responsive to the wishes of their membership and usually advance positions favored by the rank and file. For example, Raymond Bauer, Ithiel de Sola Pool, and Lewis Dexter have observed that the officials of groups like the Chamber of Commerce and the National Association of Manufacturers are usually very solicitous of their members and generally attempt to pursue policies acceptable to all elements in the organization: "Since such organizations represent a wide range of interests in a wide range of businesses, special efforts are taken to avoid generating any avoidable internal conflict. Cautious procedures are employed for reaching a policy position and spokesmen are confined to stating that position without elaboration." They also pointed out that the chamber polls its members on controversial issues. The stand advocated by the chamber is usually that position favored by a majority, "but there is a general understanding that no stand will be taken if opinion is sharply divided."[29] This practice of consulting the rank and file is by no means limited to the Chamber of Commerce. John Bunzel has found in his study of the National Federation of Independent Businesses that the organization polls "the members to learn their opinions on a variety of domestic and international issues." The federation then uses the published reports of its internal referendums to lobby for those government programs that its constituents believe will benefit them.[30]

The desire to represent and advance the interests of the rank and file is not limited to business associations alone. Ironically enough, while McConnell argues in *Private Power and American Democracy* that organizational elites often pursue their own interests to the detriment of the membership, he does not find any evidence of such behavior in his study of the American Farm Bureau.[31] On the contrary, he observes that the leadership of the bureau is conscious of the fact that its members have diverse goals and is eager to harmonize these differences. "The outstanding achievement of the Farm Bureau," he declares, "has been to weld the dominant economic interests of the Middle West and the South" together.[32] The Farm Bureau, like the NAM, "must reconcile the different claims of various producing groups within its own ranks; this necessarily results in compromise and a greater degree of temperateness in its own demands."[33] However, while the members of the Farm Bureau who grow different crops have different objectives, the organization has enjoyed a certain degree of unity because it is primarily oriented toward the more affluent members of the farm community. Although McConnell deplores the narrow class outlook of this organization, he seems to imply that the leadership has faithfully represented its constituents' wishes. He notes that "the Farm Bureau, in the words of its own publication, is an 'organization of superior farmers.' Moreover, the record of its actions shows that it has served as the spokesman of these 'superior farmers.'"[34]

The same pattern of responsiveness seems to characterize yet other organizations. In particular, several researchers have observed that there is often widespread participation and competition in political parties and clubs. Seymour Martin Lipset's study of the Cooperative Commonwealth Federation in Saskatchewan does not find an organization dominated by either our second or third variety of oligarchy. On the contrary, Lipset argues:

Though the forces making for bureaucratic control of the farmer's movement exist in Saskatchewan as they do elsewhere, the structural conditions for rank-and-file participation and for resistance to such control are stronger there than in most other areas. . . . The secondary leaders of all the farm groups are working farmers who are just as much affected by economic pressures and general currents of opinion as are the rank and file. Unless these leaders express the feelings of their neighbors, who have chosen them, they will be replaced by others who do. The extent of direct participation means that the farmers' movement must always be receptive to the needs of the members.[35]

In a similar vein, James Q. Wilson finds in his study of amateur democrats and socialist parties that organizations based on ideology—as opposed to patronage—tend to have very responsible leaders.[36] "Political amateurs in this country and perhaps generally," he notes, "are vitally interested in mechanisms to ensure the intraparty accountability of office holders and party leaders."[37] This concern is reflected in the fact that "ideological parties and amateur clubs are alike in their reluctance to vest discretionary authority in their leaders."[38]

But even nonideological parties that vest more authority in the hands of their officials are not free of all internal checks and balances. In his study of the Detroit Republican and Democratic parties, Samuel Eldersveld has stressed the high degree of factionalism that exists in both parties.[39] On the basis of such studies, Wilson observes that "few parties, and indeed few large organizations of any kind, are monolithic structures free of disagreement and faction." "Indeed," he argues, "parties, being voluntary associations, are especially likely to be a coalition of subgroups that operate in uneasy alliance with one another."[40] This observation can be easily confirmed by anyone who witnessed the chaotic proceedings of the 1972 Democratic convention. It would be difficult to argue that the national Democratic party was ruled by an autocratic or unchecked elite since such notable party officials as Mayor Daley were defeated on the convention floor by insurgent groups led by the McGovern forces.

In other groups as diverse as Common Cause, state teachers' associations, or the American Medical Association, we likewise find evidence that the leadership is representative of its members. Common Cause, for instance, establishes its legislative priorities on the basis of a referendum it conducts among its members each year. In order to maintain and expand its membership, the association tries to focus its energy on those issues that most trouble its rank and file. Among educational groups there is often a similar desire to reflect the needs of constituents. Nicholas Masters's, Robert Salisbury's, and Thomas Eliot's study, "The School Men in Missouri," notes that the Missouri State Teachers' Association "takes great care to avoid actions that will result in divisions in the education lobby." MSTA believes that the educational lobby will be most effective if it can present a united front to the state legislature. "Nothing would be more damaging to MSTA's standing as an expert than to have rival experts on the legislative scene."[41] Rather than acting as an imperious, self-serving bureaucracy, MSTA tries to be a broker, reconciling and exhorting divergent groups to support a unified legislative program.

And finally, even in the American Medical Association there is evidence that the organization's officials are highly responsive to membership wishes. However, in contrast to the other associations we have looked at, the AMA leadership does not seem to be informally checked by the need to reconcile diverse interests nor formally checked by genuinely meaningful electoral mechanisms. Despite the absence of these constraints, the organization's leadership still appears not to have misused its authority for its self-enrichment. On the contrary, many critics would no doubt willingly agree that the AMA has vigorously defended the economic interests of the profession. Elton Rayack, for instance, maintains in his study of the medical profession that "evidence leads to the general conclusion that the American Medical Association, on socio-economic issues related to medical care, does in fact truly reflect the will of the overwhelming majority of physicians in private medical practice." Rayack concludes:

Revolts against the leadership of the AMA are not indicative of general discontent with organized medicine's policies. The "revolts" have been sporadic, rather widely spaced in time, short-lived, and generally ineffective. Furthermore, except on the relatively minor issue of social security coverage for physicians, the dissidents have been unable to muster any widespread support. For the most part, the opposition has come from physicians outside private practice—from physicians in medical schools, in research organizations, in large hospitals, and in government service. There is no significant evidence to indicate any meaningful opposition to the AMA leadership among the private practitioners who make up 75 percent of the medical profession and probably about 90 percent of the AMA membership. On the contrary, whatever evidence is available points to the conclusion that the policies of the leadership are consistent with the wishes of the vast majority of AMA membership. [42]

Contrary to what pluralism's critics claim, we can see that there are numerous organizations that are not served by officials solely interested in their own self-aggrandizement (oligarchy three). In addition, the preceding examples demonstrate that many groups have leaders who are either informally checked by the need to harmonize heterogeneous interests in their organizations or more formally checked by referendums and other electoral constraints (oligarchy two).

Besides asserting that organizational elites pursue goals that diverge from those of the rank and file, critics like Kariel and

McConnell at times imply that such tendencies are inherent or inevitable in all large organizations. However, as we shall soon see, the explanation they offer to account for the rise of our more pernicious varieties of oligarchy seems more relevant to certain kinds of organizations than to others.

Inquiries into the origins of our second form of elitism usually focus on certain external and internal characteristics of the group in question. For instance, the nature of an organization's external environment seems to play an important role in influencing how the association is internally governed. Richard Simpson and William Gulley have shown that if an organization must constantly bargain with other groups to realize its objectives, it will tend to involve its members more fully in the decision-making process. [43] In a study of 211 different organizations they found that the more an organization is dependent on other parties in the community, the more it is "relatively decentralized with initiation of activity concentrated at the local level and with a strong concern for grass roots membership involvement and internal communications." [44] The reasons for such a relationship are relatively self-evident. Simpson and Gulley argue that when an organization needs the consent of other groups to realize its goals, the leadership feels it is essential to communicate with the rank and file about the obstacles facing the organization. In addition, in order to enhance their bargaining position with other elements in society, the leaders need to have the full support of their membership. The officials of such a group thus have a tendency to involve the grass roots as fully as they can in the activities of the organization. The more knowledgeable and supportive the membership is, the more effective the leadership can be in pursuit of the group's objectives. Simpson and Gulley's findings also suggest that the more competitive the political system becomes, the greater the probability that organizational leaders will keep in touch with the wishes of the rank and file. In a society based on partisan mutual adjustment, an organization that appears not to speak for its members will wield little or no influence with opposing interests.

If organizations that need to strike bargains with other groups to achieve their ends are often run by leaders who are solicitous of the rank and file, organizations that feel severely threatened by the larger society tend to be governed by officials who are hostile to any kind of internal checks and balances. Kariel suggests that one reason many labor unions have been run by unchecked elites is that they initially faced a tremendous degree of hostility from the business and political community. "Unions were inevitably forced to develop tactics and organizational arrangements that would assure their survival," Kariel notes. "Somehow they had to respond to the potent antagonistic forces in their environment: to ideology, public law, and the sheer violence of business."[45] Since unions encountered a great deal of antagonism from other groups in society, it was only natural that their leaders became adamant about maintaining internal unity. Likewise William Leiserson has observed that labor leaders who had to fight for the very survival of their organizations have often regarded internal opposition as a threat to the existence of the labor movement.[46] In times of stress these officials believe that the course of action they themselves prefer is the only conceivable policy the organization can follow, and they therefore tend to resist any rank-and-file attempts to set limits on their power. However, if Kariel and Leiserson are correct, then we can expect groups that do not feel their survival is jeopardized by the counterclaims of other organizations to have leaders who are more willing to debate the group's goals and strategies. In fact, most of Kariel's references are to labor unions, which historically have encountered bitter opposition from other interests in society. In contrast, most of the groups cited above, which are more tolerant of internal opposition, have not been forced to contend with such hostile opposition.

While the external pressures confronting an organization are highly important in shaping the attitudes of its leadership, the inclinations of its membership also tend to have a bearing on whether an organization has a checked or unchecked elite. For example, the reasons people choose to join a group and the diversity of their demands seem to affect the discretionary power exercised by group officials. As mentioned before, Wilson finds in *The Amateur Democrats* that individuals who join a group for ideological or purposive reasons are very insistent that they be involved in the deliberations of the organization.[47] In contrast, people who join an interest group or support a political machine because they expect patronage or tangible economic rewards may be relatively indifferent to how the organization is internally governed. As long as the association satisfies the rank-and-file's desire for material rewards, the membership may not care whether there are formal checks on the leadership's authority. When the rank and file are concerned only with the goods or services an organization can provide, it stands to reason that they may be unconcerned how the leadership goes about delivering those goods. However, the lack of formal checks does not mean that officials have a completely free hand in running the association. The quiescence of the membership may not last if the organization is no longer able to meet the expectations of the rank and file.

These informal restraints on group elites are likely to be more apparent in associations made up of diverse elements. If a group has a heterogeneous membership with multiple and, in some cases, divergent goals, the leadership will be under more pressure to negotiate with the rank and file. Unlike an organization that has a homogeneous membership and a limited number of objectives, a diverse organization with multiple goals will have a more difficult time satisfying its members' preferences. Such associations are likely to go to greater lengths to consult with their members and to avoid taking stands on issues that might divide their rank and file. The behavior of the Chamber of Commerce, the NAM, and the Farm Bureau clearly illustrates this point. As noted earlier, Bauer, Pool, and Dexter as well as McConnell have shown that these groups have often tempered their proposals and avoided issues they felt might disrupt the unity of the organization. Similarly, Simpson's and Gulley's study found that organizations that seek to achieve multiple goals as well as organizations that must deal with numerous external parties tend to "stress loyal, active involvement of rank and file members in their activities."[48] The more faction-ridden an association is, the harder it is for the leadership to govern in a centralized, autocratic fashion.

However, as should be obvious, merely because the rank and file want to influence their leaders is no guarantee that they will always succeed. Even if an association has members who have joined for purposive reasons or has members who wish to achieve divergent goals, we cannot necessarily conclude that the rank and file will be able to restrain the actions of their officials. Besides analyzing the intentions of group members, we must also look at the opportunities they have to challenge their leaders and at their ability to do so.

According to Albert Hirschman, individuals who are dissatisfied with an organization's activities have two different options open to them, "exit" or "voice."[49] That is, if people are dissatisfied, they can either withdraw from the association or they can stay and actively voice their opposition to the group's existing policy. As should be expected, the more options or resources an organization's rank and file possess, the easier it is for them to hold their officials accountable if they so desire. For instance, an organization that has a heterogeneous rank and file who are not unwilling to terminate their association with the group would be likely to have leaders who are solicitous of membership wishes. And if we may refer to the Farm Bureau and the NAM again, such seems to be the case. McConnell points out that the Farm Bureau must constantly face the prospect that wealthy growers who produce specialized crops may quit and join narrower commodity associations. Since the 1930s the bureau has been "alive to the dangers of commodity-ism"[50] and has fought such tendencies by attempting to represent the wishes of its constituents in a forceful manner.[51]

Similarly, Richard Gable has observed in his study of the NAM that the organization has been apprehensive about its fluctuating membership and has tried to focus on issues, like labor relations, about which it believes its supporters are most concerned.[52] "As a voluntary organization the Association must formulate policies that are acceptable to the members and are felt essential to their well-being and [to] achieving group objectives. If it does not, the members may withdraw." He goes on to note the "the fluctuations of membership indicate that the NAM's labor policies have been essentially reflective of members' desires, because membership has swollen during campaigns of union opposition."[53] The threat of exit thus appears especially potent as an informal check on the leadership when the organization relies on a heterogeneous and somewhat volatile constituency. Officials who blatantly ignore the sentiments of the membership may find that they have few resources to command and even fewer followers to lead.

However, as Hirschman points out, not all individuals exit when they become dissatisfied with existing programs. Either because of necessity or loyalty, many elect to stay in an organization and protest actions they deem undesirable. But the success with which the rank and file can oppose their leaders is again dependent on a variety of factors. For instance, Michels suggested that the unique background of workers has a bearing on whether union leaders can insulate themselves from membership pressure. Michels argued that the leaders of the SPD were able to acquire uncontested power because the great majority of the rank and file lacked the political skills to monitor the decisions of their officials. Both the manner of their educational training and the nature of their work prevented them from acquiring the talents necessary to play an active role in the affairs of the party. [54] Even if they became agitated over an issue or disagreed with the direction the organization was pursuing, they lacked the ability to make their objections effectively known. Lipset, Trow, and Coleman provide confirming evidence of this point, noting that those unions such as the ITU or the Actors' Guild which draw from the best-educated segments of the working class are internally the least oligarchically structured. [55] Untrained and uneducated members often seem to go hand in hand with unchecked organizational power. If such is the case, then working-class groups like labor unions, which have constituents who often lack both verbal and organizational skills necessary to oppose their leaders, are more likely to be run by unchecked elites than are associations dominated by a more educated and articulate membership. The success with which an association's officials can develop into our second form of oligarchy is in part dependent upon the abilities of the rank and file.

However, even if the rank and file have the ability to challenge their leaders, the success of their efforts may also be influenced by the structure of the organization, in particular, by the number and kind of subunits within the organization and by the way in which the parent body formally or informally interacts with its subunits. David Truman suggests that a useful distinction that "can be applied to political organizations in the United States is that between federated and unitary forms." [56] The first type of structure formally divides power between its subunits and the larger, more inclusive body, as in a national organization that has relatively separate and independent state or even county associations. In many cases membership in the larger organization is indirect in the sense that the individual joins the parent body via his participation in the smaller subunit. In contrast, a unitary association is a "single organization that may, and usually does, have subdivisions to carry on various functions."[57] In this type of association, individuals usually belong directly to the parent organization and participate in the activities of local affiliates only if their needs or preferences so dictate.

This variation in types of organizational structure can often be important to dissident groups wishing to oppose the leaders of the parent group. Obviously, a federated structure offers any parties who might wish to challenge the larger organization a more secure and independent base from which to launch their attack. When state or county units are formally independent of the parent organization, they can criticize the association with only minimal fear of punishment. The record of many federated interest groups indicates that state associations have often opposed the leaders of the national organization. Truman notes that even in the AMA various state societies and even some county societies have on occasion opposed the policies of the parent organization. And he remarks that "the national organization once was reduced to petulant complaints that it was not permitted to state its position in the pages of the California Medical Association's journal."[58] The Farm Bureau has also experienced similar internal disputes. John Heinz has observed that "state bureaus of the AFBF often appear at Congressional hearings to oppose the position of the national organization when it conflicts with the interests of crops in their own states."[59] Similarly, McConnell has pointed out that the Ohio and Vermont federations came to the support of the Farm Security Administration at a time when the national organization was severely attacking it.[60]

Even in more unitary organizations we find that a tradition of local independence facilitates internal diversity and dissent. For instance, in the 1960s a group of so-called young Turks challenged the leadership of the NAACP, arguing that the organization should place more emphasis on protest activities and less stress on legal action in order to bring about social change. While this insurgent group gained some support, it was never able to dominate the organization, at the height of its power controlling only twelve of the sixty seats on the NAACP's board of directors.[61] However, even though these more impatient reformers never succeeded in altering the official objectives of the organization, they did succeed in controlling a number of the association's branch offices. In Milwaukee, for example, Father Groppi led NAACP youth councils in mass protest activities against that city's segregated housing patterns, while in Mississippi Charles Evers organized local campaigns against the practice of Jim Crow. The autonomy of the NAACP's branch offices enabled the insurgents to pursue policies on a local level that the parent organization and its leadership refused to advocate on a national level.

While the preceding discussion is not meant to be an exhaustive treatment of the topic or a definitive survey of the existing literature, it nonetheless reveals that (1) the nature of a group's environment, (2) the inclinations of its rank and file, and (3) the capabilities of its membership to exit or voice are crucial in determining whether or not an organization's elites are restrained. This is not to deny, of course, that leaders and led come to possess differences in outlook by virtue of their differing roles in the organization. However, as noted above, there is a good deal of evidence suggesting that such a gap does not necessarily lead to the emergence of unchecked leadership. Institutionalized opposition such as that found in the two-party system of the ITU seems to be relatively rare (incidentally, such a system seems to be evolving in the American Political Science Association, of which McConnell and Kariel have been members) but nonetheless there are a number of other formal and informal restraints operating in many interest groups to prevent the rise of unchecked power.

In addition, we must also remember that even if an association's leaders do come to wield unchecked power (oligarchy two), there is no reason for assuming that they will automatically utilize their authority to advance their own private objectives (oligarchy three). Kariel, McConnell, and even Michels imply that leaders who wield unchecked power may at times scrupulously attempt to act in the best interests of their rank and file. If that is the case, then we need to ask what conditions give rise to our third form of elitism. Unfortunately, the situation is not all that clear. In large part, because so few studies find organizational leaders who advance their welfare at the expense of the membership, there are few insights into why such a phenomenon might arise. However, both Kariel and Michels at times insist that elites do misuse their power, and they account for its occurrence in such a fashion that we cannot believe it happens very frequently. In fact, their explanation of our third form of elitism focuses on factors that are likely to trouble primarily lower-class organizations. Kariel observes that misused power is most likely to occur in working-class organizations, like labor unions, where the status differences that separate the leaders of a group from their members are great. When individuals who become officials in an organization acquire wealth and prestige that they never could enjoy as members of the rank and file, they are often reluctant to surrender their power since it would entail a dramatic alteration in their life style. Similarly, Michels stresses the fact that SPD officials who were of working-class origins were not eager to be thrown back into the factories from which they had just escaped. After enjoying the perquisites associated with being union or party officials, they knew it would be a major readjustment to take up the life of a factory worker again. Instead of struggling unremittingly to advance the interests of their followers, the leaders often behaved in a conciliatory fashion toward business and the state for fear of jeopardizing the status of the organization and their own position within it. [62]

However, the very reasons Kariel and Michels use to explain the rise of our third form of oligarchy should give us reason to believe that it is not a very prevalent form of organizational elitism. The stark differences Kariel and Michels paint between the status of a union official and the life of an average factory worker are not to be found in most interest groups today. In many of the associations that are dominated by middle-class people, the salary and life style of the officials are not likely to diverge much from the patterns of the rank and file. Whereas the leaders of the SPD had no separate skills by which they might earn an income or enjoy the status they knew as union leaders, the officials of business associations or reform groups like Common Cause or the Sierra Club are usually lawyers or professionals of some type who could easily find lucrative employment elsewhere. They thus lack the incentives to misuse power that Kariel and Michels have attributed to working-class leaders.

Furthermore, even among organizations like labor unions, which are most likely to be subject to our third form of elitism, there are reasons for believing that the worst forms of oligarchy may be less prevalent in the future. First of all, in contrast to workers at the beginning of the twentieth century, present-day union members have dramatically increased their level of education and are thus less likely to be apathetic, uninformed, or unable to monitor or override the decisions of their leadership. Secondly, in many unions, college-educated or professionally trained individuals are replacing former factory workers in positions of leadership. This new core of industrial leaders lacks the incentive its predecessors might have had to abuse power for fear of being thrown back into the factory if displaced from office.

Pluralism's Remedies for Oligarchy

Even if the more pernicious forms of oligarchy are not extensive, we must still ask how pluralism would deal with those situations in which group officials have in fact misused their power. When individuals within groups feel they have come to be dominated by our second or third form of oligarchy, we need to know what options are open to them. Logically, there are two positions that have been espoused. First, laissez-faire pluralists have usually suggested that the option of exiting is sufficient to protect an individual's rights. As soon as a person feels the leadership of an organization he is affiliated with ignores his interests or pursues policies detrimental to his wishes, he can always voluntarily choose to terminate his relationship with the group in question. Voluntary associations are qualitatively different from the state—they exercise no sovereign authority over the individual. While the state will legally expect a certain degree of compliance with its directives and impose penalties on those who seek to sever their ties with the polity, most private associations are not in a comparable position to levy sanctions against departing members. Interest groups are concerned with far fewer aspects of an individual's life than is the state, and it is thus far easier for a person to disassociate himself from a group than from the state and to suffer no serious consequences. If a substantial number of people terminate their ties to a particular interest group, the ability of that group to wield power in society at large is bound to suffer. And in fact, as noted earlier, the very possibility that members might withdraw has made many organizations like the NAM, the Chamber of Commerce, and Common Cause more sensitive to the wishes of the rank and file.

However, if the option of severing one's relationship with an interest group may be a viable one for many people, it must be admitted that it is less than a totally satisfactory solution to the problem of organizational elitism. On some occasions membership in an organization is not a mere luxury an individual can indulge in to satisfy his personal needs or to achieve a particular social goal; on the contrary, it may be a prerequisite for a person to earn his very livelihood. A doctor who loses his right to practice in a hospital because of AMA sanctions has no meaningful option to leave the organization and go elsewhere. Similarly, with the rise of the union shop, individuals who voluntarily terminate their association with the union simultaneously terminate their prospects for gainful employment in that field.

If the individual option of leaving the group is not a completely satisfactory answer to our worst form of organizational oligarchy, a second and perhaps more effective solution is to have the government oversee or regulate the internal affairs of particular interest groups. For instance, when private associations have the legal right to limit or deny people's access to certain occupations or professions, the state can certainly insure that the officials of these organizations do not abuse their power or abridge the prerogatives of the rank and file. Thus doctors denied the use of hospital facilities should have the right to appeal that decision to a court of law. In order to guarantee that valid professional reasons, as opposed to political or personal considerations, are invoked, the state should be able to regulate a group like the AMA, which itself exercises quasi-regulatory power. Similarly, labor dissidents should be able to count on government supervision of union elections if the threat of fraud is a genuine possibility.

If, as a public pluralist would point out, the distinction between public and many so-called private associations is at best a tenuous one, there is ample justification for government regulation of the internal as well as the external affairs of many organizations. Especially when groups purport to regulate their members for reasons of public safety or when groups have used the power and authority of the state to advance their own interests, it is difficult for these same associations to claim immunity from some degree of public scrutiny. This is especially true of the types of organizations most likely to develop our third form of oligarchy, namely, unions and Community Action groups or poverty associations. In return for government assistance during the initial organizing stage, the government should have the right to require that the officials of these associations not misuse their positions of power.

In fact, over the past several decades there have been several attempts to pass legislation that would give the government the authority to oversee the activities of various private groups. OEO, for instance, has the power to stipulate when and how poverty officials are elected as well as the authority to oversee the spending of money by local Community Action groups. Likewise, the two major postwar pieces of labor legislation, the Taft-Hartley Law and the Landrum-Griffin Act, authorize the Departments of Justice and Labor to intervene in union affairs if it appears that the rights of the rank and file are being violated. While the Taft-Hartley Law insures that the members, rather than the officials, of a union have the final say on whether a union strikes or stays on the job, the Landrum-Griffin Act goes even further by (1) granting to union members a bill of rights comparable to that of the federal Constitution, (2) regulating the timing as well as the manner in which elections are held, and, finally, (3) requiring union officials to make extensive reports on their financial activities. [63]

However, the impact of such legislation has been uneven. As pointed out in the previous chapter, Greenstone and Peterson generally have praised the operation of the OEO poverty programs. Rather than finding a self-serving elite, they note that poverty leaders in Detroit and New York attempted to "increase community control over social welfare institutions." [64] They also insist that even in those cities where poverty officials were less than vigorous in pursuing community goals, the problem was not inevitable and might have been easily avoided if OEO had insisted on different methods of recruiting and selecting staff to run the local organizations.

Government efforts to limit the abuse of power by union officials have met with more mixed results. But in many cases the failure of public officials to check the abuses of labor leaders has been a result more of their lack of concern and motivation than of insufficient legal power. This point is dramatically illustrated by the attempt of dissident forces to oust Tony Boyle from the presidency of the United Mine Workers. In the initial campaign between Boyle and Chip Yablonski, the Yablonski-led insurgents repeatedly asked the Department of Labor to invoke its authority under the Landrum-Griffin Act to supervise the union's election; either because of indifference or political considerations, the Nixon administration decided not to intervene. Unfortunately, it was not until the murder of Yablonski that the Department of Labor did take action to guarantee that the election between Boyle and Arnold Miller was an honest one. As this case graphically illustrates, once political elites are willing to implement the laws presently on the books, it is possible for flagrant abuses of power in private associations to be contained.

Interestingly enough, critics of pluralism like Kariel recognize that such government intervention in the internal affairs of many organizations can be successful in preventing the misuse of elite power, but they tend to see such action as a denial—rather than merely an extension—of pluralistic doctrine. [65] This error stems in large part from a failure to recognize that there are a variety of forms of pluralism. Historically most laissez-faire pluralists have seen the concentration of power in the hands of public officials as the chief threat to the liberties of the individual. But if today we recognize, as a public pluralist would, that private groups may at times likewise pose a threat to the interests of their members, we can easily argue that government checks on groups may be needed to supplement associational restraints on government. If the government can limit the misuse of power within associations without at the same time hindering the ability of interest groups to challenge government activities, the vitality of the pluralistic process can be maintained. This is especially the case if, as in the Landrum-Griffin Act, the government regulates the internal procedures of an organization but refrains from dictating the goals or the policy objectives of the association it supervises. It is the presence of checks and balances on concentrated forms of power rather than the protection of what are in many cases only semiprivate groups that constitutes the essence of public pluralism. On those few occasions when either our second or third forms of oligarchy have appeared, judicious public regulation of the internal affairs of troublesome organizations may be necessary to curtail the misuse of a group's trust. If the more pernicious forms of organizational elitism do not succumb to the increasing skills and education of the constituents who make up most interest groups, or to the growing acceptance of most groups in the political system, or to the changes in the composition of most organizational elites, then government assistance may provide the members of a group with one more means of checking their elected officials.

NOTES

1, Henry S. Kariel, *The Decline of American Pluralism*, pp. 3-4.
2. Grant McConnell, *Private Power and American Democracy*, p. 120.
3. See Juan Linz, "Robert Michels," p. 268, for an alternative attempt to clarify what the word oligarchy means.
4. Kariel, *Decline of American Pluralism*, p. 4.
5. Ibid., p. 20.
6. Ibid., p. 33.
7. Ibid., pp. 51-52.
8. Ibid., p. 55.
9. Ibid., p. 52.
10. Ibid., p. 51.
11. Ibid., p. 64.
12. Ibid.
13. McConnell, *Private Power and American Democracy*, p. 122.
14. Ibid., p. 122.
15. Ibid., p. 153.
16. For example, see ibid., pp. 148-49.
17. Ibid., p. 152.
18. Robert Michels, *Political Parties*, p. 70.
19. Ibid., p. 111.

20. Ibid., p. 288.

21. Philip J. Cook, "Robert Michels' "Political Parties in Perspective," pp. 773-96; John May, "Democracy, Organizations, Michels," pp. 417-29.

22. P. J. Cook, "Robert Michels' *Political Parties,*" pp. 792-94.

23. McConnell, *Private Power and American Democracy,* p. 121.

24. Ibid., p. 151.

25. Kariel, *Decline of American Pluralism,* p. 68.

26. Ibid.

27. Seymour Martin Lipset, Martin A. Trow, and James S. Coleman, *Union Democracy.*

28. See for example, Harmon Zeigler, *Interest Groups in American Society;* H. R. Mahood, ed., *Pressure Groups in American Politics;* Raymond A. Bauer, Ithiel de Sola Pool, and Lewis Anthony Dexter, *American Business and Public Policy.*

29. Bauer, Pool, and Dexter, *American Business and Public Policy,* p. 333.

30. John H. Bunzel, "The National Federation of Independent Business," p. 113.

31. Grant McConnell, *The Decline of Agrarian Democracy.*

32. Ibid., p. 140.

33. Ibid., p. 148.

34. Ibid., p. 170.

35. Seymour Martin Lipset, *Agrarian Socialism,* p. 204.

36. James Q. Wilson, *The Amateur Democrat.* See also *Political Organizations.*

37. Wilson, *Political Organizations,* p. 107.

38. Ibid., p. 108.

39. Samuel J. Eldersveld, *Political Parties.*

40. Wilson, *Political Organizations,* p. 114.

41. Nicholas A. Masters, Robert H. Salisbury, and Thomas H. Eliot, "The School Men in Missouri," p. 223.

42. Elton Rayack, *Professional Power and American Medicine,* p. 17.

43. Richard Simpson and William Gulley, "Goals, Environmental Pressures, and Organizational Characteristics," pp. 344-50.

44. Ibid., p. 345.

45. Kariel, *Decline of American Pluralism,* p. 51.

46. William Leiserson, *American Trade Union Democracy,* p. 55.

47. Wilson, *Amateur Democrat,* pp. 180-87.

48. Simpson and Gulley, "Goals, Environmental Pressures, and Organizational Characteristics," p. 345.

49. Albert Hirschman, *Exit, Voice, and Loyalty.*

50. McConnell, *Decline of Agrarian Democracy*, p. 76.

51. Ibid., p. 80-91.

52. Richard Gable, "NAM, Influential Lobby or Kiss of Death?" pp. 250-66.

53. Ibid., p. 260.

54. Michels, *Political Parties*, pp. 85-98.

55. Lipset, Trow, and Coleman, *Union Democracy*, p. 320.

56. David Truman, *The Governmental Process*, p. 115.

57. Ibid., p. 116.

58. Ibid., p. 117.

59. John Heinz, "The Political Impasse in Farm Support Legislation," p. 195.

60. McConnell, *Decline of Agrarian Democracy*, p. 157.

61. Wilson, *Political Organizations*, p. 179.

62. Michels, *Political Parties*, pp. 172-88.

63. Sanford Cohen, *Labor Law*, p. 265.

64. J. David Greenstone and Paul E. Peterson, *Race and Authority in Urban Politics*, p. 309.

65. Kariel, *Decline of American Pluralism*, pp. 252-72.

Chapter

8

Pluralism Vs.
Participatory Democracy:
The Purpose of Participation

In the preceding chapters I have tried to show that alternative theories of democracy have very different notions of what role the citizenry should play in the political arena as well as very different conceptions of who constitutes the relevant public. While polyarchal democrats have argued that the public's role should be limited to choosing among competing elites, both populists and pluralists have insisted that the electorate should have some say in the formulation of government policy. However, populists and pluralists have often vigorously disagreed with one another over who constitutes the relevant citizenry. Populists have envisaged the people as the majority of citizens and have insisted that they should express their views through referendums, while pluralists have usually argued that the numerous issue publics in society should be the relevant public to decide important issues, and they have argued that these interests should exercise their say primarily through the give-and-take of political bargaining.

Because it has been argued that many people do not belong to any groups, or that marginal or public interest groups have difficulty gaining access to the bargaining table, or that groups are dominated by a handful of elites, a number of academicians have often voiced reservations about pluralism's conception of the public. Yet, we have seen in the last several chapters that many of these criticisms seem unfounded. Through a policy of public regulation of interest-group activity, it is possible to insure that the members of all issue publics have some meaningful say in the formulation of government programs.

In this chapter it is necessary to analyze one final alternative to pluralism, that of participatory democracy. The term participatory democracy has been applied to several different variants of democratic theory, all of which share the belief that devolution of power to smaller units of government will maximize opportunities for public participation. In the following chapter I shall examine in more detail the assumptions of community control, a variety of participatory democracy that has gained widespread support among those who seek to make governmental institutions more responsive to minority interests. In this chapter, however, I wish to look at what I have chosen to call *communitarian democracy*, a variant of participatory doctrine that is concerned less with governmental responsiveness to local needs than with the broader functions of participation in a communal setting.

Communitarian democracy's commitment to widespread participation is reflected in its criticism of pluralism. Participatory democrats like Robert Paul Wolff, Peter Bachrach, and David Ellerman believe that pluralism, like most other theories of democracy, fails to appreciate the inherent benefits of public participation as an end in and of itself.[1] While pluralists have tended to view political involvement as a means by which the individual might secure certain tangible benefits, communitarian democrats argue that the very act of participation leads to individual moral growth and development and thus is desirable apart from any instrumental benefits it may provide.

Examples and Assumptions of Communitarian Democracy

Although communitarian forms of democracy have enjoyed great popularity in recent years, the doctrine is rooted in a long and venerable tradition. Examples of communal participation have varied greatly in time and place, ranging from the New England town meeting to the utopian settlement of nineteenth-century

America, from the Israeli kibbutz movement to the experiments in industrial democracy in Yugoslavia. Likewise, spokesmen for participatory democracy range from eighteenth-century political philosophers like Rousseau to more recent advocates like Wolff, Ellerman, and Bachrach. Beneath these variations, however, it is possible to discern certain common values implicitly shared by all communitarian democrats.

First of all, the advocates of communitarian forms of democracy usually insist that the overwhelming majority of individuals want to play a more active role in guiding and shaping their own lives. They argue that intermittent political participation is inadequate if individuals are to exercise control over their own destiny and fulfill their basic human need for social interaction. According to this line of reasoning, instead of merely holding elites accountable at election time or influencing policy indirectly via group bargaining, members of the public should partake in the actual deliberations of the community. However, communitarian democrats often express varying degrees of optimism about man's present degree of readiness to take this kind of an active part in the political process. While some like Wolff write as if the citizenry is currently prepared to assume a more prominent role, others like Carole Pateman concede that people may presently be apathetic about political matters but insist that this apathy stems from the realities of the political situation today.[2] That is, people are indifferent to politics because they know they have no real opportunities to influence the outcome of most issues; but if institutional changes were made to facilitate participation, then they would chose to involve themselves more actively. Still other communitarian democrats like Ellerman argue that the citizenry's unwillingness to participate actively in politics is an outgrowth of a false consciousness created and sustained by our capitalist economic system.[3] Like Ellerman, many participatory democrats are socialists who maintain in Marxian fashion that economic changes are necessary for the complete realization of communitarian democracy. In their view, only an egalitarian society in which the means of production are publicly owned is likely to instill in individuals the proclivities necessary to make a political system based on intensive participation a genuine possibility.

Secondly, most participatory democrats insist that it is only in small communities that individuals will have the opportunity to deliberate matters of social importance. In the eighteenth century Rousseau argued that the city-state rather than the nation-state was the best vehicle to maximize citizen involvement. Today, in a similar vein, Wolff calls for the creation of small communities where people can share in the common political life, and Bachrach advocates the development of new centers of participation within factories and other places of work. Likewise, communitarian democrats with socialist leanings insist that centralized state planning must be replaced by decentralized forms of decision making that will allow individuals to assume control over their own lives. Participatory democrats, whether socialist or not, view large-scale units of government as too remote to allow for the kind of intensive individual involvement they deem desirable.

Thirdly, most communitarian democrats believe that once people are given the opportunity to become involved in politics, the quality of public life will improve dramatically. They insist that the issues that divide men are not fundamental in nature or incapable of resolution; on the contrary, they believe that if people are given the chance to meaningfully debate the problems that trouble them, they will be able to resolve their differences peacefully and harmoniously. Through the give-and-take of communal assemblies individuals can search for the common interests that unite them and upon this basis forge an affective sense of community.

Finally, as noted above, communitarian democrats tend to view the fact of participation as a desirable end in and of itself. Advocates of participatory democracy like Wolff and Pateman believe that the individual will be likely to develop his capabilities to their fullest only when he has an opportunity to share in the deliberation of important social issues. Individual fulfillment and public involvement are thus seen as inextricably linked. Regardless of the instrumental gains to be secured, participatory democrats believe that a person will emotionally and morally benefit from immersing himself in the social affairs of his community. Rousseau, for example, thought participating in a democratic state "could elevate men and turn them into moral and intelligent human beings."[4] Similarly, as Terrence Cook and Patrick Morgan point out, many participatory democrats believe that public involvement will make people both more knowledgeable about important events and less selfish in their attitudes toward others. [5] Rather than being a necessary burden an individual must bear in order to accomplish other substantive goals, participation in the life of the community is seen as a beneficial objective in and of itself.

Assumptions and Reality

The four points outlined above constitute the cornerstone of the participatory argument, yet it is interesting to note that communitarian democrats by and large neglect to demonstrate whether these assumptions are in fact valid. Many participatory democrats muster very little data in support of their arguments, and those who do attempt to offer empirical evidence often end up citing data that undermine their own position. In order to determine the workability of the communitarian model, an analysis of relevant empirical evidence needs to be undertaken. However, it should be pointed out that the data to be examined in this chapter are diverse and heterogeneous in nature, ranging from studies of participation in American politics to analyses of Yugoslavian factories, Israeli kibbutzim, and other experiments in participatory democracy. While some might argue that experiments like the kibbutzim are not always identical with the communities they would like to see built, we must recognize that such sources represent the best and in fact only evidence available. All too often, people like Bachrach or Wolff who favor communal experiments have neither participated in building such communities nor cited examples of communities that they think were successful. Unless we are willing to argue that there is no way of ever empirically determining whether the assumptions of participatory democracy are valid, we must look at those cases that most clearly approximate the participatory/communal model.

As we shall soon see, an examination of these kinds of sources, which modern participatory democrats have all too often ignored, reveals that communitarian forms of government are not necessarily as workable as advocates like Pateman et al. would like to believe. First of all, while participatory democrats like Wolff have insisted that people are intensely interested in political matters, much of the recent empirical evidence on participation in American politics suggests otherwise. Instead of being eager to immerse themselves in community affairs, most individuals appear to want to participate in a narrow and segmented fashion. As mentioned earlier, students of public opinion and voting behavior have shown that the vast majority of people are concerned about only a limited range of issues. Philip Converse, Sidney Verba, Norman Nie, and David RePass, among others, have found that instead of consti- tuting a single cohesive body, the electorate is fragmented into numerous issue publics whose interest and involvement in politics seem to fluctuate back and forth between peaks of activity and inactivity.[6] When issues of importance to particular individuals are in the news or elicit government reaction, certain segments of the populace become highly involved in politics, but as old disputes recede and new ones come to the fore, different issue publics be- come activated.[7]

Perhaps even more damaging to the participatory cause is the fact that even within these rather narrow issue publics, many individuals choose not to play an active role in advancing their own interests. While people may be willing to join and financially support an interest group, they often want the officers of the asso- ciation to assume most of the responsibility for the day-to-day operations of the group. In this way individuals can pursue the policies they deem desirable without incurring too many demands on their scarce time or energy. By participating in only a limited fashion in a group's activities, an individual can receive the psycho- logical benefits of supporting a cause he believes in, as well as the tangible benefits the organization may happen to secure, without having to exhaust his own spare time. Thus, many groups become elitist in nature because the rank and file want to consolidate power in the hands of their leadership. Even though people may be willing to join interest groups and may want to play a more active role in public affairs, they often have very clear reservations about becom- ing too absorbed in the give-and-take of political life. Rather than viewing intensive participation as an ennobling process, many individuals simply see it as too great a burden to shoulder. In place of a *gemeinschaft* community where all directly partake in the deliberations of the group, people often prefer a centrally run association that places fewer demands on their leisure time.

However, as noted earlier, some participatory democrats like Pateman argue that people are indifferent to community affairs because the present structure of the political system does not provide any meaningful opportunities for expanded participation. Once people become socialized into accepting a passive political life, they will inevitably show little concern with public affairs. But Pateman maintains that if institutional changes were made to facilitate more public involvement, attitudes toward participation would likewise change.[8] Individuals as diverse as David Ellerman, Charles Hampden-Turner, and the authors of the Port Huron Manifesto of SDS take Pateman's argument one step further, insisting that the economic realities underlying our present political system also work to the detriment of greater public concern with political affairs.[9] They contend that the traditional voting studies of academic political scientists are so parochial in their design and execution that they provide us with few insights into the ultimate capabilities or interests of the average citizen. According to communitarian democrats of a socialist bent, altering the capitalist nature of our economy will do away with the conditions that have led the individual to become politically apathetic.

While this argument has a certain degree of plausibility, we must be careful to interpret it in the proper context. By undertaking certain institutional changes we may very well encourage more people to participate in politics, but the individuals who are stimulated to participate may choose to involve themselves in a limited, rather than an all-encompassing, fashion. The record of a variety of experiments that best seem to approximate the participatory model—including communal movements in the United States in the nineteenth and twentieth centuries, Israeli kibbutzim, worker councils in industrial societies, and self-managed factories in Yugoslavia—indicates that the overwhelming majority of people are not enamored with intensive participation over a prolonged period of time. In many respects, these experiments are appropriate subjects of study, for they all have attempted to develop a cooperative, communal environment on a small scale. In addition, many of the American communes, most of the Israeli kibbutzim, and certainly all of the Yugoslavian factories are institutions that are not based on capitalist assumptions. If participatory democrats of a socialist inclination are correct in insisting that the present economic make-up of American society either prevents or discourages people from wanting to participate actively in a communal setting, we should expect these alternative forms of political life based on different economic principles to enjoy considerable success in recruiting people to participate in their affairs.

However, such is not the case. If we look first at the evidence on the utopian communities established in the United States between 1820 and 1870, we cannot fail to note that most of them lasted for only a relatively short period of time. In a fundamentally sympathetic examination of American utopian movements, Rosabeth Kanter has studied over ninety-one communal ventures that left some kind of historical record and finds that "less than a dozen of the ninety-one known groups lasted more than sixteen years; for the majority, the average life-span was less than four years." Furthermore, she admits, "such well known communes as New Harmony and Brook Farm were among the short-lived groups. . . . Brook Farm ended after six years despite support from leading intellectuals of the time." On the basis of this data Kanter notes that "building viable utopian communities has proven to be difficult: translating the utopian dream into reality is fraught with issues that in time may even distort the original vision."[10]

If these communes supposedly tapped a deep-seated human desire to participate intensely in the affairs of a *gemeinschaft* community, one must ask why they were unable to sustain themselves over a longer period of time. Institutionally the opportunities existed for individuals to participate more actively in a communal setting, but very few persons seemed to have taken advantage of them. Moreover, even when people did decide to join a commune, their commitment was often halfhearted. As Kanter points out, most of the utopian settlements had to worry constantly that the lure of the larger, impersonal world outside the confines of the group would lead their members to lose interest in sustaining new forms of communal living. In fact, many communes frequently acted under the assumption that people would not voluntarily choose to remain in *gemeinschaft* organizations. The settlements that were most successful depended on a series of "commitment mechanisms" to promote a sense of communal solidarity. These included renunciation, sacrifices, mortification, the application of sanctions, mutual criticism sessions, and the institutionalization of the power and authority of the leader.[11] Kanter observes that many groups required people to relinquish "relationships that . . . [were] potentially disruptive to group cohesion, thereby heightening the relationship of individual to group."[12] The communities that were most successful usually formulated elaborate sets of rules to minimize the contact between their members and the outside world. Even personal relationships between two individuals within the commune were often viewed in a less than favorable light for fear that they might detract from the individual's commitment to the larger group.

Besides isolating their members from outside contact, many utopian settlements also undertook systematic efforts to break down or transform the values of their recruits. Kanter notes that a number of communes relied on the commitment mechanism of mortification to maintain the allegiance of their followers. The essence of mortification was to "strip away aspects of an individual's previous identity, to make him dependent on authority for direction, and to place him in a position of uncertainty . . . until he learns and comes to accept the norms of the group."[13] To achieve this goal the successful communes usually forced their members to undergo extensive periods of self-criticism or they applied direct sanctions to deviant members in order to make them uncertain about their status in the larger community. Kanter remarks that in successful nineteenth-century communities

the individual "bared his soul" to social control, admitting weaknesses, failings, and imperfections. The individual humbled himself before the group. . . . No part of his life was left unexamined and uncriticized, since all belonged to the system. The group might probe and pry into the most intimate matters, indicating its right to be a significant presence in the internal life of the individual. These mortification practices thus indicated to members that even their innermost "selves" were being "watched" by others.[14]

When mutual criticism failed to work, the community often used sanctions designed to "embarrass the member before the community and indicate to him that his membership status in the organization is always in question."[15]

Rather than proving that people will automatically choose the benefits of an affective, communal form of life if only they have the opportunity to experience them, the record of most nineteenth-century communes seems to indicate otherwise. By limiting the group's relations with outsiders and relying on a variety of often harsh conversion mechanisms, many utopian communities sought to resocialize people so that they would want to participate more intensely in the group's activities. Yet even these efforts proved to be unsuccessful in the great majority of communal experiments. If intensive socialization could have remolded people to accept the dictates of communal existence, as participatory democrats have often argued, one would have expected the second generation to remain with the utopian settlements. However, Kanter points out that even in those few communes, such as the Shakers' settlement, that lasted for any length of time, "most of the children . . . did not remain in the community when [they were] old enough to leave."[16] Ironically, most offspring of the original founders chose not to support the communal form of life in which they had been raised, despite the fact that they had experienced only minimal contact with the outside world.

David and Elena French have pointed out that support for communal life underwent several modifications during the nineteenth century. They argue that there were two distinct periods in the communal movement, one lasting from 1824 to 1846 and the other spanning the period from 1847 to 1866.[17] The first period, which they label the *Owenite era*, witnessed a basic concern with building a very intensive form of communal life in which all shared equally their possessions, ideas, and emotions. But the people who participated in these early experiments were ultimately to discover that the "interpersonal demands of communal life were more than they were prepared to accept," and "in the exhaustion and disillusionment that followed, people became more cautious, approaching social organization with sharply limited assumptions as to what it could offer them."[18] As a result, French and French argue, the second period of communal building, which they call the *Fourieristic era*, was more limited in its scope and more individualistic in its outlook: "In the flight from 'communes' with their overtones of total sharing and familial bonds, people were moving towards looser 'communities,' in which relationships were to be more partial and contractual."[19] Interestingly enough, French and French, who themselves are advocates of communal forms of living, recognize that the same shift away from all-encompassing to more limited communities has characterized the American "alternative" movement of the last fifteen years. This shift in emphasis is epitomized in the swing from the "commune" of the 1960s to the "community" of the 1970s as the basic social unit. "At least symbolically, the commune had been a place for total, intimate experience within a relatively small group of people." However, they note, "in the communities of the 1970s . . . relationships were to be segmented and muted. . . . The structure of life was increasingly reminiscent of American society prior to the convulsions of the 1960s."[20]

If the record of communal societies in the United States provides little, if any, evidence in support of the participatory argument, it does not necessarily mean that the communal ideal cannot be realized in other countries with different economic and political traditions. For example, a participatory democrat could argue that communitarian patterns of democracy seem to be fluorishing in the kibbutz movement in Israel. Some of the earliest settlements trace their origins back to 1910, even though a majority of the existing 230 kibbutzim were founded in the early 1950s during the birth of the Israeli state.[21] While most of the communal settlements are relatively small, averaging around 400 members, their population has grown by about 1 percent during the decade of the 1960s.

Despite the longevity of some of the kibbutzim, it is questionable whether the evolution of these settlements would completely satisfy the expectations of a communitarian democrat. It must be kept in mind that many of the kibbutzim were founded by long-time Zionists and Jewish socialists who were extremely hostile to what they perceived to be the commercialism and crass individualism of modern capitalist society. In establishing enclaves in which all individuals could directly participate in building and running a communal enterprise, the founders of the kibbutzim felt that they were developing an alternative pattern of living that would be quickly emulated throughout the state of Israel.[22] These aspirations have by no means been fulfilled. At its high point, over 7.5 percent of the total Israeli population was tied to the kibbutz movement, with 50 percent of the rural population living in a settlement; today less than 3.5 percent of the overall population and less than 25 percent of rural inhabitants belong to a kibbutz.

In fact, in contrast to the late 1940s, when a whole series of new kibbutzim were created, the last several years have seen the creation of only a handful of communes. Contrary to the hope of its Zionist and socialist founders that the kibbutz would be a form of political existence appealing to a great majority of Jews, such appears not to be the case. Only a very small minority of the Israeli population have found the intense atmosphere of the kibbutz to their liking, and even the many defenders of the kibbutz recognize that the attractiveness of their movement is based as much upon the role the kibbutz has played in Israeli history as it is upon the organization's political and social principles. Dan Leon argues that "there can be little doubt that the rapid development of all the major kibbutzim . . . can only be explained in terms of the pioneering role which the kibbutzim played in the upbuilding and defense of Jewish Palestine." He acknowledges that "the Israeli commune would have gone the way of other communal experiments . . . were it not for the fact that . . . the kibbutzim played a vanguard role in the Jewish national and social revival in Israel." The kibbutz was constantly in the "forefront of every phase of the struggle for political independence against the . . . Arabs."[23] As substantiating evidence, it is interesting to note that the few additional kibbutzim that have been created in recent years have generally been established in the land the Israelis won in the 1967 Arab war.

If the relatively small number of people who presently belong to a kibbutz raises the question of whether the great majority of individuals could ever be induced to embrace participatory ideals, the lack of participatory fervor within the kibbutz itself raises even more nagging doubts on this subject. The major institution in the kibbutz for making decisions is the general assembly, which usually convenes on a weekly basis. In addition to this meeting, where the majority of members have the power to set policy, there are within the kibbutz numerous committees and elected officials whose job it is to attend to specialized problems facing the commune. While the kibbutz is thus theoretically a pure form of participatory democracy, the practice of kibbutz democracy often falls far short of the communitarian ideal. In the general meeting, for instance, participation is often halfhearted and limited in nature. Avraham Ben-Yosef notes:

The one serious weakness in the practical application of kibbutz organization is the sporadic attendance of most members at general meetings. There is a tendency for the general meeting to fall, all too fixedly, into the hands of a certain body of stalwarts who almost always attend. . . . It is clear that these phenomena detract not a little from the reality of kibbutz democracy, and although they may be natural enough, they are none the less deplorable. It may well be contended that a member who does not attend the general meeting fairly regularly has no real conception of the kibbutz as a framework for life. [24]

Ben-Yosef adds that "an average attendance of three-quarters of the total membership . . . certainly seems to be desirable, instead of the mere one-third or one-half which usually forms the actual quorum."[25] A small percentage of people who choose to live in a kibbutz—who in turn are a small portion of the Israeli population—indicate a desire to participate fully in the affairs of the commune.

The lack of attendance at the general assembly is only one indication of membership apathy in the kibbutz. Ben-Yosef observes it is often extremely difficult to get people to serve on the various committees within the kibbutz settlement, remarking that the nominating committee, which has the task of choosing people to do service work, "has one of the hardest tasks of all in the kibbutz, for members by no means rush to offer their services."[26] Even with expanded opportunities to become involved in the deliberations of their community, many people elect not to take advantage of them. For supporters of kibbutz democracy such as Ben-Yosef, this lack of public interest raises many problems. He points out that "the kibbutzim insist that their democracy be all embracing," yet he notes that "there is a tendency for a rather narrow leadership group to rotate the many posts among themselves most of the time. . . . These members . . . undoubtedly form a kind of elite."[27] H. Darin-Drabkin has argued that this tendency has become more pronounced over time: "The most conspicuous development has been the shift in the field of policy making from the general assembly to the secretariat and its committees. . . . If we compare the present relationships in the kibbutz with the situation in the 1920s, we find that the general assembly's scope has considerably diminished." In contrast, he notes that the power of the secretariat, the committees, and other executive institutions has been augmented and cautioned that "the strengthening of the centralist forces in the kibbutz and the shift of power to executive institutions contain some inherent dangers to kibbutz democracy which cannot be ignored."[28]

The problems facing the kibbutz are not only political but also social in nature. Besides attempting to build an organization in which all individuals share in the exercise of political power, the kibbutz has tried to develop communal living and educational arrangements. But in recent years the membership's desire to forego their own private lives in order to participate in such communal activities seems to be waning. French and French note that parents increasingly choose to take their meals in their own apartments rather than in the communal dining rooms. Moreover, in contrast "to the established tradition of communal child rearing, many parents are taking their children home for the night rather than leaving them in the communal children's house."[29] In other cases people complain about the joint purchases of goods and services and insist that there be more individualized consumption. When the kibbutzim were relatively unmechanized and poor, people were more willing to adopt a standardized, communal pattern of living. But as French and French remark, "with greater wealth comes increasing opportunity for individualized consumption, and the kibbutz experience indicates that this can be damaging to communal solidarity."[30] Presently the kibbutzim are toying with the idea of allowing personal budgets, but Haim Barkai has observed that this proposal has become the subject of "one of the most heated debates the kibbutz movement has ever come on."[31] Many people perhaps rightly feel that the movement towards more personalized comsumption will jeopardize the very basis of kibbutz solidarity. To observers like Leon, the kibbutz has begun to yield to the dangerous tendency "for the centrifugal forces . . . to grow and for the individual to be so occupied with his own work, his own family, his own social circle and his own interests that he loses sight of the organic totality of kibbutz life."[32] In the opinion of many commentators, the kibbutzim are gradually evolving towards a less collective form of living. French and French even conclude that "the future of collective settlements in Israel would seem to be unclear. The kibbutzim remain alive and well today; it remains to be seen how long this will continue to be true."[33]

If the Israeli kibbutz represents an attempt, however flawed, to build the kind of community that participatory democrats often seem to advocate, it by no means exhausts the possibilities for enhanced individual participation. Many communitarian democrats, including Bachrach, Pateman, and Ellerman, suggest that the most feasible way of building participatory communities in the United States or in any industrial country, for that matter, is through worker control of industry. This is especially true of participatory democrats with socialist leanings, who believe that economic changes need to precede or accompany attempts at increasing individual participation. In fact, the idea of worker participation has gained such popularity that even pluralists like Robert Dahl have affirmed the importance of experimenting with new forms of worker involvement in factories.[34] Yet Dahl has recognized, as many communitarian democrats have not, that perhaps the greatest obstacle to more participation in the work place may be the relative indifference of the average wage earner.

In discussing worker participation, we must distinguish between worker interest in lower-level, or job-centered, issues and in higher-level, or managerial, decisions. Lower-level activities refer "broadly to those management decisions relating to control of day-to-day shop floor activities, while the higher level refers to decisions on investment, marketing and so forth."[35] As Paul Blumberg has shown in a survey of the literature on industrial relations, most workers are interested in having some say in industrial decisions that directly affect them in the shop.[36] As is to be expected, workers appear to prefer democratic managers who treat them with respect to authoritarian supervisors who preside over the shop by fiat. But merely because workers are interested in job-centered problems does not necessarily mean that they want to participate in higher-level, managerial decisions. There is considerable evidence from experiments in a variety of countries indicating that workers are apathetic about such forms of participation.

For example, since 1951 the West German government has attempted to increase worker participation in the operation of the steel and mining industries. By law the government has required firms in these industries to set up workers' councils in which labor shares equally with management the right to make decisions governing vacations, work rules, the administration of plant welfare facilities, and the time and method of wage payments. These same councils also have some say in the determination of pay scales and in the hiring and firing of employees. Most observers of the German workers' councils, including Daniel Kramer and Hardy Wagner, find that the authority of the councils is substantial and that they vigorously exercise the statutory powers granted to them.[37] However, despite the apparent presence of an effective vehicle to govern their factories, most workers appear indifferent to the councils. On a visit to one firm Kramer found that only 15 percent of the work force attended a plant personnel meeting of the workers' council. "It does appear," he notes, "that the reaction of the ordinary employee to the doings of the councils is one of almost total unconcern." Kramer quotes the chairman of another workers' council as saying that "the workers in our place are really not interested in their works councils. They come to us quickly enough if they have a pay question or a dispute about hours with management. They are concerned only with what they can get out of it."[38]

Efforts in other countries to involve workers more fully in industrial decisions have repeatedly fallen short of their objectives. In Israel the attempt to provide for more worker participation in factories has met with even less success than in Germany. The Israeli case is interesting because the enterprises that have attempted to introduce more worker participation are owned by the General Federation of Labor (the Histadrut), an organization that officially describes itself as committed to socialist principles. Between 1945 and 1967 the Histadrut leadership made three major attempts, all of which proved to be unsuccessful, to institutionalize worker participation in the industrial sector.[39] This failure cannot be attributed to any single cause, but worker apathy seems to have been a contributing factor blocking implementation of the program. Keitha Fina concludes that the program failed to work because of "managerial resistance . . . worker reluctance to vary well established norms without drastic technological changes in evidence, and worker apathy towards activities other than those related to setting norms and premiums."[40] In a similar vein, Pateman cites a survey of Norwegian workers by H. Holter that found that only "16% of blue collar and 11% of white collar workers wished they had more participation in decisions concerning the management of the whole firm."[41]

On the basis of a series of instances such as those described above, Paul Blumberg, who is himself an advocate of workers' control, has admitted:

Workers' indifference cannot be overcome simply by involving them directly. And here we must take note of the record of joint consultation bodies, miscellaneous plant committees, and other advisory councils in England, France, Belgium, Sweden, . . . Israel and elsewhere. While these have involved workers directly or through representatives close to home, they have generally proved very disappointing and have failed to arouse workers' sustained interest. . . . In Britain, France, Israel, and India these bodies have achieved the most meager results, at best, and discussions of these forms sound like nothing so much as funeral orations.[42]

The repeated failure of so many efforts to involve labor more fully in the work place thus seems to raise numerous doubts about the feasibility of Pateman's and Bachrach's calls for more worker control.

However, participatory democrats who are also socialists insist that the data we have looked at by no means definitively prove that individuals cannot become interested in the running of their factories. They argue that in a profit-oriented, capitalist system, workers become so socialized into being passive tools of management that they are never likely to want a larger voice in running their own lives. In the view of Ellerman et al., the trouble with

Pateman's argument is that merely expanding political opportunities is insufficient to change the attitudes of the public. The very economic base underlying the political system must also be altered if we expect workers to embrace the goals of participatory democracy. The assumption of Ellerman et al. is that unless the structure of large-scale capitalism is replaced by small-scale political and economic institutions, individuals will lack the incentives necessary to exercise a greater role in shaping the forces that govern them. The inability to grasp this point, a participatory democrat might argue, even accounts for the mistaken belief that the problems we have identified in American communes or Israeli kibbutzim are likely to recur in all communal experiments. Even if communes or factories are based on socialist principles, they are not likely to survive if they exist in a larger capitalist economy.

While this argument has a certain degree of appeal, it is a rather difficult proposition to test. All too often, radical communitarian socialists seem inclined to suggest ad infinitum that if only an additional political or economic change were made, the public would respond as participatory democrats believe they should. Since the prospect of creating a decentralized socialist system in the U.S. is not very promising, it is difficult to predict how people would behave under changed economic conditions. Fortunately, however, the fact that Yugoslavia has adopted a highly decentralized socialist system of government does provide us with some means of examining the thesis of the more radical participatory democrats.

In 1950 Yugoslavia established an economic system that has sought to avoid both the pattern of large-scale capitalism found in the West and the pattern of state socialism practiced by the Soviet Union. In place of a command economy, in which a few elites make decisions, Tito has attempted to create a decentralized system in which a great deal of economic and political power is devolved to individual factories. Up until 1970 the state required every economic enterprise to set up a workers' council to be elected by the employees. While workers' councils, which usually consisted of twenty members, were theoretically to retain primary responsibility for running the enterprise, most elected a smaller management board and appointed a director to assume operating responsibility for the factory. Since the Yugoslavian model seems to satisfy the conditions stipulated by communitarian socialists, we should expect to find more workers displaying interest and participating in the operation of the factories. However, as in many nonsocialist countries, the data on Yugoslavian worker participation are not very encouraging. First of all, it should be pointed out that worker control of factories is a highly indirect, formalistic process. To alter conditions in their enterprises, employees must work through their elected representatives on the workers' councils. But as Kramer has noted, many workers' councils often ignore the demands of their own constituents: "A questionnaire circulated by . . . [the journal] *Borba* showed that only fifty-six per cent of the workers who completed the form said that their work council had disclosed to them what it was trying to accomplish."[43] Secondly, even when the councils do stay in closer contact with workers, it is an open question whether they actually exercise much power. Opinion on this subject is split. Fred Neal has argued "that the meaningfulness of worker management varied from enterprise to enterprise."[44] In some plants he found workers' councils that were in control of factory operations, while in other cases he encountered councils that were not coming to grips with any important managerial problems. In contrast, in several studies of worker perceptions of influence within their factories, Josip Zupanov and Arnold Tannenbaum have observed that the director, rather than the workers' council, wields the most power.[45] Similarly, Jiri Kolaja conducted content analysis of numerous council meetings and has concluded that the plant director and not the workers' council is the key figure in the Yugoslavian factory.[46] In one plant, for instance, he found that in the course of a year the director seemed responsible for initiating over sixty-six decisions while the councils seemed responsible for only nine.

Even if workers' councils were more active in running their factories than the present evidence indicates, we still need to know (1) whether workers think self-management is an important goal to strive for and (2) whether they as individuals are willing to spend their time participating in such self-management councils. Until recently, most observers have found that workers said it was important to strengthen the power of workers' councils—or at least paid lip service to such a goal. However, Veljko Rus has pointed out that in recent years public support for all-powerful councils has abated. By 1968, he noted, most workers argued that the managers should have about the same amount of power as that exercised by the councils.[47] Likewise, Gerry Hunnius has observed that after a constitutional amendment was passed in 1970, relaxing the standards for worker participation in factories, many firms became more centralized in their operations.[48] The Yugoslavian government undertook the constitutional revision in order to enhance the flexibility of individual factories, allowing the amount of power that enterprises parcel out to workers' councils to be a matter of their own choosing. In order to maximize the plant's efficiency and productivity, many workers have taken advantage of the new constitutional provisions to concede more power to their own corps of professionally trained managers and to deemphasize the importance of the workers' councils.

When we inquire whether most workers themselves are eager to participate in the operations of the councils, the evidence is negative. In 1965 Josip Obradovic undertook an extensive survey of worker attitudes in Yugoslavia, interviewing over 537 workers in twenty different plants.[49] On the basis of his survey he "concluded that participation in self-management should not be overemphasized as a source of satisfaction."[50] He noted that workers mentioned wages, working conditions, and possibilities for advancement highest in their list of desired job characteristics. In contrast, participation on workers' councils rated fifth with participants and sixth with nonparticipants. Many other observers of Yugoslavian factories have often remarked that the average worker is indifferent to participation in self-management. Ichak Adizes relates the conversation of one worker, who told him, "Let someone else manage; I want good pay." He observes that instead of eagerly participating in the affairs of their council, many individuals complain of the constant round of meetings and political activities as a drain on their time.[51]

Sharon Zukin arrives at a similar conclusion in her study of public attitudes in Yugoslavia, noting that "Yugoslavians tend to see self-management more in terms of economic benefits than ideological goals."[52] In an extensive set of discussions with numerous Yugoslavians, she finds that "self-management as an ideological goal has little relevance to people's everyday lives" and that most "appear preoccupied with the standard of living. . . . The two decades of self-management are perceived as a given institution, a formalism from which the ordinary Yugoslav derives only such benefits as he can see and spend."[53] Similarly, Kolaja observed that Yugoslavian workers are often highly selective in their participation, displaying little or no concern about many of the general industrial problems facing their factories but great interest in more personal questions, such as how many apartments their plants will build and who will be assigned to them.[54] In fact, on the basis of studies such as Kolaja's, Pateman admits that among average Yugoslavian factory workers "there is evidence of a more general lack of knowledge of, and interest in, the basic working of the system."[55] However, later she tries to argue that "the Yugoslav experience gives us no good reason to suppose that the democratization of industrial authority structure is impossible, difficult and complicated though it may be."[56] Whether the evidence she herself cites warrants such optimism is another question.

As has been true of experiments with worker control in Germany and elsewhere, the Yugoslavian effort to increase participation has not met with complete success. While communitarian socialists claim that changes in the economic structure will precipitate alterations in worker attitudes and behavior, the record seems to indicate otherwise. Over a quarter of a century of decentralized socialism in Yugoslavia appears to have had no appreciable impact on the willingness of its citizenry to participate actively in industrial affairs. A few Yugoslavian socialists like Dragan Markovic argue that the "consciousness of workers formed in capitalist relations of production—when the means of production have been separated from producers—is changing very slowly,"[57] but they overlook the fact that workers appear to be becoming less, rather than more, concerned with self-management, the longer socialism exists in Yugoslavia. Even when there are ample opportunities to become involved, people seem unable to sustain any long-term interest in inclusive forms of communal or industrial participation, preferring instead to restrict their involvement to matters of more direct and personal concern.

If workers often choose not to participate more fully in communal activities, participatory democrats of a socialist persuasion always have the convenient argument of claiming that the public is still suffering from "false consciousness." Many communal socialists seem to fall into the trap of insisting that there is a one-to-one relationship between a country's economic system and its political institutions. But as anyone knows after even a cursory look at the diverse array of governments in various countries where the means of production are publicly owned, the link between politics and economics is not always that apparent. Moreover, it should be stressed that even if we accept the participatory socialist critique as valid, it would still be possible to question the feasibility of implementing the communitarian model. If the creation of a more decentralized, egalitarian socialist community would change public attitudes towards community involvement, one must ask how participatory socialists expect to build a socialist society in a country they believe to be dominated by capitalist interests. The socialist variety of participatory democracy seems flawed in that it lacks a meaningful theory of social change. While communitarian democrats have a vision of the kind of society they would like to build, they provide few if any viable suggestions as to how that vision will finally be attained. To insist that people will change only if certain economic or political reforms are instituted begs the question of how those alterations are to be implemented in the first place.

The Nature of Communal Life

There are still other difficulties that plague a participatory form of democracy. It is certainly not clear from the record of previous experiments in communal living whether small communities are the most suitable form of government for encouraging meaningful public debate. Nevertheless, most communitarian democrats have insisted that small political units provide the individual with more opportunities for meaningful participation than do larger bodies of government. Through the vehicle of the town meeting or communal gathering, scaled-down units of government supposedly afford every citizen the chance to discuss the whole range of issues facing the community. Unfortunately, however, the practice of small, face-to-face communities often falls short of their promise. Indeed, there seems to be considerable evidence that such communities tend to inhibit public debate rather than to facilitate it. Edward Banfield, James Q. Wilson, Arthur Vidich, Joseph Bensman and A. H. Birch have observed that people in small communities usually go out of their way to avoid discussing controversial issues.[58] City councils in small towns are often noted for their ability to ramble on indefinitely without ever coming to grips with the issues before them. Instead of directly confronting potentially troublesome problems, most seek to avoid dealing with the issues as long as possible, and when they finally do make decisions, they usually formulate proposals in such a way as to gain the support of every member of the council. Vidich and Bensman reported that in the two years they observed a small town government at work, "all decisions brought to a vote were passed unanimously. The dissent, disagreement, and factionalism which existed in the community [were] not expressed at board meetings."[59]

In a similar vein, utopian communities and kibbutz settlements often develop norms that lead to the repression, rather than the expression, of alternative points of view. Kanter has noted that many of the utopian experiments of the nineteenth century went out of their way to ostracize persons who deviated in the slightest way from the established norms of the community.[60] Rather than encouraging individuals to question the prevailing style of life, most communes sought to resocialize their members to conform to existing patterns of behavior. Even when communities held assemblies to formulate policy, their purpose was often less to hear and act upon the grievances of their members than to instill the kinds of attitudes that would prevent them from complaining in the first place. Robert Hine has observed in his study of utopian colonies in California over the last hundred years that those communes that lasted for any length of time were often extremely authoritarian, requiring "unquestioning obedience to leadership."[61] Similarly, Bruno Bettelheim has pointed out that there are well-defined restraints on meaningful debate in the Israeli kibbutz. Bettelheim argues that kibbutz children are trained not to deviate from the norms of the community and that while they can criticize certain practices of the settlement, they come to realize that there are clearly defined limits beyond which they should not venture.[62]

Likewise Melford Spiro claims that "although the regimentation that certain critics of socialism regard as intrinsic to a planned society is not characteristic [of the kibbutz] there can be no doubt that one's choices are restricted in a social system of this type."[63] He points out that "group censure, informal though it is, is highly effective in a small community" in dampening the expression of unpopular ideas. [64]

There are a variety of possible explanations that may account for the restricted political life in these types of communities. Kanter at times suggests that the lack of genuine debate and participation in many of the nineteenth-century utopian settlements was an accident of their precarious situation. [65] Since many communities faced an uncertain existence, they went to great lengths to reinforce the commitment of their followers by limiting the influx of new ideas and by pressuring members to internalize the prevailing norms of the group. This explanation suggests that the very scarcity of people who wanted to belong to an affective community may in part account for the fact that many communes chose to restrict, rather than expand, the scope of public debate.

However, at other times Kanter, as well as scholars like Bettelheim and Boris Stern, have implied that the hostility of communal settlements to internal debate was inherent in their very conception of community and public participation. [66] Stern has remarked that the socialist founders of the kibbutz considered "the movement to represent the highest form of social organization as yet devised by human beings. As such the kibbutz community cannot tolerate deviations, revisionism, or internal revolutionary changes." "All educational and cultural activities of the kibbutz," he noted, "are designed to transmit to the children the importance of preserving the kibbutz and its social and moral values."[67] Communal movements like the kibbutz have been founded on the belief that public participation will lead to individual moral growth and self-development since it will allow the individual to identify with the higher moral purposes embodied in the community. Participation is not simply a mechanism for achieving compromises among competing private interests; on the contrary, it is a means for the individual to overcome his selfish concerns by involving himself with the welfare of the community as a whole.

However, in specifying the ways in which men should benefit

from participation, many communal movements have ended up restricting the scope of public debate. If participation should lead to individual moral development, as they have believed, then participation cannot be a completely open-end process. Utopian communities and kibbutz settlements have had no reason to tolerate—let alone encourage—a diversity of opinions since they have believed they know how men should develop in the first place. If people will morally grow only when they become less concerned with their own private affairs, there seems to be little justification for tolerating what has often been interpreted as self-serving criticism on the part of individual participants. When people have argued over the goals of the group, it is only natural that participatory settlements have seen it as a failure of communal spirit. Because utopian communities and kibbutz settlements have believed that citizen involvement is a means of making people more public minded, it is perhaps inevitable that they have insisted participation reinforce, not challenge, the norms of the group. In the process these communities have inverted the purpose of participation by insisting that individuals involve themselves in community affairs, not to debate the objectives of the group, but to internalize community goals that have already been formulated.

This conception of participation was summed up well by Rousseau's notion of the "general will."[68] Rousseau believed that the individual could attain moral self-development through participation in the life of the community, but he shared with many modern participatory democrats some definite notions about which forms of citizen involvement were permissible and which were not. Although at times he suggested that people should be free to participate as they wished, he also insisted that they ought to "will the general will," that they should affirm the standards best suited to the larger community.[69] Since Rousseau believed that an individual would not morally grow or develop unless he chose what was in the common interest of all, he did not believe that public participation could be a process of totally unrestricted give-and-take. Like the members of the utopian settlements and kibbutzim, Rousseau regarded popular participation less as a means for identifying and resolving public differences than as a vehicle for realizing higher moral purposes.

Although many participatory democrats have espoused very limited conceptions of participation, other advocates of communal forms of democracy entertain less restrictive views on this subject. For instance, unlike many of his predecessors, Wolff repeatedly stresses the need for communities to develop elaborate procedures to guarantee full and complete discussion. [70] Wolff is eager to build a theory of participatory democracy that does not specify in a priori fashion the benefits that will accrue to individuals from participating in public affairs. In contrast to Rousseau and the builders of the utopian communities and kibbutz settlements, he envisions the creation of a polity that normatively will tolerate the expression of a diversity of opinions. The question we need to ask, however, is whether empirically it is possible to have much meaningful debate in a small community. Even if the founders of participatory settlements do not equate individual development with the internalization of group standards, strong pressures may inevitably develop within the community to choke off debate.

The avoidance of controversy in small towns is instructive in this respect. Students of urban politics have often argued that the reluctance of small communities to tolerate dissent may reflect their fear of public conflict. As the unit of government in which people interact becomes smaller, the problem of dealing with discord becomes more acute. This observation raises troublesome problems for one of participatory democracy's most cherished beliefs, that the differences that divide men are not serious in nature. In contrast to pluralists, who insist that there are always likely to be disagreements between individuals that can be compromised but never completely eliminated, participatory democrats have been much more sanguine about the possibility of eliminating conflict. They have argued that by scaling down the size of the political community it will be possible for people to resolve their differences amicably and decide upon mutually satisfactory policies. But ironically enough, many observers, including George Simmel, Lewis Coser, and Banfield and Wilson, suggest that the opposite relationship may be true: the closer the ties between people become, the more likely intense conflict will occur. [71] Thus when the unit of government becomes smaller, the danger that disagreement will become intense and uncontainable increases rather than diminishes. In small communities there is no way to segment or isolate differences between individuals. As Simmel notes:

The more we have in common with another as a whole person, the more easily will our totality be involved in every single relation to him. Therefore if a quarrel arises between persons in an internal relationship, it often . . . will be . . . passionately expansive. [72]

Similarly, as Coser points out, if people constantly interact with one another, the possibility exists "that conflict would mobilize the entire affect of [an individual's] personality" and totally disrupt his personal relations. [73] Banfield and Wilson observe that when conflict does arise in small communities, it is often difficult to contain since by their very nature small localities have no formal structure for dealing with dissension in an impersonal manner. It is precisely because of this danger that small communities have a tendency either to avoid or to suppress situations of potential conflict. The generally accepted rule of unanimity and the rambling, pointless style of discourse characteristic of many small towns are effective ways of insuring that individuals are not put on the spot or forced to clearly examine their differences with others. [74] Besides tacitly agreeing not to disagree, the only other option is for communities to pressure their members into internalizing certain common standards of behavior.

While many of the utopian settlements or kibbutzim may have restricted public debate because they had a particular conception of the benefits of participation, their policies also helped to prevent potentially dangerous disagreements from breaking out. Hine has noted in his study of California communes that the most democratic organizations were the ones least likely to last. In those organizations that established general assemblies to foster debate, "tremendous conflicts" arose "which usually proved quickly fatal." [75] Perhaps inevitably, then, most participatory experiments have attempted to avoid or suppress debate and conflict, for when they occur, their impact on the group is difficult to limit. If issues ever do break through these social restraints, they are apt, as Banfield and Wilson note, "to polarize the community into hostile camps." [76]

The Internal Dilemma of Participatory Democracy

Even if participatory communities did encourage more internal debate, there are additional reasons for being skeptical about their ability to foster meaningful citizen involvement. As a basic tenet, participatory democrats have wanted to increase both the individual's ability to participate and his power to control the events that trouble him. However, as Dahl has pointed out, a conflict may exist between maximizing opportunities for individual involvement and maximizing the ability to actually implement one's wishes.[77] If we want to expand individual participation, we must, as most communitarian democrats have long recognized, limit the size and population of the political unit. Naturally, as the number of members in a community begins to grow, the ability of each individual to influence the shaping of policy must decline correspondingly.

As a way of illustrating this point, we might try to estimate how many people could be expected to play a moderate to active role in the deliberations of a community. If we take as our model the New England town meeting, which two or three hundred persons might attend, we would soon see that the limits of time would severely restrict the actual number of participants who could voice their opinions. If the community held a meeting once a week for four hours, and if the time allotted to each individual was ten minutes, only twenty-four people would be able to state their views. These individuals would represent less than one-tenth of the total number of people gathered in the assembly. As the community became smaller, the percentage of people who could play a direct role would naturally begin to grow. Thus the size of the political unit and the degree of citizen involvement are inversely related. However, as the size of the community diminishes, so do the resources and power it can draw on to cope with problems that are regional or national in nature. The smaller the jurisdiction of the political unit, the less its "government can regulate aspects of the environment that its citizens want to regulate, from air and water pollution and racial justice to the dissemination of nuclear weapons."[78] In their quest for effective or meaningful participation, communitarian democrats thus seem to confront an unresolvable paradox. By reducing the size of the polity, they increase the opportunities for individuals to participate; but by increasing the opportunities for citizen involvement, they run the risk of trivializing its importance. The smaller the unit of government, the less significant become the issues that the individuals within the political community can effectively influence.

This dilemma is best seen in the work of Wolff, one of the most articulate defenders of communitarian democracy. In "Beyond Tolerance" Wolff talks of the need for developing policies that will deal with pressing collective problems such as poverty, public order, and pollution. [79] However, his solution to these problems is not to centralize power but to fragment it among many independent communities. While these units may afford numerous opportunities for the individual to participate in politics, Wolff provides no hint as to how they will be able to deal effectively with the social ills that alarm him. Since most of the issues he mentions transcend narrow political units, any established participatory government would lack jurisdiction for effectively alleviating these problems. Likewise, if independent communes were not subject to the authority of a larger political entity, the danger might arise that one unit's answer to an issue like pollution would be unacceptable to other localities.

The Costs and Benefits of Intensive Participation

It is also possible to argue that the psychological costs of intensive communal participation often outweigh their assumed benefits. Nevertheless, communitarian democrats have frequently defended active citizen involvement for just the opposite reason. They insist that pluralism, like most other theories of democracy, fails to appreciate the value of participation as an end in and of itself. In their view, public involvement itself is a means of realizing man's fullest moral and emotional potential and is thus desirable apart from any instrumental benefits it might provide.

However, most participatory democrats have mustered very little evidence in support of their contention that communal life has a beneficial effect on the individual personality. Indeed, if we look at analyses of the impact of communal life in the Israeli kibbutz on the psychological makeup of its members, we find evidence which, although fragmentary in nature, suggests that intensive forms of participation may entail very high costs. Scholars like Murray Weingarten, Yonina Talmon, Bruno Bettelheim, A. I. Rabin, and Melford Spiro—who are by no means unsympathetic observers of the kibbutz—have found that communal forms of life often stifle, rather than enhance, an individual's sense of freedom and self-fulfillment.[80] Even though the kibbutz may envelop the individual in an affective community and successfully socialize him to look after the interests of the larger whole, it appears to impoverish his outlook on life. Bettelheim has noted that

in . . . striving to undo social alienation on the one hand and too much family closeness on the other [members of the kibbutz] have gone way out in seeking a solidarity of equals. But having enjoyed collective closeness for a while now, they seem to find it hard to bear at times.

Precisely because they share so much of daily life with each other, they have a great need, like turtles, to withdraw into their shells. Though they greet each other with a "Shalom!" or "How's things?" twenty times or more each day, they really have little to talk about, since everyone knows everything about everyone else—good reason to withhold the really important things for oneself and to share them with no one.[81]

In a similar vein, Murray Weingarten has pointed out that the word *matzuv raah* ("depression") is very popular in a number of kibbutzim. Because life in a communal setting places heavy demands on a person's time and energy, many individuals consciously or subconsciously feel overburdened by community affairs. Rather than being fulfilled by the intensity of their affective ties with other members of the settlement, they become depressed by their inability to have a life apart from the kibbutz. Weingarten notes that in recognition of this problem, some kibbutzim have formulated an individual bill of rights in order to provide people with a private outlet for the expression of their own needs.[82]

Likewise, Yonina Talmon has observed that most members of the second generation are very ambivalent about the continuity of the kibbutz movement. While they believe that they have an obligation to their parents and to the kibbutz that raised them to stay and help the movement survive, they often see communal activities as restricting, rather than enlarging or enriching, their lives. Regardless of the sense of security that the closely knit community provides, many feel a sense of claustrophobia within the kibbutz settlement. Talmon notes that the decision to remain a part of the community is often a difficult one.

The duty to stay on in the native village engenders a deep fear of closure because it implies blocked mobility and a curtailment of life chances. It imposes a drastic limitation on free choice of domicile, of career or associates, and of friends. The cultivation of external contact and the period of service outside the kibbutz mitigate local closure but at the same time accentuate the problems involved in local continuity. Many second generation members are loath to sever their external ties and to forego the more variegated opportunities offered by life outside their kibbutz. They feel cut off and hemmed in. [83]

In addition to limiting the individual's freedom to act as he pleases, the closeness of the kibbutz also seems to retard the creativity of its members. Because children are taught to be concerned about the welfare of the community, they are often discouraged from entertaining ideas that challenge well-engrained attitudes. The spirit of loyalty and commitment that the kibbutz attempts to instill in its members frequently tends to kill off any spark of originality or uniqueness in its children. A. I. Rabin has observed that "the kibbutz subject's own goals are rather short range, characterized by a short future time perspective."[84] He maintains that "this trend is primarily due to the fact that the kibbutz does not hold out the freedom of vocational and occupational choice to its membership; individual goals of a long range are determined by the collectivity."[85] In a similar vein, Bettelheim argues that the "personality of the kibbutz-born generation seems depleted compared to the complexity and richness in some of the first generation."[86] To further confirm this point, we may note that soldiers from the kibbutz often seem to lack the ability to make flexible and spontaneous adjustments to ever changing situations. In the opinion of many Israeli officers, children of the kibbutz are committed and courageous fighters who will endure countless hardships to protect their country, but they are unable to adapt effectively to situations with which they have had no prior experience.[87] The environment from which they come seems to have provided them with limited capacity to deal with the vagaries of new and complex developments.[88]

Even though life in a kibbutz often seems to result in a sense of claustrophobia, lack of a private life, and diminished creativity, it still is possible to argue that the friendship and warm, supportive environment of the commune more than compensate for any of these deficiencies. In an intensive, affective organization we would expect few members to suffer from human isolation or lack of close personal ties. However, in an important study, *Children of the Kibbutz*, Melford Spiro raises serious doubts about the veracity of this claim. On the basis of his examination of kibbutz children, he notes:

Very few *sabras* [those born and raised in a kibbutz] have intimate friends. Even in the high school the "chum" or "buddy"—the inseparable same sex friend that is so characteristic of American adolescent behavior—is all but nonexistent. Moreover, the ordinary close friend is also infrequent. . . . The situation is no different from the adult *sabras*. . . . The *sabras* not only avoid deep emotional relationships with a few, but they maintain an attitude of psychological distance with the many.[89]

Spiro insists that these traits are not endemic in Israeli culture nor found among Jews in general, for he claims that "since this syndrome is not characteristic of the *sabra's* parents, we may further assume that such experiences are a function of kibbutz socialization."[90]

Ironically enough, many communitarian democrats advocate the creation of a collective form of politics because they believe that the atomistic nature of early liberalism has had damaging psychological consequences for the individual. They argue that because the highly individualistic outlook of liberalism ignores man's social needs, it has led to the alienation, rather than the fulfillment, of the individual. What participatory democrats have failed to see is that their own proposals to create a tightly knit community can likewise have serious psychological repercussions. While extreme individualism seems to lead to social isolation or anomic behavior, a small, cohesive political and social organization seems to restrict a person's opportunities to develop his own personality. Even though children in a participatory setting may be more community minded than individuals raised on the outside, they frequently end up paying a relatively high price. In exchange for the alleged benefits of affective ties with others, they often must curtail their imagination and control their creative instincts. Instead of being ennobling, participation in a communal form of politics seems to be a restricting experience that limits the overall development of the individual. While communitarian democrats claim that pluralism fails to appreciate the beneficial effects of participation as an end in and of itself, the actual record of participation in the types of communities described above shows that involvement in such communities frequently has its offsetting psychological costs.

A Reassessment of the Data

Despite the critical implications of the empirical studies cited above, a variety of commentators have questioned whether it is valid to evaluate the prospects for participatory democracy on the basis of past historical examples. Some proponents of communitarian participation maintain that empirical data can never undermine or refute what is basically a normative theory of democracy. Graeme Duncan and Steven Lukes insist that "to claim that sociological findings can show these . . . political theories to be demonstrably invalid is seriously to misunderstand the most basic features of much political theory, which often touches reality only at the edges."[91] They maintain that participatory democrats are not so much proposing an empirical theory of government that is readily attainable as offering a normative ideal that they hope people will eventually aspire to fulfill. Advocates of communitarian democracy regard their theory as a critique of the status quo and look upon intensive participation as a goal that men should constantly try to attain. While they recognize that people fail to live up to the assumptions of the communitarian model, they see no need to abandon the goal itself. On the contrary, because intensive participation is an ideal, communitarian forms of democracy are valid as a standard for measuring and evaluating the worthiness of our present political institutions. The gap between the assumptions of the participatory model and the behavior of the public is thus less an indication of the model's failure than a sign of the need for political reform. The theories of communitarian democracy "are a critique of reality in terms of a vision of human nature and possibilities, and for this reason cannot simply be refuted on the grounds that people do not satisfy the required standards."[92]

While the above line of reasoning may seem persuasive, it is flawed in two respects. First of all, even if we accept the participatory argument as a radical critique of the status quo and a statement of a more egalitarian ideal, it is still important to ask if the vision of communitarian democracy can ever be achieved. Unless advocates of communal politics such as Duncan and Lukes are willing to agree that their conception of democracy is merely a utopian goal with no chance of ever being realized, it is important to empirically assess the feasibility of building a participatory community. All social critics must eventually decide if their proposals are merely wistful propositions that perhaps only "true believers" may find interesting, or if they are serious calls for reform that will one day become a reality. Secondly, and even more importantly, Duncan's and Luke's argument seems to be based on a misunderstanding of what the empirical evidence actually shows. They suggest that merely because the data indicate that it is not presently feasible to implement the goal of communitarian democracy, we should not jettison the participatory ideal. But an important question to ask is whether the ideals of communitarian democracy are worth achieving regardless of whether or not they are feasible to implement. To make that assessment we need to know if the achievement of certain values, such as a sense of community, compromises other important values, such as individuality or creativity. While studies such as Bettelheim's or Weingarten's cannot tell us how to rank order different sets of objectives, they can certainly provide some insight into the costs of realizing alternative sets of values. The dichotomy that Duncan and Lukes implicitly make between a feasible and a normative argument does not undermine the relevance of empirical data for evaluating the claims of communitarian democrats. In this sense, the collection of empirical data is central to a proper assessment of the benefits and drawbacks of participatory democracy.

It should also be pointed out that even if we accept the proposition that the empirical data on participation are unfavorable, other critics have suggested that evidence from past experiments in communitarian democracy does not necessarily imply anything about the future. Merely because some attempts at achieving more intensive participation have been flawed does not logically mean that all future attempts must likewise fail. However, even though the thrust of this argument is basically correct, it seems somewhat beside the point. The possibility exists that in certain cases people might be able to sustain an interest in a participatory settlement that provided its members with a satisfying, rather than restrictive, communal existence. The limitations of other experiments do not rule out that eventuality. But it is necessary to stress that the available data indicate that the outlook for building such communal forms of democracy on a widespread scale is not very promising.

NOTES

1. Robert Paul Wolff, *In Defense of Anarchism*; Robert Paul Wolff, *The Poverty of Liberalism*; Peter Bachrach, *The Theory of Democratic Elitism*; David Ellerman, "Capitalism and Workers' Self-Management," pp. 3-20.

2. Wolff, *Poverty of Liberalism,* pp. 185-95; Carole Pateman, *Participation and Democratic Theory,* pp. 79-101. See also Arnold S. Kaufman, "Human Nature and Participatory Democracy," pp. 178-201.

3. Ellerman, "Capitalism and Workers' Self-Management," pp. 3-20.

4. Jean Jacques Rousseau, *The Social Contract*, p. 20.

5. Terrence Cook and Patrick Morgan, *Participatory Democracy*, p. 10.

6. Philip Converse, "The Nature of Belief Systems in Mass Publics," pp. 206-61; Sidney Verba and Norman Nie, *Participation in America*, p. 106; David E. RePass, "Issue Salience and Party Choice," pp. 389-400.

7. Gabriel Almond and Sidney Verba, *The Civic Culture*, pp. 337-75.

8. Pateman, *Participation and Democratic Theory*, pp. 79-101.

9. Ellerman, "Capitalism and Workers' Self-Management"; Charles Hampden-Turner, "The Factory as an Oppressive and Non-Emancipatory Environment," pp. 30-45; Paul Jacobs and Saul Landau, eds., *The New Radicals*, p. 154.

10. Rosabeth Moss Kanter, *Commitment and Community*, p. 63.

11. Ibid., pp. 75-125.

12. Ibid., p. 82.

13. Ibid., p. 103.

14. Ibid., p. 106.

15. Ibid., p. 107.

16. Ibid., p. 146.

17. David French and Elena French, *Working Communally*, pp. 65-67.

18. Ibid., p. 67.

19. Ibid., p. 69.

20. Ibid., p. 103.

21. Dan Leon, *The Kibbutz*, pp. 1-24.

22. Ibid., pp. 1-24.

23. Ibid., p. 15.

24. Avraham Ben-Yosef, *The Purest Democracy in the World*, pp. 33-34.

25. Ibid., p. 34.

26. Ibid., p. 29.

27. Ibid., p. 32.

28. H. Darin-Drabkin, *The Other Society*, p. 109.

29. French and French, *Working Communally*, p. 135.

30. Ibid., p. 137.

31. Haim Barkai, *The Kibbutz*, p. 40.

32. Leon, *The Kibbutz*, p. 73.

33. French and French, *Working Communally*, p. 135.

34. Robert Dahl, *After the Revolution*, pp. 120-40.

35. Pateman, *Participation and Democratic Theory*, p. 70.

36. Paul Blumberg, *Industrial Democracy*, pp. 70-138.

37. Daniel Kramer, *Participatory Democracy*, p. 78; Hardy Wagner, *Erfahrungen mit dem Betriebsverfassungsgesetz*, pp. 82-90.

38. D. Kramer, *Participatory Democracy*, p. 82.

39. Keitha Sapsin Fine, "Worker Participation in Israel," pp. 226-67.

40. Ibid., p. 238.

41. Pateman, *Participation and Democratic Theory*, p. 85.

42. Blumberg, *Industrial Democracy*, p. 3.

43. D. Kramer, *Participatory Democracy*, p. 81.

44. Fred Neal, *Titoism in Action*, p. 138.

45. Josip Zupanov and Arnold S. Tannenbaum, "The Distribution of Control in Some Yugoslav Industrial Organizations as Perceived by Members," pp. 98-99.

46. Jiri Kolaja, *Workers' Councils*, p. 34.

47. Veljko Rus, "Influence Structure in Yugoslav Enterprise," p. 150.

48. Gerry Hunnius, "Yugoslavia," p. 267.

49. Josip Obradovic, "Participation and Work Attitudes in Yugoslavia," pp. 161-69.

50. Josip Obradovic, as summarized by Gerry Hunnius, "Workers' Self-Management in Yugoslavia," p. 303.

51. Ichak Adizes, *Industrial Democracy*, p. 219.

52. Sharon Zukin, *Beyond Marx and Tito*, p. 97.

53. Ibid., p. 98.

54. Kolaja, *Workers' Councils*, pp. 45-50.

55. Pateman, *Participation and Democratic Theory*, p. 99.

56. Ibid., p. 102.

57. Dragan Markovic et al., *Factories to Their Workers*, p. 18.

58. Edward C. Banfield and James Q. Wilson, *City Politics*, p. 25; Arthur J. Vidich and Joseph Bensman, *Small Town in Mass Society*, pp. 111-15; A. H. Birch, *Small Town Politics*.

59. Vidich and Bensman, *Small Town in Mass Society*, p. 112.

60. Kanter, *Commitment and Community*, pp. 75-126.

61. Robert Hine, *California's Utopian Colonies*, p. 170.

62. Bruno Bettelheim, *Children of the Dream*.

63. Melford Spiro, *Kibbutz*, p. 204.

64. Ibid., p. 99.

65. Kanter, *Commitment and Community*, pp. 71, 75-90.

66. Bettelheim, *Children of the Dream*, pp. 13-28, 303-17; Boris Stern, *The Kibbutz That Was*, p. 117.

67. Stern, *The Kibbutz that Was*, p. 117.

68. J. L. Talmon, *The Origins of Totalitarian Democracy*.

69. See also Patrick Riley, "A Possible Explanation of Rousseau's General Will."

70. Wolff, *Poverty of Liberalism*, pp. 3-51.

71. Banfield and Wilson, *City Politics*; Lewis Coser, *The Functions of Social Conflict*.

72. George Simmel, quoted in Coser, *Functions of Social Conflict*, p. 67.

73. Coser, *Functions of Social Conflict*, p. 69.

74. Banfield and Wilson, *City Politics*, p. 25.

75. Hine, *California's Utopian Colonies*, p. 170.

76. Banfield and Wilson, *City Politics*, p. 25.

77. Robert Dahl, "Democracy and the Chinese Boxes," p. 374.

78. Ibid.

79. Robert Paul Wolff, Barrington Moore, Jr., and Herbert Marcuse, *A Critique of Pure Tolerance*, pp. 49-53.

80. Murray Weingarten, "The Individual and the Community"; Yonina Talmon, *Family and Community in the Kibbutz*; Bettelheim, *Children*

of the Dream; A. I. Rabin, *Growing Up in the Kibbutz*; Melford Spiro, *Children of the Kibbutz*.

81. Bettelheim, *Children of the Dream*, p. 251.
82. Weingarten, "The Individual and the Community," p. 519.
83. Y. Talmon, *Family and Community in the Kibbutz*, p. 160.
84. Rabin, *Growing Up in the Kibbutz*, p. 209.
85. Ibid., p. 294.
86. Bettelheim, *Children of the Dream*, p. 294.
87. Ibid., p. 294.
88. Ibid., p. 264.
89. Spiro, *Children of the Kibbutz*, p. 424.
90. Ibid., p. 429.
91. Graeme Duncan and Steven Lukes, "Democracy Restated," p. 197.
92. Ibid., p. 199.

PART **III**

The Issue of Decision Making

The previous section of this book has analyzed in considerable detail how various theories of democracy have viewed the problem of public participation. In this third and final section, we need to deal with one remaining issue in democratic theory, the problem of decision making. The reason for focusing on this issue is undoubtedly obvious since most people choose to participate in politics in order to affect the outcome of public decisions. For analytic reasons we have separated the problem of decision making from that of participation, but we must recognize that for all practical purposes the two issues are intimately linked. The scope of popular participation is bound to affect the content of any publicly made decision. As we shall see, most theories of democracy implicitly—if not explicitly—contain a theory of decision making that complements and reinforces its theory of participation. The alternative approaches to democracy that we have considered disagree not only on the capabilities of the individual to participate in politics but also on the consequences of public involvement for governmental decision making.

To explore these differences in a more systematic fashion, chapter 9 will examine the proposals various democratic theorists have advanced for altering the decision-making process. While pluralists want to share power between government officials and the numerous interest groups in society, polyarchists want to concentrate authority in the hands of elected officials and participatory democrats want to disperse power among smaller communities and neighborhoods. These theories of democracy often rely on radically different arguments for justifying the restructuring of the decision-making process. By analyzing a variety of studies of community decision making, I hope to demonstrate that the proposals of participatory and polyarchal democracy fail to achieve their stated objectives even when judged by the criteria they themselves suggest are important. In contrast, I hope to show how a pluralistic form of decision making, involving mutual adjustment among numerous parties, can yield many of the benefits that more centralized or decentralized decision-making procedures are purportedly capable of achieving.

Finally, chapter 10 will focus on the problem of policy implementation, or public administration. Not only do alternative approaches to democratic theory have radically different assessments of what kinds of decision-making procedures are apt to be effective; they also disagree with one another over what kinds of institutional or administrative procedures are apt to be successful in translating publicly determined goals into workable policy. Polyarchal and populist democrats believe it is possible to prevent public policies from being distorted or altered at the administrative stage if the goals of government agencies are clearly defined and their discretionary powers are strictly limited. While these versions of democracy tend to view organizations in Weberian terms as rational, neutral instruments for achieving externally determined goals, pluralist democrats recognize that administrative bodies are highly political and on occasion even pathological in their behavior, and they argue that a process of partisan mutual adjustment is necessary to limit and neutralize these organizational tendencies. In the pluralist view, the give-and-take of interest-group bargaining can improve the implementation of public decisions as well as contribute to their formulation.

Chapter

9

Pluralism and the Problem of Decision Making

Because most theories of democracy have different estimates of people's ability to participate in politics, it is important to know how public involvement affects the content of government policies. Besides determining to what extent people are capable of participating in politics, a normative theory of democracy must decide to what extent popular participation has beneficial or deleterious effects on the output of the political system. Some scholars believe a tradeoff exists between participation and effective policy making, while others insist that the two complement and reinforce one another. In part, this chapter will attempt to determine which of these claims is the more accurate and defensible position.

Community control advocates like Alan Altshuler or Milton Kotler—who represent a variety of participatory democracy differing from the one considered in the preceding chapter—argue that the decision-making process should be decentralized to allow for greater popular involvement on the local level.[1] They insist that politicians elected in city, state, or national elections are too remote to understand the needs of localized neighborhoods and that as a result many people no longer feel they can trust in the honesty or impartiality of their officials.[2] In the participatory view, political power will never be wielded in an equitable fashion unless local neighborhoods gain effective control over important institutions, like the police or schools. In contrast, polyarchal democrats like Theodore Lowi and Robert Crain maintain that popular participation leads to an excessive fragmentation of political power.[3] They contend that the crisis facing the political system stems less from the public's mistrust of high officials than from the government's inability to develop effective solutions for complex social problems like pollution, transportation, or poverty. In their opinion, power must be concentrated in the hands of political elites if the state is to engage in the kind of long-range, comprehensive planning necessary to solve these troublesome social issues. In contrast to both polyarchists and participatory democrats, pluralists argue that the decision-making process should be neither highly centralized nor highly decentralized. They advocate a mixed form of policy making in which power is divided among political elites and the myriad number of interest publics that make up society. Rather than devolve power to autonomous units of government or centralize authority in the hands of a few officials, they favor a middle course that incorporates the benefits of popular participation but avoids the pitfalls of excessive fragmentation.*

---

*Like polyarchists, many populists—Michael Harrington, for one—seem sympathetic with efforts to engage in long-range planning. But in comparison with the other forms of democracy that we have examined, populism's theory of decision making is not always clearly stated. While populists insist that the public should play an important role in the decision-making process, they never clearly spell out the relationship between comprehensive planning by the state and public involvement in policy making. In Harrington's book *Toward a Democratic Left*, we are never certain whether the public is merely to have the final say over options that a political elite may formulate or whether the majority is actually to be involved in the formulation as well as the final selection of policy (pp. 63-88). In either case, populism's theory of decision making cannot be considered unique. If it favors centralized elites developing comprehensive plans, its view of decision making does not radically differ from that of polyarchy. If, in contrast, it wants the public to have some say in the formulation and the ratification of decisions, it is apt to accept many of pluralism's assumptions about the desirability of numerous policy makers. In evaluating populism, we must stress that its main contribution to democratic theory seems to lie in its theory of participation. Regardless of how decisions are made, populism has insisted that the majority should express its approval in periodic referendums. As should be obvious, this theory of participation is logically compatible with either a centralized or a decentralized style of decision making.

Before attempting to evaluate the relative merits of these competing theories of decision making, we must recall that the proponents of various approaches to democracy often suggest radically different criteria for measuring success. Because commentators cannot always agree on the main problems confronting the political system, they naturally tend to stress the importance of realizing different values. This very wealth of standards makes it difficult to compare alternative patterns of decision making since there is no commonly accepted criterion of accomplishment or failure. As we shall soon see, some authors think the poverty-race issue is of such importance that decision-making procedures should be evaluated primarily by their ability to alleviate the worst consequences of ghetto life. Other critics stress criteria that are broader in nature, focusing on values that are not necessarily beneficial to any one particular group in society.

Among the criteria that have been cited, the following seem to have received the most attention. First, many authors, including Altshuler, claim that decision-making procedures should be evaluated primarily in terms of their ability to generate a sense of confidence and trust among the public.[4] Advocates of community control insist that this issue is an especially troublesome problem in the inner city, where many residents no longer see the exercise of political power as legitimate and noncoercive in nature.

A second type of criterion by which to compare various forms of decision making is to ask which pattern can most effectively achieve a sense of efficacy among presently disorganized segments of the population. Again, this is a criterion that focuses primarily on the problems of the ghetto. As many commentators have noted, the sense of despair that accompanies poverty often leads people to inaction, which in turn feeds on and reinforces their initial despair.[5] Using this criterion of efficacy, we might ask to what extent a pattern of decision making can help people to break out of this vicious cycle and gain a sense of mastery over their own lives.

A third standard, which has somewhat broader consequences than our first two, is to determine to what extent a decision-making pattern can increase government responsiveness to public demands. This criterion, as should be obvious by now, raises the issue discussed in part II of this book: determining who constitutes the relevant public.

A fourth criterion is to ask which pattern of decision making is most likely to minimize spill-over effects among different units of government. In many cases the costs and benefits of public services may accrue to people who live outside a political unit's boundaries. This issue is an important one because when benefits spill over beyond a government's boundaries, an insufficient quantity of a good may be provided; but when costs spill over, the level of services may be carried on at too high a level. [6]

A fifth alternative is to evaluate different forms of policy making on the basis of their ability to achieve significant economies of scale. As we shall see, the price that residents of a community must pay in order to obtain certain basic public amenities may depend on the size of the unit providing the service. [7]

A sixth criterion, which critics like Robert Crain think is important, might be labeled the standard of social justice. [8] That is, to what degree can a pattern of decision making implement needed social programs or achieve a more equitable redistribution of goods and services among the various segments of society? In large metropolitan areas, there is often a mismatch between the financial needs of the inner city, where the poor and minorities have congregated, and the economic resources of suburban neighborhoods, where white middle-class professionals have taken up residence. The key issue is how to design a decision-making procedure for linking together these needs and assets.

Finally, a seventh alternative is to judge a form of policy making by its ability to generate innovative as well as effective solutions to pressing social problems. Using this criterion we might ask what forms of decision making have been most successful in developing new policies. In contrast to our sixth criterion, we are less concerned with whether the solution restructures or redistributes resources than with how quickly and creatively it can act. [9]

Although all democratic theories would no doubt agree that the above mentioned criteria are important, they would rank these values in a different fashion. Participatory democrats often seem to deemphasize the importance of economies of scale or innovative policy making (criteria five and seven) in order to maximize the legitimacy, efficacy, and responsiveness of the political system (criteria one, two and three). Elitist democrats have appeared more interested in developing a form of decision making that will minimize spill-over effects and promote social justice and innovative policy making (criteria four, six, and seven). Polyarchists like Lowi seem willing to sacrifice some of the values that participatory democrats stress in order to build a political system that can act decisively to meet the country's social problems. In contrast, pluralists seek to strike a balance among our various criteria. They believe that the political system faces a serious legitimacy problem that requires more intensive citizen involvement in the policy-making arena; but at the same time they feel that the polity needs to develop more innovative policies for dealing with problems like pollution, energy conservation, and urban deterioration.

In order to assess these rival models of decision making, it will be necessary to examine how each would handle the criteria that alternative theories cite as being important. Even if a certain style of policy making achieves the objectives it hopes to realize, we must know what the price of that success is in terms of alternative values foregone. It will also be necessary to evaluate each theory by the standards it chooses to stress. If a model of democracy gives up certain values in order to realize others but cannot achieve the objectives that it regards as important, then we must judge it as deficient.

The Participatory Option

Proponents of community control—including scholars interested in the problems of the ghetto, advocates for the poor, and black civil rights leaders—are primarily concerned with overcoming the alienation of the inner city. As Altshuler has convincingly argued, a large part of the urban problem in the United States stems from the unfortunate fact that many poor and black residents of large cities feel powerless to exercise any control over their own lives. [10] Ghetto dwellers believe that the government is insensitive to their needs and that as a result their life situation can never be altered for the better. This problem of trust and responsiveness is intimately related to the paucity of power enjoyed by most communities. Many residents of the inner city have no faith in the bureaucrats they come in contact with precisely because they know they do not have any control over the institutions to which these bureaucrats are answerable.

The participatory solution for this crisis of authority is to devolve political power to the local level. Participatory democrats believe confidence in public authority can be restored if neighborhoods within large cities are allowed to assume control of institutions like the schools or police that are important in shaping the lives of urban residents. Advocates of community control also contend that the dispersal of power to local neighborhoods will help to instill a greater sense of self-esteem in low-income people. While many individuals in the inner city presently suffer from a low sense of efficacy, the acquisition of controlling power over key institutions is likely to alter their perceptions of themselves. As advocates of participatory democracy have noted, granting power to the powerless is one of the most obvious ways to break people's sense of dependency. This shift in attitudes, in turn, is likely to result in the development of a new set of local leaders who will possess the confidence necessary to seek further improvements in community institutions. Likewise, the enhanced sense of efficacy that is apt to grow out of community control efforts is bound to lead to an increased sense of self-regulation within local neighborhoods. A well-organized community that actively participates in the running of its own institutions is more likely to discourage deviant behavior than an atomized neighborhood debilitated by the psychological consequences of poverty and powerlessness.

Although these arguments merit serious consideration, they also raise some significant doubts. There is no denying that the problems cited by participatory democrats are real and must eventually be dealt with, but the question is whether the proliferation of numerous independent government entities is either the proper or the complete solution. Regardless of whether participatory democracy is a success by the criteria it wishes to be judged by, it is a form of decision making that may entail some very high costs. In looking at our criteria for evaluating policy making, a strong case can be made that a very decentralized manner of formulating decisions will be relatively unsuccessful in developing policies that promote social justice (criterion six), foster innovative and effective decision making (criterion seven), limit spill-over effects (criterion four), or minimize the unit costs of delivering services (criterion five).

The most glaring weakness in the decentralization effort—particularly in the movement for community control of schools—is its apparent inability to achieve an equitable distribution of goods and services in society as a whole (criterion six). Neighborhood management of institutions like the school system might make the personnel of those organizations more sensitive to the needs of their constituents, but it is difficult to see how devolving more power to local school boards will guarantee that inner city schools receive an equitable distribution of funds in the first place. Given their limited resources, many ghetto schools will undoubtedly be hard pressed to provide adequate compensation to their faculty or adequate facilities to their students without some kind of outside assistance. To achieve a just distribution of goods within the larger society, policy decisions must be made on a macro rather than a micro level. In dispersing more power to neighborhoods, all the advocates of community control can ever hope to accomplish is to give local residents the opportunity to revise the way resources in their neighborhoods have traditionally been allocated. In contrast to a pluralistic or polyarchal form of decision making, community control will not provide inner city residents with any means of increasing the benefits that they receive from the larger political system. By its very nature, participatory democracy is more suited to altering the internal allocation of benefits within a single community than to altering the distribution of resources within society as a whole.

Similarly, community control may have the unintended consequence of eroding the basic rights of many minority groups. Even if local management of institutions like schools, police, or welfare departments will make these bureaucracies more responsive to the needs of the ghetto, where blacks or the poor constitute a majority, it may very well have adverse consequences for minority members who live in predominantly white areas. A police force that is sensitive to the needs of blacks in a ghetto might in another context just as easily be sensitive to the wishes of whites who want to halt the advance of civil rights. It is perhaps ironic that a doctrine related so long to calls for white separatism is now advanced as a radically new proposal for improving the situation of minority groups. While community control may provide some tangible benefits for blacks who live in the ghetto, it may very well hinder the efforts of minority members to secure nonprejudicial treatment outside the inner city. And even within minority neighborhoods, there is the danger that white ethnic groups might find themselves the victims of a reverse form of racism, as occurred with the anti-Semitism that often surfaced in the Ocean Hill-Brownsville controversy.

Aside from problems in protecting minority rights or in achieving a redistribution of social resources, a decentralized form of decision making might also encounter difficulties in formulating innovative policies (criterion seven). On the basis of a variety of studies, it appears that the development of independent communities inhibits, rather than fosters, the adoption of new policy options. In a survey of the literature on organizational innovation, James Q. Wilson has noted that the number of innovations generated is directly related to the diversity of an organization (i.e., to the complexity of its tasks and its incentive systems), while the number of innovations implemented is inversely related to these factors.[11] Although Wilson's observations refer to individual organizations, they can easily be applied to the political system as a whole, as Samuel Huntington has argued, if we equate organizational diversity with the dispersion of political power.[12] That is, the more political power is dispersed, the more likely we are to see a variety of proposals for policy innovations, but conversely, the less likely we are to see many new policy adoptions. Similarly, when power is highly centralized, we are apt to see few new policy suggestions but quite a few adoptions of the proposals that are put forth. Thus whenever power is either highly dispersed or highly concentrated, the rate of innovation will tend to be low. It is only when a political system contains both a diversity of groups and a sufficient concentration of power to implement new ideas that the policy-making process is bound to be receptive to program innovations.

However, this conclusion needs to be qualified in one important respect. As will be argued in more detail later on, there are theoretical as well as empirical reasons for believing that the number of innovations generated is related not only to how many decision-making parties there are but also to how often these parties interact with one another. Charles Lindblom and Michael Aiken, among others, have pointed out that the interaction among groups serves both to stimulate the creation of new ideas and to encourage their diffusion. [13] The optimal form of decision making for encouraging new policy options is thus one that contains both (1) a multiplicity of parties interacting with one another to generate new ideas and (2) adequate power to implement the policies that happen to be formulated.

Participatory democracy is deficient in both these respects. Since the very notion of community control entails the concentration of power in the hands of locally elected officials rather than the sharing of power among different levels of government, there is likely to be little interaction among political units. While it is possible that locally controlled communities might attempt radically different kinds of programs when they first acquire power, the process would probably be short-lived. Without suitable interaction with groups or other units of government, community control experiments would lack the necessary degree of interchange to compel further policy innovation. Moreover, even if neighborhoods did generate new proposals for dealing with issues that transcend their own boundaries, they would have neither the power nor the jurisdiction to implement their decisions. In terms of Wilson's argument, community control definitely occupies that end of the continuum where organizations lack the capability to adopt any policy innovations that might conceivably be developed.

In addition, a segmented form of decision making runs the risk of undermining the effectiveness of any form of policy making regardless of its degree of creativity. Whenever local communities attempt to deal with problems that are regional in nature, their solutions may turn into someone else's problems. As the decision-making process becomes more fragmented, individual neighborhoods will have few incentives to weigh the spill-over effects or external costs that accompany the implementation of a particular policy (criterion four). It is thus possible that community control could result in a rather inequitable system of decision making in which individual localities would pass on part of the costs of their decisions to other units of government. If every decision of a community affected only that community, there would naturally be no objection to autonomous units of government. However, since problems often cross politically determined boundaries, independent localities might easily ignore the costs and gains to other communities and produce too much or too little of a certain service or good. If a local government builds and maintains an extensive park system, residents from other districts who have not borne the cost of the parks through taxation may nonetheless come and use them. Or if a community takes a lax attitude towards the prosecution of crime, its actions may adversely affect surrounding neighborhoods. Similarly, if a municipality decides to alter its zoning laws in order to attract heavy industry, it may result in polluting the air in the whole region. Given a system of autonomous units of government each with its own zoning power, there would be no way either of prohibiting such actions or of extracting benefits from the offending community.

Finally, the creation of multiple, autonomous units of government has the added drawback that it may entail unnecessarily high costs for the performance of certain functions (criterion five). In the production of government services it is often possible to realize noticeable economies of scale; i.e., the average cost of producing a good or service may decline as the output of that good or service is increased. On the basis of a number of economic studies undertaken in the 1950s and 1960s, Werner Hirsch has argued that air pollution control, sewage disposal, public transportation, power, water, public health services, and hospitals are likely to enjoy major economies of scale.[14] If separate neighborhoods try to operate their own transportation departments or run their own public health programs, they may have to pay more than they would if a larger unit of government provided the same service. Whether the possible economic costs of such fragmentation are more or less important than the psychological benefits received from running one's own neighborhood is a separate question that cannot be dealt with here. But it must be kept in mind that regardless of the extent to which community control restores a sense of trust or efficacy among residents of a community, it has its definite costs.

In recent years, however, some economists have insisted that there are no economies of scale to be realized in municipal services that are labor intensive. Unlike transportation, air pollution, or utilities, which involve large amounts of capital investment, many municipal services, such as education, fire or police protection, require little or no capital. In fact, in a recent study of the Indianapolis police department and surrounding law enforcement units, Elinor Ostrum has indicated that there may be large-scale diseconomies when service organizations become too large.[15] Unfortunately, as Robert Bish and Hugh Nourse have argued, studies such as Ostrum's are "plagued with the difficulties of output measurement and thus cannot be used to indicate whether or not the governments analyzed were producing efficiently."[16] Unless there is an adequate measure of outputs, it is difficult to control for the quality of services provided by various units of government. Also, as will be shown in the next chapter, in order to minimize the costs in running a large organization facing heterogeneous tasks, it is imperative that the organization decentralize its operations and grant considerable discretion to lower-level administrators. Thus to adequately compare the costs of running police departments, it is necessary to compare an efficiently run, large unit that has administratively decentralized its operations and an efficiently run, smaller department. Unfortunately, most of the present cost comparisons of municipal departments fail to control for such variables.

It should also be pointed out that research by Peter Blau, Richard Schoenherr, and S.R. Klatzky indicates that as an organization gets larger, its staff personnel and administrative overhead decline regardless of whether the organization is capital or labor intensive.[17] If these findings are reliable, the costs of providing a unit of service could conceivably be lower for large labor-intensive organizations like police departments. Given the present difficulties in much of the literature and the fact that some of the data are internally inconsistent, it is still an open question whether or not there are diseconomies of scale in labor-intensive organizations.

On the basis of the above discussion, we can thus argue that community control is an incomplete solution to the problems that face the political system. In fact, it is interesting to note that some proponents of community control, such as Altshuler, seem willing to concede this very point. Altshuler has modified his advocacy of community control in two important respects. First, in order to promote the redistribution of resources from wealthier to poorer areas and to prevent communities from passing on part of the costs associated with their decisions to other localities, he appears willing to accept a federated system of decision making. Altshuler calls for the creation of a two- or three-tier system of government, in which local communities would formulate policies dealing with institutions like the schools while larger units of government would decide policies that had redistributive consequences or spill-over effects on other communities.[18]

Secondly, in addition to espousing community control, Altshuler implicitly endorses a variant of public pluralism as a strategy for improving conditions in the inner city. Besides calling for neighborhood self-government, Altshuler talks of the necessity of mobilizing the poor so that they can deal more effectively with city hall.[19] He argues that organizing the poor will serve a dual purpose: not only will it enable them to take charge of neighborhood government, but it will also allow them to bargain more effectively with other interests in the city. While Altshuler groups both these activities under the rubric of community control, it is questionable to what extent the notion of political bargaining remains true to the kind of local autonomy envisioned by most participatory democrats. More importantly, in making the distinction between self-government on the neighborhood level and interest-group pressure within the larger political system, Altshuler implies that community control is only a partial, and not a complete, solution to the urban problem. In order to supplement the deficiencies of neighborhood self-government, he falls back on the kind of interest-group politics that public pluralists advocate.

Although Altshuler's eclectic approach to decision making answers many of the objections raised earlier about community control, it leaves yet other issues unresolved. To be fair to community control, we must evaluate it by a variety of standards, including the criteria its advocates think are important. If participatory democrats like Altshuler implicitly admit that community control is only a partial solution to the urban crisis, they nonetheless argue that it constitutes a necessary complement to other forms of decision making. The issue at hand, then, is not whether community control fails to take other costs or values into account but whether it is capable of realizing the values that participatory democrats themselves have deemed important. As pointed out previously, most proponents of community control believe it is essential to make government officials more responsive to the wishes of the public (criterion three). The question is whether community control is either the only way or necessarily the best way to achieve this objective.

Contrary to the claims of its proponents, it can be argued that community control might inhibit government responsiveness to a diverse array of groups. To argue that decentralization will make the government more responsive to the public necessitates defining who constitutes the public. As pointed out in chapter 6, whenever there are separate decision-making points for different policy areas, such as education or law enforcement, it becomes much easier for the dominant interest in the field to limit the scope of conflict and the array of forces opposing it. Instead of doing away with isolated and segmented decision-making centers, the establishment of community control would probably lead to their proliferation. As a result, the ability of one particular group to monopolize the formulation of policy would be enhanced rather than curtailed. In the case of education, it would be members of the various communities who would have the dominant voice, to the detriment of other groups such as teachers' unions. Whether the decision-making process is divided into isolated segments by function (as is presently the case with school policy) or by territory (as the proponents of participatory democracy suggest), the number of groups that can participate in the political system will be limited. To argue that decentralization will make the government more responsive to the public is to argue that the government should be responsive to a different segment of the citizenry. Community control will undoubtedly increase the receptivity of certain institutions to the needs of the neighborhood community, but in the process it will make the same institutions less responsive to other elements in society.

However, many economists argue that this fragmented and isolated pattern of decision making is desirable because it allows individual political units to cater to the needs of specialized groups. Charles Tiebout, Robert Bish, and Hugh Nourse insist that autonomous communities are necessary both in the inner city and in suburban areas in order to adequately satisfy individual preferences for public goods.[20] They maintain that large units of government must cater to the demands of a relatively heterogeneous public. In a large jurisdiction "we would expect public good provision to approximate that preferred by the median voter."[21] Either through a process of voting or bargaining, the political system would produce an array of goods and services that not all members would individually like to see provided. However, when the metropolitan area is fragmented into numerous, smaller units of government, municipalities can cater to more homogeneous populations with similar tastes. Citizens are likely to achieve a higher level of welfare since they no longer have to pay for goods and services they do not want. The more homogeneous the preferences of the population, the more likely it is that individuals who fit the local norms will find all of their wants amply satisfied.

Despite the apparent attractiveness of these proposals, there are certain empirical and normative questions that need to be faced. First, given the high degree of daily mobility in the metropolitan area and the fact that most people work, live, and shop in a variety of different jurisdictions, it seems questionable whether individuals would maximize their preferences by participating in only one governmental unit. Usually people consume public services in a variety of places but have the opportunity to express their political preferences in only one jurisdiction.[22] Secondly, it should be pointed out that the creation of autonomous, homogeneous communities is not solely the result of like-minded individuals voluntarily clustering together. Through restrictive zoning and subdivision regulation, many suburban communities have made it legally and financially difficult for people of heterogeneous backgrounds to settle within their boundaries. Rather than maximizing the opportunities for people to live in the jurisdiction that best satisfies their preferences, the proliferation of suburban townships has often resulted in a diminution of life chances for many persons. Unquestionably there are numerous individuals of modest income in the inner city who prefer the mixture of public goods and services provided by suburban neighborhoods. But they recognize, as Tiebout, Bish, and Nourse often do not, that their place of residence has more to do with the legal and financial barriers that the suburbs have placed in their path than with their own preferences for public goods. Instead of assuming, as many urban economists do, that the growth of numerous municipalities will result in "better performance satisfaction" for all citizens, we must recognize that it may lead to the maximization of satisfaction for only the more affluent residents of suburban communities.

Besides arguing that community control will lead to greater responsiveness, critics like Altshuler have maintained that devolution of power to local units of government will create an enhanced sense of trust and efficacy within the inner city (criteria one and two). If local management of institutions like schools or police can provide better service to neighborhoods, then public trust in government will be restored. Likewise, if power is turned over to the inner city, there will likely develop a new corps of leaders who feel efficacious enough to seek additional changes that will alter the status of the inner city for the better. Unfortunately, however, the available evidence suggests the need for caution in accepting these claims. In a study of experiments in decentralization in the cities of New York and New Haven, Douglas Yates has found that an inverse relationship exists between the extent of power a community exercises and the degree of success it enjoys in either improving local services or in building a sense of efficacy among its members. [23] While his terminology is different from that used in this book, Yates has arranged the experiments he observed along a continuum with highly specific (what we would call pluralistic) groups at one end and more diffuse (what we would call community control) projects at the other end. The pluralistic experiments were designed to provide a very limited service to the neighborhood or to monitor or bargain with a specific government agency over its programs in the community. In contrast, the experiments at the opposite end of the continuum entailed local neighborhoods actually governing complex institutions like the school system. When Yates attempted to determine which approach fostered the greatest sense of efficacy among local residents, he found that community control experiments had the lowest ratings, while more pluralistic and functionally specific efforts had the highest ratings. [24] A similar pattern emerged when he attempted to see which approach most improved services to the neighborhood. Contrary to what the advocates of community control had argued, he found that as the power of the neighborhood increased to the point where it was actually governing local institutions, its ability to improve services did not increase correspondingly. However, when neighborhoods were organized into advocate groups to secure tangible benefits from city-wide bureaucracies, their record was substantially better.

The explanation for this discrepancy reflects the nature of the tasks confronting the two different kinds of experiments. As soon as members of a community attempted to govern institutions like the local schools, they became overwhelmed by the number and the complexity of problems facing them. In some cases they were not certain what they wanted to do with their grant of power once they had acquired it. As a result, community-controlled school boards often undertook very few initiatives and had very little impact on the institutions they ostensibly administered. For similar reasons, many of the participants on locally controlled school boards became so disillusioned and discouraged about what they had accomplished that their sense of political efficacy did not significantly improve. However, when groups were organized to achieve more limited and specific goals, they were more likely to achieve their objectives, and this fact in turn reinforced the confidence they had in their ability to influence the decision-making process.[25] If a group was interested in applying pressure on a city agency to improve the delivery of municipal services to its neighborhood, its goals were clearly focused and its task was minimal in comparison to the burdens borne by organizations that had day-to-day administrative duties. It was thus much easier for advocate groups to build a record of success than it was for their community control counterparts.

Yates's study is highly significant in that it is one of the first efforts to determine whether the claims of participatory democrats are supported by the evidence. Yates suggested that if we want to promote a sense of efficacy or trust among inner city residents, a pluralistic, rather than a community control, approach may be the most feasible alternative. By organizing the poor for political action, pluralism can greatly increase the ability of ghetto residents to influence the conditions that govern their lives. But if people are expected to assume responsibility for running institutions with which they have little experience, it should not be surprising that they easily become frustrated and disillusioned. The problem with the program of participatory democrats is that merely turning power over to the poor will not automatically guarantee that they will be able to use it either wisely or effectively.

The Polyarchal Option

While participatory democrats have called for the dispersal of power to local neighborhoods, polyarchal democrats have argued that authority should be concentrated in the hands of elected officials. Polyarchists like Lowi maintain that the major problems facing the United States stem less from inner city alienation than from the government's inability to implement comprehensive plans for dealing with issues like pollution, mass transportation, or poverty. They insist that the problems of the inner city reflect the inability of the larger city to deliver effective services to individual neighborhoods rather than a shortage of power within local communities themselves. In the polyarchal view, authority is so fragmented that the political system is forced to pursue a strategy of muddling through, of dealing with troublesome issues in a piecemeal, rather than a comprehensive and innovative, fashion.[26]

To remedy this situation, polyarchists insist that the institutional power of publicly elected officials should be strengthened so that they can deal quickly and effectively with the myriad problems that face the nation.[27] On a national level, elitist democrats usually favor an active president who possesses the authority to override the veto power wielded by agencies and interest groups. The need for a vigilant judicial branch is also seen by many, especially Lowi, who insists that the Supreme Court must restrain Congress's propensity to parcel out its authority to administrative agencies and to special interests. On a local level, polyarchists have endorsed efforts to consolidate metropolitan governments and to eliminate the present fragmentation of political units. In place of multiple, overlapping lines of authority, they favor the simplification of the decision-making process and the concentration of official responsibility at the top. In the polyarchist view, if political elites can be insulated from the direct pressure of interest groups, they will be able to engage in systematic as well as effective long-range planning. "Planning requires law, choice, priorities, moralities," Lowi has argued.[28] Public involvement, or more specifically, public bargaining over policies, is seen as the antithesis of this orderly process. Like many other elitist democrats, Lowi maintains that the compromises and logrolling of pluralism are a corruption of, rather than an aid to, the rational process of establishing priorities and formulating options.

Although polyarchists have often vigorously stated their case, it is debatable whether the available evidence supports their call for more centralized policy making. Before determining the extent to which elitist patterns of democracy can actually realize the values polyarchists stress as being important, we must see how this form of decision making deals with alternative standards of performance. Even if concentrating power in the hands of elected officials can minimize spill-over effects (criterion four) or lead to more equitable social programs (criterion six) or more innovative policies (criterion seven), we also need to know whether it can offer any answer to the kinds of problems Altshuler and other participatory democrats have so graphically described. It is possible that polyarchy, like community control, is at best only a partial solution to the numerous difficulties confronting the political system.

For instance, it can be argued that the treatment of the poverty problem in a book like *The End of Liberalism* raises serious doubts about polyarchy's solution to the urban crisis. Lowi in particular seems to have overlooked the gravity of the situation Altshuler has described, for nowhere in his study does he address the problem of alienation and apathy that many commentators claim is widespread among residents of the inner city. Perhaps because of this oversight, Lowi fails to show how concentrating power could ever restore a sense of legitimacy (criterion one) among the poor. In fact, there are reasons for believing that the polyarchal call for centralized authority might very well exacerbate the prevalent attitude of alienation found in the ghetto. As Altshuler has argued, residents of the inner city often reject the legitimacy of the political system because they feel that they have little or no influence over its actions. Thus concentrating power in the hands of a few elected officials would make the poor feel even more estranged from the decision-making process. However, Lowi insists that consolidation of power could strengthen respect for authority if it were coupled with stricter enforcement of the law.

While Lowi does not specifically address the problem of alienation among the poor, he does confront the larger issue of cynicism about government among the general population. Lowi concedes that the public has grown increasingly cynical about political institutions in recent years, and he contends that it is the capriciousness of a discretionary system of administration, rather than the remoteness of centralized institutions, that is responsible for this crisis of legitimacy. Because lower-level bureaucrats have been given considerable leeway in interpreting the intent of officially made laws, the administration of justice has become less than evenhanded.[29] In Lowi's opinion, public confidence in government will be restored only when this discretionary pattern of administration is replaced by stricter enforcement of the law. While this line of reasoning at first appears persuasive, it seems somewhat beside the point. Many residents of the inner city seem to be complaining less about the administration of the law than about the content of the law itself. The decline of public authority is as much a problem of people feeling excluded from the policy-making process as it is of the law being unevenly applied. Even if centralization of power were accompanied by more stringent enforcement of the law, it might very well contribute to, rather than alleviate, the problem of public distrust. In making the decision-making process more remote from the residents of the inner city, polyarchy makes it difficult for local citizens to have any say over the decisions that affect their daily lives.

If consolidating power in the hands of elected officials is not likely to restore a sense of trust among lower-income residents, it is likely to encounter even more difficulties in reviving dormant neighborhoods and in instituting a sense of efficacy (criterion two) among the poor. Polyarchal democrats like Lowi often overlook the importance of helping the poor to become more active in helping themselves. Lowi maintains that poverty is essentially a problem of limited work opportunities and inadequate welfare funds; and to cope with this issue, he repeatedly praises what he calls the "old system of welfare," in which the government doles out month-ly payments to the indigent.[30] Rejecting the "new system of wel-fare," which tries to organize the poor for political action, he argues that the old system meets the needs of the poor at the same time that it preserves the rule of law.[31]

However, this whole approach seems to stem from a mispercep-tion on Lowi's part of the nature of urban social problems. He fails to take account of the work of scholars like Dorothy James, Ken-neth Clark, and Milton Greenblatt, among others, who argue that poverty is as much a psychological as an economic problem.[32] These studies have shown that prolonged exposure to ghetto condi-tions seem to have a corrosive effect on the personalities of the poor; when people are unable to escape from the restraints of poverty, they often experience a pervasive sense of hopelessness and depression, which in turn makes it more difficult for them to break out of the cycle of poverty. When the effects of racial dis-crimination reinforce the conditions of economic want, the damage to the psychology of the individual becomes magnified even more. Centralized attempts to increase employment opportunities or to increase the size of welfare handouts can thus be considered only partial solutions to the problem. If individuals suffer from a low sense of efficacy, they are often unable to take advantage of eco-nomic opportunities even when these are present in large numbers. Similarly, if people feel they are unable to control their own lives, strengthening the old system of welfare will tend to reinforce, not change, that attitude. A sense of self-respect is not likely to be generated within an individual by treating him as an object of a centralized welfare program; on the contrary, such measures will serve only to reinforce his feelings of dependence. Indeed, the centralized, dole-oriented system of welfare that Lowi praises was widely criticized in the early 1960s for precisely this reason. Its most glaring fault, as critics pointed out, lies in the fact that it attacks the surface manifestations of poverty rather than its under-lying causes.[33]

Despite the claim by Lowi and other polyarchists that concen-trating power in the hands of political elites is necessary to deal with the country's social problems, we can argue, then, that at best it is only an incomplete solution. Polyarchists like Lowi seem to misread the problems of the inner city, in particular, and the problems of poverty, in general. While centralized planning may be desirable in some policy areas, it seems inadequate as a method of restoring a sense of efficacy or trust among lower-income residents.

But as was the case with participatory democracy, we must also judge polyarchy by the criteria that its supporters stress as being important. To be fair, we must keep in mind that advocates have defended centralization of political power on the grounds that it will minimize externalities (criterion four) and lead to more socially just (criterion six) as well as more innovative policy making (criterion seven). A polyarchist would point out that political elites could prevent local units of government from passing on part of the costs of their decisions to neighboring communities if they had the power to engage in comprehensive planning. Similarly, elitist democrats like Lowi insist that the political system would be able to deal effectively with redistributive problems by limiting the proliferation of government units and concentrating power in the hands of a few elected officials. Only a centralized form of government would have the authority to transfer payments from one segment of society to another when an inequitable distribution of resources had occurred. In contrast to the decentralized, participatory model, a polyarchal form of decision making would never lack the power to equalize the funds that suburban and inner city schools could spend on education. As the power and jurisdiction of a unit of government were increased, its ability to affect the allocation of resources in society as a whole would likewise increase. Similarly, expanding the policy-making arena would insure that basic civil rights were protected in a uniform fashion. A centralized administration would have sufficient power to insist that every community guarantee certain essential liberties to all individuals regardless of their ethnic background. Finally, by concentrating authority in the hands of a few, the political system would be able to experiment with the adoption of novel approaches to traditional social problems and to thwart the efforts of veto groups seeking to stall needed social change. Only a centralized form of decision making, freed from the endless process of interest-group bargaining, would have the time to develop innovative social policies.

Merely because a centralized form of policy making could theoretically achieve these objectives does not mean that it necessarily will accomplish them in practice. Even if we assume that most political elites are eager to limit externalities, promote redistributive goals, and introduce innovative social programs, there are a variety of structural reasons for believing that centralized decision making will retard, rather than advance, these objectives. [34] The polyarchal view of decision making seems to be based on an exaggerated view of man's information-gathering and problem-solving abilities. If this were a world of costless information, it is conceivable that a few political elites might be able to detect any inefficient or inequitable distribution of social services. However, since most decision makers have limited cognitive abilities, it is not surprising that centralized elites often encounter serious difficulties in identifying and creatively resolving these kinds of problems. If there are externalities associated with a program, the parties that are affected are not necessarily in a position to alert public officials to the need for change. Similarly, when power is centralized at the top and direct involvement of the public is minimized, political elites cut themselves off from a great deal of information about the distribution of a program's costs and benefits. Those individuals who are most affected by an inequitable distribution of resources or a breakdown in the protection of civil liberties may not have an avenue for airing their grievances. Once power is concentrated, it becomes more difficult for dissenting views, which might expose these social costs, to get through to key decision makers.

Likewise, centralization of authority may retard the development of new ideas in that it alters the incentives for proposing radically new policies. In delegating more power to upper levels of government, polyarchal democrats would dramatically change the costs and rewards for innovative behavior facing personnel at lower levels. If decisions were made exclusively at the top, subordinates would not find it very rewarding to consider alternative ways of solving problems because they would not have any say over the final decision. No agency or interest group would consider wasting its resources developing new ideas if it had no real influence in the policy-making process. Similarly, interest groups and agencies would be less inclined to criticize the proposals of other groups since their suggestions would not carry much weight with decision makers at the top. Moreover, the lack of competition and interaction among agencies and interest groups would reinforce the propensity of agencies to play a cautious, rather than creative, role in the policy-making process. As Roland McKean has noted, bureaus with a relatively high degree of centralization probably face fewer threats of innovation by rival groups and greater reprimands for making mistakes. [35] If major decisions were made on a centralized level, agencies would no longer have to fear competitive bureaus instituting overlapping programs to rival or threaten their domains.

Although we may not fully appreciate this fact, the possibility that one agency might preempt the activities of another and infringe on its jurisdiction has been one of the greatest spurs to innovative policy making. The development of the Polaris missile by the navy probably played a bigger role in stimulating the army to reduce the vulnerability of its Minuteman than did any comprehensive, rational planning. Similarly, competition between the EPA and the AEC (and, later, its successor, the Nuclear Regulatory Commission), has done more to insure the safe disposal of radioactive material than any degree of centralized, long-range planning. If the influence of various lower- or middle-level bureaus were dramatically curbed, the bargaining and competition among agencies would likewise decrease. Bureaus would be rewarded for complying with, rather than challenging, major policy decisions. Such a state of affairs would not be likely to stimulate the development of either innovative or socially just programs.

The impact of centralization may just as significantly affect the creative capacities of upper-level officials as that of interest groups and lower- and middle-level bureaucrats. Polyarchal democrats have often overlooked the fact that the bargaining and interaction of private and public groups serve to lighten the load confronting government officials. Once political power becomes concentrated, public officials acquire responsibility for devising policies that were previously decided by private groups. The attempt to limit the influence of interest groups may impose such immense demands on the cognitive abilities of a few decision makers that it will eventually prove to be self-defeating. As McKean has argued, when there is a dramatic escalation in the number of decisions that must be made, political officials will "find it advantageous—indeed imperative—to screen alternatives rapidly, apply crude rules of thumb and quick judgments, and in general simplify the decision making process, because they would have to make a thousand instead of a hundred decisions per day."[36] As the authority for making decisions becomes increasingly concentrated, elites have no choice but to minimize the attention they give to each problem before them. Given the limited time and ability of most decision makers, the only way they can handle an increased work load is to speed up the consideration of various policy options.

The resulting simplification of the decision-making process is likely to have two adverse consequences. First, rather than surveying all possible options and rationally weighing the alternatives, centralized political elites will tend to neglect important social values. As pointed out earlier, when government officials are not subject to the pressures of the bargaining table, they are less likely to perceive the objectives and needs of people other than themselves. Even if they have the best of intentions, they are apt to fall back on simple decision-making rules in generating their proposals. Secondly, the centralization of the decision-making process is likely to result in a loss of flexibility. If the number of demands facing political officials forces them to adopt crude rules of thumb, policies may be formulated arbitrarily instead of being tailored to meet local conditions. However, if political elites attempt to correct this problem by spending an inordinate amount of time on any one particular issue, the decision-making process as a whole could very well grind to a halt. This is especially likely to be the case if, as Lowi suggests, political elites grant only limited discretion to lower-level officials.[37] Instead of risking the wrath of their superiors by exercising their own judgment, lower-level bureaucrats will play it safe and refer more and more matters to their superiors for final consideration. But the inevitable consequence of referring more and more issues to the top is that the decision-making process will be troubled by additional delays and slowdowns. Regardless of what polyarchists say about centralized planning, it is a form of policy making that could result in a loss of flexibility and quickness.

Finally, the advocates of centralized planning have often overlooked the fact that small groups of decision makers can fall victim to what Irving Janis has called the problem of "groupthink." Whenever small numbers of officials have sole responsibility for making important decisions, the danger exists that they may develop informal norms that effectively suppress the expression of dissenting opinions and the examination of conflicting evidence. [38] This danger is especially likely to emerge when political officials have responsibility for making vital decisions that pose threats of social disapproval and self-disapproval, such as committing the nation to a course of war. [39] As Janis has shown in several case studies of foreign policy making, political elites often do not have completely accurate information about the problems under study, nor do they necessarily want to be exposed to such information.

For instance, in making the Bay of Pigs decision, Kennedy believed that there were widespread pockets of opposition to Castro, and as a consequence he assumed that the Cuban army was ill prepared to repulse an armed attack. Intelligence experts in both the State Department and CIA knew that these assumptions were totally inaccurate. Unfortunately, however, they were never consulted. In fact, when the head of the State Department's intelligence section asked Dean Rusk if his experts could scrutinize the invasion plan, he was turned down. [40] Once the decision to attack Cuba gained momentum, no one in Kennedy's inner circle of decision makers seemed eager to question its wisdom. As Janis has argued, given the controversial nature of the plan, Kennedy's aides did not want to disturb their self-confidence by raising policy alternatives or by examining troublesome evidence. However, if the various government bureaus concerned with foreign policy had been able to criticize and contest the assumptions of Kennedy's advisors, it is possible that the Bay of Pigs fiasco could have been avoided.

We can thus see that for a variety of reasons consolidation of power in the hands of a few officials may not always be desirable. If we want the political system to act in a creative fashion, centralized planning may actually hinder the accomplishment of that goal. So far we have primarily relied on theoretical arguments to support this contention, but there are a number of empirical studies of organizational behavior and comparative city government that likewise indicate that multiple, rather than centralized, decision makers tend to foster innovative policy making. As mentioned earlier, Wilson has found in a survey of the literature on organizational innovation that an inverse relationship exists between the degree of centralization and the number of new policy ideas generated.[41] Similarly, in a series of studies on community decision making, several authors, including Robert Lineberry, Edmund Fowler, Terry Clark, Michael Aiken, and Robert Alford, have discovered that as the number of decision makers increases, so does the number of policies enacted. Instead of simply asking whether cities are ruled by an elite or by a plurality of groups, these authors have attempted to determine what effect various patterns of decision making might have on the outputs of a city. Generally, they have found that cities with centralized decision making are apt to be less active and innovative than municipalities with more pluralistic or diffuse patterns of government.

Lineberry and Fowler have compared the performance of reformed city governments, which tend to be highly centralized, with non-reformed city governments, which tend to be more open and responsive to group demands, and have discovered that centralized municipalities are more likely to have low levels of taxation and expenditures.[42] Contrary to the polyarchal argument, centralized reform cities seem to provide fewer services to their citizens. Similarly, Clark hypothesized that centralized policy making will lead to more program outputs, but in a comparative study of 51 cities he found just the opposite.[43] Considering public participation in the three policy areas of urban renewal, air pollution, and poverty, Clark discovered that as the number of groups involved increases, the city's level of expenditures also increases. Instead of hindering the city's ability to get anything done, group involvement seems to stimulate the city to become more involved in public-related activities. In another study, Aiken characterized the power structure of 31 cities as being either pyramidal, factional, or amorphous and compared the impact of these various power structures on the policy areas of poverty, urban renewal, and low-rent housing. Like Clark and Lineberry and Fowler, he found that as more groups participate in city politics, the municipality is more likely to initiate programs in these policy areas.[44] Finally, in two separate studies, Aiken and Alford compared 675 cities for the degree of innovation in the areas of poverty and public housing. They discovered that two variables are especially important in predicting whether a city will attempt to develop a program in these areas: the number of power centers in the city and the degree of interaction among these various power coalitions. [45] Once again, cities that have pluralistic, rather than centralized, decision-making arrangements are more likely to implement innovative programs.

In the comparative literature on urban government, the only study that finds that centralized communities are more likely to implement innovative policies is Robert Crain's, Elihu Katz's, and Donald Rosenthal's examination of the fluoridation issue. [46] Why their data are so at odds with the work of Aiken and Alford, Clark, and Lineberry and Fowler is not readily apparent. Clark has suggested that the type of issue might have some bearing on the success of different forms of decision making: "For less fragile decisions, the more centralized the decision making structure, the lower the level of outputs." [47] In contrast, when a municipality deals with a highly controversial issue, like fluoridation, a more centralized political system may be necessary to implement new programs. However, one would certainly be hard pressed to explain why the issue of fluoridation is more of a "fragile decision" than public housing, welfare, or tax levels. An alternative explanation would focus on the types of public participation involved in each issue. On close examination it is evident that the findings of Crain et al. do not contradict our previous studies because they compare elitism with referendums, or populistic forms of decision making. In contrast, Aiken et al. looked at group-oriented forms of participation, focusing on the number of actors involved in each issue and the scope and extent of their interaction with one another. Instead of simply asking whether centralized or noncentralized cities are most likely to be receptive to new ideas and programs, we must also distinguish between the behavior of different types of noncentralized communities. When centralized communities are contrasted with municipalities that rely on multiple actors to make decisions, the evidence still indicates that a participatory style of policy making results in higher levels of outputs.

Thus even if we use the criteria polyarchal democrats themselves have stressed as being important, the performance of centralized decision making is less impressive than advocates have led us to believe. Although polyarchists like Lowi often insist that pluralistic interest groups serve as veto groups that limit and frustrate efforts of the political system to provide more outputs, the record seems to indicate otherwise. It is centralized cities—not pluralistically oriented municipalities—that have difficulty generating and adopting new programs. In implying that a trade-off exists between rational planning and public participation, polyarchists fail to see that public participation can simplify the tasks confronting political elites as well as stimulate elected officials to engage in more creative social planning. The process of partisan mutual adjustment among groups is not antithetical to long-range, innovative planning; on the contrary, it is essential to the success of any form of decision making.

The Pluralistic Option

The difficulties with both the participatory and polyarchal forms of decision making serve only to illustrate in greater detail the benefits of a pluralistic style of government. Critics of pluralism have failed to see that the troubles confronting the present political system stem both from a feeling of alienation and mistrust in the ghetto and from a lack of innovative and creative planning. Besides restoring a sense of legitimacy and confidence in its operations, the political system needs to offer more guidance to various groups seeking to shape the outcome of policy deliberations. Unfortunately, the participatory and polyarchal alternatives seem incapable of simultaneously providing for inner city involvement and effective, long-range planning. The defenders of community control, who claim their style of resolving issues can handle the problems of trust, self-esteem, and responsiveness, seem to have difficulty dealing with larger problems such as economies of scale, spill-over effects, social justice, and innovative policy making. Conversely, the advocates of centralized decision making, who claim their form of planning can achieve more innovative and more equitable policy, often seem oblivious to the problems cited by participatory democrats as well as ill prepared to cope with them.

In contrast, the doctrine of public pluralism, which advocates a dual policy of organizing the poor from the bottom up and regulating the interplay of interests from the top down, seems to have the potential for dealing with both sets of issues. On a national level, the decision-making process can be vastly improved if the chief executive shares his power more fully with Congress and the various federal agencies and their clientele groups. If for one reason or another there is minimal interaction among these institutions, the executive branch must play the divergent roles of advocate, custodian, and manager of the political arena, fostering competition among these parties. On a local or metropolitan level, it is necessary to foster the development of a federated or multi-tier system of government with multiple, overlapping units. Rather than devolving more power to autonomous political entities in the suburban ring and in the inner city, or concentrating authority in a single, hierarchically structured metropolitan government, it would be preferable to develop a more diverse and complex political structure that would:

(1) Assist the formation of neighborhood organizations, especially among residents of the ghetto;
(2) Tolerate the development of multiple government units with varying jurisdictions and responsibilities;
(3) Arrange the above units of government in an overlapping, federated fashion so that the ability of communities to isolate themselves from neighboring communities would be limited;
(4) Provide some government body such as the Councils of Government, which came into being as a result of federal prodding in the late 1960s, with the power to review and veto the actions of smaller government authorities.

The reasons for advocating such a system of decision making are by now readily apparent. If the government encourages and assists the poor to organize themselves, it is possible to restore a sense of trust among inner city residents as well as to increase their ability to help themselves (criteria one and two). When the poor attempt to manage large and unwieldy organizations like the school system, they are less likely to realize their objectives than when they participate in a more limited and segmented fashion. Especially for political novices, the running of an institution with which they have little or no experience can actually serve to retard a sense of personal efficacy. But as Yates has shown, when the residents of ghetto neighborhoods join specific, functionally oriented groups, they are apt to feel a heightened sense of confidence both in their own ability and in the political system's ability to improve the condition of their lives. [48] Moreover, the organization of neighborhood residents is likely to improve the delivery of services to the public and thus increase the responsiveness of government institutions to citizen demands (criterion three).

Similarly, by allowing a variety of jurisdictions within a metropolitan area to maintain a certain degree of autonomy, it will be possible to enable citizens with relatively homogeneous preferences to purchase varying amounts of goods according to their priorities. In this fashion the production of government amenities will be more in accordance with the diverse array of citizen wants found in an urban community. And if additional research should show more convincingly than do the present data that there are no large economies of scale in the provision of those municipal services which are labor intensive, resources can be saved by allowing the existence of a variety of different-sized jurisdictions. Large units can provide services in which economies of scale are realizable, while smaller jurisdictions can perform any functions that are more economical when carried out by smaller administrative bodies (criterion five). However, to minimize the possibility of any one community passing on part of its costs to other districts, it is necessary to include smaller political units in a larger, federated metropolitan government that can check or veto the decisions made by its constituent parts. The existence of extensive overlap in political boundaries and the ability of communities to seek redress of grievances at more inclusive levels of government would provide a favorable environment for the resolution of spill-over effects among different units of decision making (criterion four). The larger units of government could impose levies on communities that fail to pay their fair share for combatting an external cost like pollution. And conversely, they could compensate those segments of the urban environment which have provided the larger community with external benefits, like recreational facilities, but have received no compensation.

Similarly, by developing a complex federal, as well as metropolitan, form of government in which one unit presides over a diverse array of smaller, overlapping jurisdictions, the political system can maximize its ability to deal with redistributive problems (criterion six). As pointed out earlier, there is often a geographical mismatch between the economic needs of our traditional municipal centers and the financial wealth of the surrounding suburban communities. As the middle classes have fled from urban centers, their place has usually been taken by the poor and minorities, who are most in need of social services. Because the more affluent classes have often isolated themselves in autonomous, satellite communities, they not only have escaped paying taxes to traditional urban centers that would support programs for lower-income individuals; they also have directly added to the costs that core cities must bear. Through the passage of exclusionary housing and land-use policies, most suburban communities have deliberately sought to prevent lower- and lower-middle-class families from moving to the outskirts. This attempt at self-isolation has reduced the financial burdens on the suburban resident at the expense of those remaining in the core city.

While economists like Bish and Nourse favor the proliferation of small communities, which can cater to the special preferences of different groups, they fail to see that such a policy has definite social consequences unless certain restraints are placed on suburban autonomy. In order to implement programs that would reduce the problems of poverty and inequality, it is necessary to create a federated urban structure that would have both the fiscal ability to levy taxes on those individuals living in the suburban fringe and the legal power to veto discriminatory housing or zoning laws. As indicated in chapter 2, the federal government presently requires all municipalities to submit applications for federal funds to area-wide review boards charged with the responsibility of harmonizing the requests of individual communities. To carry out such directives most cities have joined Councils of Government. Because these institutions are still in a state of evolution, it is difficult to tell whether they will undertake redistributive policies or assume responsibility for compensating municipalities that are the recipients of negative spill-over effects. The eventual power wielded by these area-wide units of government will depend on how strongly the executive branch insists that municipalities practice some form of regional planning. Left to themselves, local communities are not likely to pick up the tab for costs they can easily pass on to other communities. But if the president and the executive branch vigorously use the financial leverage of federal assistance to develop a multilevel form of regional government with veto power over the subunits within its jurisdiction, there is a genuine possibility that the spill-over and redistributive problems that plague local units of government can be minimized.

Finally, by using COGs to develop a centrally guided form of pluralistic decision making, it may be possible to stimulate the development of creative and innovative policy making (criterion seven). In an expanded, overlapping form of decision making, there will be plenty of incentives, as well as opportunities, for interest groups and local units of government to voice their opinions on policies that directly bear on them. The possibility of public officials succumbing to groupthink or ignoring important information is thus likely to be minimized. And if the president or the OMB on the national level and Councils of Government on the local level acquire enough power to supervise the interaction of these multiple participants—as public pluralists hope will eventually be the case—the political system will be able to implement the policies generated by a diverse number of groups. Unlike a polyarchal form of decision making, where power is concentrated in the hands of a few officials, or participatory democracy, where it is fragmented among numerous autonomous units, a supervised form of pluralism seeks to realize that middle ground which Wilson believes is most conducive to innovative policy making.

Whether we compare alternative forms of decision making by their ability to promote a sense of public trust, efficacy, and responsiveness, or by their capacity to achieve economies of scale or minimize spill-over effects, or by their success in stimulating social reform and innovative policy making, a public form of pluralism seems to have many advantages. Pluralism has been criticized by the advocates of centralized and decentralized power for opposite reasons, but in many cases these criticisms do not seem justified. According to the numerous criteria we have looked at, a pluralistic system of decision making often seems preferable to its competitors. That is no mean achievement when we consider that pluralism's detractors suggested many of the criteria in the first place.

NOTES

1. Alan Altshuler, *Community Control*; Milton Kotler, *Neighborhood Government*.

2. Altshuler, *Community Control*, p. 16.

3. Theodore J. Lowi, *The End of Liberalism*; Robert L. Crain, Elihu Katz, and Donald Rosenthal, *The Politics of Community Conflict*.

4. Altshuler, *Community Control*, p. 15.

5. Douglas Yates, *Neighborhood Democracy*, p. 26.

6. Robert L. Bish and Hugh O. Nourse, *Urban Economics and Policy Analysis*, pp. 111-13.

7. Ibid., pp. 107-11.

8. Crain, Katz, and Rosenthal, *Politics of Community Conflict*.

9. James Q. Wilson, "Innovation in Organizations," pp. 193-218.

10. Altshuler, *Community Control*, pp. 13-65.

11. Wilson, "Innovation in Organizations," pp. 193-218.

12. Samuel P. Huntington, *Political Order in Changing Societies*.

13. Charles Lindblom, *The Intelligence of Democracy*, pp. 165-274; Michael Aiken and Robert Alford, "Community Structure and Mobilization," p. 63.

14. Werner Hirsch, *The Economics of State and Local Government*, pp. 189, 178-83.

15. Elinor Ostrom et al., *Community Organization and the Provision of Police Services*.

16. Bish and Nourse, *Urban Economics*, p. 133.

17. Peter Blau and Richard Schoenherr, *The Structure of Organizations*; S. R. Klatzky, "Relationship of Organizational Size to Complexity and Coordination."

18. Altshuler, *Community Control*, pp. 123-90.

19. Ibid.

20. Bish and Nourse, *Urban Economics*, pp. 129-31; Charles Tiebout, "A Pure Theory of Local Expenditures," pp. 416-24.

21. Bish and Nourse, *Urban Economics*, p. 129.

22. James Heilbrun, *Urban Economics and Public Policy*, p. 345.

23. Yates, *Neighborhood Democracy*, p. 66.

24. Ibid., p. 105.

25. Ibid., p. 67.

26. Lowi, *End of Liberalism*, p. 101.

27. Crain, Katz, and Rosenthal, *Politics of Community Conflict*, p. 13.

28. Lowi, *End of Liberalism*, p. 101.

29. Ibid., p. 127.

30. Ibid., pp. 217-26.

31. Ibid., pp. 226-39.

32. Kenneth B. Clark, *Dark Ghetto*, pp. 63-80; Milton Greenblatt, ed., *Poverty and Mental Health*; Dorothy B. James, *Poverty, Politics, and Change*.

33. James, *Poverty, Politics, and Change*, pp. 148-58.

34. Herbert A. Simon and James G. March, *Organizations*; Lindblom, *Intelligence of Democracy*.

35. Roland McKean, *Public Spending*, p. 149.

36. Ibid.

37. Lowi, *End of Liberalism*, p. 302.

38. Irving L. Janis, *Victims of Groupthink*.

39. Ibid., pp. 196-97.

40. Ibid., pp. 14-50.

41. Wilson, "Innovation in Organizations," pp. 193-218.

42. Robert L. Lineberry and Edmund P. Fowler, "Reformism and Public Policies in American Cities," pp. 707-09.

43. Terry Clark, "Community Structure, Decision Making, Budget Expenditures, and Urban Renewal in Fifty-one American Cities," p. 594.

44. Michael Aiken, "The Distribution of Community Power: Structural Bases and Social Consequences."

45. Aiken and Alford, "Community Structure and Mobilization"; Michael Aiken and Robert Alford, "Community Structure and Innovation," pp. 843-64.

46. Crain, Katz, and Rosenthal, *Politics of Community Conflict*.

47. T. Clark, "Community Structure, in Fifty-one American Cities," p. 587.

48. Yates, *Neighborhood Democracy*, p. 65.

Chapter

10

Pluralism and the
Problem of Public Administration

In this chapter we need to deal with one final problem facing every theory of democracy, that of public administration. Besides determining how decisions should be made, the advocates of various theories of democracy must decide how agreed-upon policies should be implemented. Even though a form of democracy may be successful in generating new ideas, its public record will be less than impressive if it cannot successfully translate its decisions into operating programs.

Any discussion of public administration is often a confusing task in American politics because government agencies perform a multitude of functions. Many play an input role in the political system, organizing clientele groups and mobilizing support for new or existing policies. In fact, some agencies—OEO, the Departments of Commerce and Labor—perform an almost exclusively representative function, for their main task is to look after the interests of their various constituencies. Others—such as HUD, HEW, or the Defense Department—play both input and output roles, lobbying for new policies as well as implementing existing programs. While earlier we discussed the role that government bureaus should play in the policy-making process, in this chapter we need to analyze how they should perform their administrative tasks. In particular, it is necessary to determine what organizational patterns are most likely to be successful in translating public policies into operating programs.

In the quest for the optimal administrative arrangements, the proponents of competing theories of democracy must often pursue conflicting objectives. On the one hand they must try to insure that the administrative arm of the executive branch has the organizational capabilities and resources necessary to achieve its objectives, while on the other they must try to prevent agencies with administrative duties from abusing their grants of public authority. The optimal administrative arrangements must strike a balance between (1) promoting organizational effectiveness and (2) achieving organizational control. Although agencies must be given sufficient authority to carry out their stated functions, at the same time measures must be taken to insure that the goals of a policy are not consciously or unconsciously subverted in the very act of implementation.

To cope with these difficulties, the advocates of various theories of democracy must decide two separate yet crucially related issues. First, they must determine how individual agencies should be administered. Should they be highly centralized with only limited discretion granted to field offices, or should they have the option of delegating considerable authority to subunits? Secondly, the proponents of different theories of democracy must decide how they wish to organize the executive branch as a whole. Should they try as Franklin Roosevelt did to build creative disorder and duplication into the structure of the federal bureaucracy, or should they follow the suggestions of the Hoover and Ash Commissions and streamline the executive branch by functionally grouping related agencies into similar departments?[1]

Advocates of community control have argued that considerable leeway and discretion should be allowed on the individual agency level. Unless lower-level bureaucrats have the flexibility to respond to immediate community problems and the discretion to tailor the substance of programs to local demands, the delivery of public services may be ineffectual in meeting constituent needs. However, because they wish to parcel out the power of the federal government to smaller political units, most participatory democrats have paid very little attention to the problems of organizing the federal bureaucracy as a whole.

In contrast, polyarchists and populists have implicitly, if not always explicitly, called for a more centralized administration of programs on both individual agency and executive levels of government. Lowi has argued that individual agencies will lack any degree of effectiveness unless they avoid dispersing their power among various subunits. In a similar vein, polyarchists and populists have sought to consolidate and streamline the organization of the executive branch as a whole, insisting that the haphazard, overlapping nature of administrative jurisdictions constitutes an inherently wasteful and inefficient manner of implementing policy.[2] Like the members of the Hoover and Ash Commissions, who have studied the makeup of the executive branch on three separate occasions since World War II, they have concluded that (1) agencies with related duties should be consolidated and the proliferation of new agencies should be held to a minimum, (2) bureaus with functionally related tasks should be grouped together in larger departments, and (3) the jurisdictions and responsibilities of agencies should be clearly defined and delineated. In Lowi's opinion, a pluralistic system of overlapping jurisdictions so weakens and fragments the administrative process that it renders the government incapable of achieving its objectives. Likewise, the granting of any appreciable degree of flexibility to lower-level officials in the interpretation of their duties leads to widespread misuse of government power. He has maintained that under a system of administration in which rules and responsibilities are not clearly delineated, lower-level bureaucrats have too many opportunities to bargain and logroll with the clientele groups that they serve. In Lowi's view, this process of interest-group bargaining leads to the displacement of agency goals and to a corruption of the whole notion of strict implementation of the law.

Because participatory democrats have failed to develop a comprehensive approach to organizational problems, this chapter will primarily focus on polyarchy's and populism's proposals for administrative reorganization. As will be explained in greater detail later on, pluralism rejects the recommendations of its polyarchal and populist counterparts, arguing that the administrative process will be enhanced by allowing for more flexibility and duplication. While pluralists share the belief in the need for effective and efficient administration, they question whether polyarchy's measures will be capable of achieving these objectives.

The Problem of Organizational Effectiveness

If we wish to maximize an organization's effectiveness, we can argue that polyarchal-populist prescriptions for administrative reform might hamper the performance of individual agencies. Like Max Weber and Luther Gulick, polyarchists and populists seem to believe that there are certain universal administrative principles that can be applied to all organizations, e. g., straight lines of authority, unity of command, and authority commensurate with responsibility.[3] They often insist that the most effective, efficient agencies are hierarchically organized with limited discretion granted to lower-level bureaucrats. In recent years, however, this attitude has been attacked by a group of scholars who have sought to replace universalistic administrative theories with contingency models of organizational structure. Starting in the late 1960s, sociologists engaged in the comparative study of organizations began to notice that a relationship exists between an agency's size, tasks, and structure. Instead of finding that certain principles of administration are suitable for all kinds of organizations, they have observed that the most appropriate arrangements are contingent upon the volume and complexity of problems facing an organization. In an important study of state employment agencies, Peter Blau has shown that as the amount of work increases, an agency finds itself under greater pressure to decentralize its operations.[4] As an organization grows in size, it becomes increasingly difficult for the agency to administer its programs in a highly centralized fashion. However, in related studies, Paul Lawrence, Jay Lorsch, Charles Perrow, and James Thompson find that the optimal administrative arrangements are as dependent on the variability in an agency's tasks as on the amount of work actually performed.[5] While these studies often differ in terminology and emphasis, they share the conclusion that a centralized, rule-oriented organization is suitable for performing only certain kinds of tasks.

Perrow in particular finds that the most desirable administrative arrangements are contingent upon two factors: the degree of variability in the problems confronting an agency and the degree to which an agency has reliable and established techniques for solving the problems facing it. By combining these two variables, Perrow has developed a typology of four different kinds of organizations, each with very different types of administrative needs (see table 4).[6]

Table 4

Technology available to agency	Nature of tasks	
	UNIFORM	COMPLEX
Solutions to problems clear	Passport Bureau	Voice of America
	Box 1	Box 2
Solutions to problems unclear	Bureau of Education	HUD
	Box 4	Box 3

Box one represents an organization like the Passport Bureau of the U. S. Department of State, which faces very routine tasks and has a fairly clear conception of how best to deal with its administrative duties. In box two we find an agency like the Voice of America, whose broadcasts must explain a great variety of phenomena but can rely on a clear idea of how to handle the issues. Box three represents an administrative body like HUD, which not only faces the complex task of revitalizing the nation's decaying cities but also must rely on a body of knowledge that as yet cannot reliably specify which programs would be most effective in furthering the agency's goals. Finally, in box four we find an organization like the Office of Education in HEW, which has a more homogeneous task than HUD yet may not be quite certain what mixture of policies will be most effective in achieving its goals.

The identification of different types of agencies can tell us in turn what kinds of organizational arrangements are most likely to lead to effective administration. Perrow argues that the centralized, rule-oriented model of organization that Lowi advocates would be appropriate only for an agency administering relatively simple, straightforward programs, such as those found in box one. While an organization that reacted in a consistent fashion to every problem would perform more than adequately if its tasks never varied, it would prove to be inordinately inept, as Lawrence and Lorsch have shown, once its administrative duties lacked uniformity. [7] As the tasks confronting an agency become more heterogeneous and the solutions to its problems become more uncertain, it will have to grant greater discretion to middle- and lower-level officials, as do the agencies in boxes three and four. When exceptions arise or unusual problems develop, a centralized organization lacks the flexibility necessary to deal with administrative problems that deviate from the usual tasks at hand. Similarly, if the state of knowledge in policy areas such as education or crime is rather undeveloped, agencies in those fields will have to forego reliance on detailed plans in order to experiment with a variety of approaches in their search for appropriate solutions. Unless lower-level bureaucrats can exercise discretion in implementing policy, their agencies will be unable to launch any creative attacks on their respective problems. The lack of certainty about how best to run a particular program rules out centralized administration.

Unfortunately, however, polyarchal and populist democrats like Lowi and Harrington seem oblivious to these findings. Like the members of the Hoover and Ash Commissions, who have insisted that centralized and well-disciplined organizations are necessarily the most effective, polyarchists and populists have fallen into the mistake of believing that there are universal principles of good management that apply to all organizations. From the recent literature on contingency models of organizational theory, we now know that when the problems bureaucracies deal with are neither standardized nor easily understood, centralized agencies may be the least effective form of administration.

For similar reasons the desire of polyarchists and populists to rationalize and streamline the executive branch as a whole may in the long run prove to be self-defeating. While polyarchists and populists have often seen the duplication and overlap of federal programs as an inherently inefficient, ineffectual way of implementing policy, it can be argued that the most effective structuring of the executive branch may be contingent on the nature of the issues that must be handled. If it is possible to isolate a relatively self-contained problem, a single agency can conceivably take sole responsibility for dealing with it. But when issues cut across the boundaries of traditional government agencies, as is becoming increasingly true in many policy areas, some blurring of agency responsibilities may be desirable.[8] As policy planners began to realize in the 1960s, programs dealing with poverty, housing, manpower training, health, education, and welfare are all intimately linked. The Johnson administration's war on poverty could not focus on a series of separate and unrelated problems, for the issue involved the activities of a variety of government agencies.

In fact, on the basis of recent administrative experience, Warren Bennis has gone so far as to suggest that established, traditional bureaucracies may be ill equipped to deal with the complexities of modern-day social issues.[9] In a similar vein, Harold Seidman has argued that because of the interdependent, overlapping nature of so many social problems, the executive branch will eventually be composed of "adaptive, rapidly changing temporary systems" organized around problem areas.[10] Although Bennis and Seidman may have overstated their case, it can nonetheless be argued that a blurring of agency jurisdictions is essential for problems that resist simple categorization. The most appropriate organizational arrangements for maximizing agency effectiveness are contingent on the issues they face. Since so many government bureaus deal with problems that are (1) heterogeneous in nature, (2) not fully understood by experts in the field, and (3) not conterminous with traditional agency boundaries, efforts to consolidate operations on the executive level may have the unintended consequence of impairing administrative effectiveness.

The Problem of Organizational Control

Regardless of the impact that centralized administration of individual agencies or consolidation of the executive branch as a whole may have on the effectiveness of various government agencies, we still need to ask if these measures will insure organizational control. While every theory of democracy must attempt to provide sufficient resources and flexibility to the administrative arm of the executive branch, it must simultaneously try to prevent agencies from consciously or unconsciously altering the goals of their respective programs. Merely because an agency has the proper administrative structure to match its tasks is no guarantee that it will faithfully and vigorously execute its responsibilities. The question that thus needs to be asked is whether polyarchal-populist suggestions for controlling individual agencies would stimulate government bureaus to remain faithful to their initial goals. While polyarchists like Lowi often insist that it is the constant bargaining an agency must undertake in a pluralistic system that leads to the displacement of goals, they fail to realize that informal norms within an organization may be just as important in accounting for an agency's failure to achieve its objectives. Polyarchists argue that by doing away with discretion and the bargaining associated with it and by instituting centralized, rule-oriented methods of organizational control, it will be possible to insure that an agency remains faithful to its original goals.

However, it can be argued that this approach to administration places too much reliance on formalized, rule-oriented modes of control. On the basis of the work of Robert Merton and the early Peter Blau, students of organizational theory have increasingly come to reject the view held by Weber and others that organizations are rational instruments that can be scientifically programmed to achieve specified objectives.[11] Merton et al. pointed out that agencies, especially centralized, rule-oriented agencies, often develop their own informal norms of behavior that sometimes act to undermine the organization's original objectives. In a study of state welfare agencies Merton has described how the top hierarchy attempted to increase the reliability of behavior within the organization by instituting a wide variety of rules. By closely regulating the conduct of its personnel, the agency believed it could provide better service to its clientele, but in fact, Merton noted, the opposite situation developed. Once the agency formulated an elaborate set of rules, its case workers became wary that they might violate some organizational regulation and thereby jeopardize their careers. To counter these feelings, employees developed their own informal norms for dealing with clients, including a reduction in the amount of personal relations between case workers and their clients and an extreme reliance on organizational rules for making decisions. One such rule was that families not be broken up, and it was enforced to the point where "a social worker in violation of his own judgment as to what would be most beneficial for the clients" would recommend that mentally disturbed children remain with their families even though the brothers and sisters would suffer as a result.[12] Ironically enough, an agency that attempted to insure better service to its clients inadvertently ended up providing worse service. The informal norms that the organization's personnel had developed in response to the internal directives of the top hierarchy resulted in the subtle yet significant displacement of the agency's original objectives. The employees became more intent on routinely applying the rules of the organization than on meeting the needs of their clients.

Peter Blau's analysis of a state employment bureau offers another illustration of the same type of phenomenon.[13] The bureau, which had the official task of helping people find employment, developed a simple and, at first glance, highly effective procedure for guaranteeing that its personnel actually attempted to find jobs for their clients. Each month placement officers were evaluated by the percentage of people they found employment for out of the total number of individuals they interviewed. Unfortunately, these rules, which were meant to make the employment agency more productive, often served to limit the usefulness of the agency to the job hunters it was supposed to assist. As was the case of the welfare bureau, employees developed informal norms of behavior to mitigate the severity of the organization's evaluation scheme. For instance, when employment officials heard of new job openings they refused to share that information with other personnel. Each placement worker would attempt to hoard as many job notices as he could until he happened to interview individuals who qualified for the positions. But even more importantly, since it was difficult to place minority members with limited education or skills, employees sought to reduce the possibility of receiving low evaluation scores by deliberately discouraging such individuals from utilizing the services of the agency. The rules the organization established to achieve its goals had the unintended consequence of impairing the ability of the agency to meet its objectives. Instead of attempting to help the people most in need of their services, i.e., indigent minority members, the personnel of the employment agency attempted to dissuade them from calling on state help in the first place. The informal norms that the employees had developed in response to evaluation procedures worked at cross-purposes to the original objectives of the agency.

Both the Blau and Merton studies indicate that internal procedures are important in explaining why agencies often fail to achieve their objectives. But even more importantly, they show that the informal norms of a bureau are most likely to subvert the original objectives of the organization when it is run in a highly centralized, formalistic fashion. While Lowi believes that limiting the discretion of lower-level bureaucrats will insure their faithful adherence to agency goals, such procedures will often have the opposite result. If bureaucratic personnel are governed by an elaborate set of rules, they may lose sight of their original objectives, as Merton has demonstrated, or subvert the intent of the established procedures, as Blau has demonstrated.

The failure of polyarchists and populists to see that their efforts to control individual agencies may have certain unintended consequences is symptomatic of a much larger problem. While informal groups within an agency can intentionally or unintentionally lead to the alteration of an organization's goals, an agency's political ties with outside clientele groups can also affect its commitment to its official objectives. Recognition of this fact is essential if we wish to properly evaluate recommendations for rearranging the structure of the federal bureaucracy. As noted earlier, polyarchal-populist suggestions for organizing the executive branch as a whole include (1) holding to a minimum the proliferation of new agencies, (2) grouping functionally related agencies together into larger departments, and (3) carefully delineating each agency's duties and responsibilities in order to eliminate overlapping programs. As we have already seen, the delineation of each agency's duties and responsibilities may not always be desirable when problems cut across traditional agency boundaries. But even more importantly, we can argue that if all of the polyarchal-populist proposals were ever fully implemented, they would restrict rather than facilitate public control of the bureaucracy. Proponents of consolidating and streamlining the executive branch often seem naive in their assumption that reorganization efforts will have little or no adverse impact on the way in which government programs are administered. As Francis Rourke, Mathew Holden, Philip Selznick, and Richard Neustadt have pointed out, agencies often acquire a political stake in the continuation of their programs.[14] This phenomenon belies the polyarchal-populist assumption, derived from Weber, that organizations are neutral administrators of the programs they oversee. Either through selective recruitment or internal socialization, most of the personnel of various government bureaus become highly committed to the policies they administer. To preserve the essential parts of their programs, agencies will generally seek out clientele groups or constituencies in order to protect themselves from the claims of competing agencies. Every bureau wishes to generate enough potential support in the larger political community so that it can fight off legislative attacks that might jeopardize the existence of its programs.

While these observations may at first seem rather obvious, they provide us with some guidelines that may be more realistic than Lowi's administrative prescriptions for guaranteeing that government agencies vigorously pursue their stated objectives. First of all, Lowi's call for limiting the proliferation of new agencies could be a serious political mistake, for, as Holden has shown, it is not advisable to ask an established bureau to administer new or controversial programs. Holden has pointed out that once an agency develops its clientele groups, it is likely to be hostile to acquiring new programs that may jeopardize its existing network of relationships.[15] If a well-established agency is forced to operate a program that may alienate its supporters, it is likely to drag its feet in implementing the new policy. In the process the original objectives of the program may very will be altered or displaced.

A prime example of this phenomenon can be found in the administration of the food stamp program, which Congress delegated to the Department of Agriculture in the late 1960s when it expanded its relief-in-kind programs. Since the Department of Agriculture is primarily oriented toward the Farm Bureau and corporate farmers rather than the urban or rural poor, its administration of the program has been less than vigorous. [16] Because Congress failed to consider the implementation of its policies carefully, it employed an organizational strategy that worked at cross-purposes to its policy objectives. It would have been more advisable to create a separate agency, since new organizations will tend to vigorously implement their assigned programs in order to overcome the precarious political position they occupy as newly established bodies. A recently created bureau without any established power base will naturally try to build a following by making sure that its policies are successfully administered. To ward off attacks from competing agencies or from hostile legislators, it must provide enough tangible or symbolic benefits to its potential supporters that they will be willing to come to the aid of the bureau in times of trouble. In order to build a viable political following, an agency will implement those policies which will earn it the consistent support of at least one constituency group.

The argument that applies to the placement of individual programs likewise applies to the placement of agencies as a whole. As Selznick has pointed out, if government programs are violently opposed by other interests in society, it may be necessary to shield them organizationally from their opponents so that they can survive politically. [17] If two separate agencies have functionally similar jobs but different and conflicting goals, it may not be advisable to place both of them in one large department since the agency that is weakest will then be much more vulnerable to interests that oppose its activities. For example, in the late 1940s the Hoover Commission called for the consolidation of the Farm Home Administration, the Farm Credit Administration, and the Agricultural Extension Service on the grounds that all these agencies were concerned with the same function of extending credit to farmers. What seemed like a logical move to end administrative duplication would in reality have worked a hardship on marginal farmers. [18] The Farm Credit Administration and the Agricultural Extension Service, which were both created at the request of the Farm Bureau, are primarily concerned with serving the needs of moderate and well-to-do farmers, while the Farm Home Administration seeks to provide special assistance to marginal farmers who might not otherwise receive any kind of credit. If the various agencies had been combined, the resulting bureau would have sought to cultivate the undivided support of at least one clientele group. Since the Farm Bureau is better organized than marginal farmers, an agency that had the responsibility for extending loans to both constituencies would probably cater to the wishes of the more organized group. In the process the goal of Congress to provide needed financial aid to marginal farmers would be attenuated, if not displaced altogether.

On the basis of the above examples, we can see why the attempts of polyarchal and populist democrats to control the federal bureaucracy not only may prove to be ineffective but also may contribute to the very practices they wish to avoid in the first place. Regardless of how centralized a bureau may be or how much discretion an agency happens to wield, its political ties to outside groups will significantly influence its ultimate behavior. While Lowi might deplore this tendency of organizations to develop political links with outside groups, he fails to see that it is possible to utilize a knowledge of this phenomenon to safeguard the implementation of government policies. If the structure of the federal bureaucracy were ever reorganized along more centralized lines, as Lowi and the Hoover and Ash Commissions have suggested, the danger of organizations displacing their goals would be heightened rather than lessened. Since established departments tend to have their personnel and programs coopted by outside constituencies, an important way to provide new or controversial programs with a chance of survival is to allow for the proliferation of new agencies. Similarly, because new or controversial bureaus are politically more vulnerable when they are placed next to bureaus that oppose their objectives, it may not always be desirable to rationalize the administrative process by grouping functionally related agencies together into larger departments. The attempts of polyarchal democrats to consolidate the executive branch would effectively foreclose reliance on these administrative strategies. Ironically enough, while Lowi often sees the profusion of government agencies and the untidy nature of the bureaucratic system as a sign of administrative weakness, it may in fact be a sign of administrative vitality. While the efforts of populists and polyarchists to operate individual bureaus in a more centralized, nondiscretionary fashion may make it more difficult to insure that agencies remain committed to their programs, their desire to streamline the executive branch as a whole may also have the same unintended consequence.

The Pluralistic Alternative

The difficulties with a centrally operated bureaucracy only cast in greater relief the benefits of a more pluralistic pattern of administration. We noted earler that pluralists are not adverse to agencies' either decentralizing their operations or exercising discretion in the administration of their programs. As Perrow convincingly argues, when the responsibilities of organizations are heterogeneous in nature and the methodology they must employ to deal with their problems is not well established, it is essential that agencies decentralize their operations. When government bureaus must respond to a series of diverse demands, centralized, formalistically run organizations may be both too slow and too rigid to provide adequate services to their clients. If the residents of large cities come to play a more active role in government, it will be imperative that city, state, and federal agencies have the flexibility to meet their demands promptly. The sense of public mistrust that is found in many communities may be difficult to overcome if centralized, rule-oriented bureaus are unable to respond quickly to local needs.

While Lowi suggests that the discretionary manner in which many laws are enforced has led to a breakdown in respect for public authority, in reality the situation may be much more complex. Residents of the inner city may not be opposed to lower-level bureaucrats exercising discretion per se so much as they are opposed to the manner in which officials have exercised that discretion in the past. Even though residents of urban areas feel that public officials have utilized their discretionary power to the disadvantage of the inner city, they may hope that bureaucrats will eventually use such authority to be more sensitive to the wishes of local neighborhoods. For example, it may be appropriate for the police to strictly enforce an ordinance against loitering or disorderly conduct in a suburban community, but it may be necessary to interpret that ordinance more leniently in an inner city neighborhood. If a residential area lacks adequate back yards or parks, it will be natural for citizens to spend more of their leisure time in the streets. As a result, behavior that a suburban neighborhood might see as undesirable might appear very differently to residents of an inner city community. If a police department attempts to enforce an ordinance uniformly in these two contrasting situations, it may alienate, rather than win the support of, the local community. How officials use their power of discretion—not whether they should have it—is the key administrative problem that needs to be confronted.

The best way to prevent agencies from abusing their discretion is to build some degree of organizational duplication and planned disorder into the structure of the executive branch as a whole. While pluralists argue that on a micro-level the decentralization of individual agencies can lead to greater administrative effectiveness, they insist that on a macro-level, agency and group competition can limit any misuse of government power that may arise. It is not discretion or bargaining per se—but the political proclivities cited by Holden et al. or the presence of informal groups trying to protect their interests in the larger organization—that causes agencies to displace their goals. To control these tendencies, a carefully designed system of organizational checks and balances is preferable to a system of rigid internal procedures and limited discretion.

First of all, when some degree of creative disorder exists in the arrangement of federal agencies, crucial programs can be more easily protected from opposing interests. Both the Roosevelt and Johnson administrations provide excellent illustrations of this point. According to the orthodox polyarchal theory of administration, Roosevelt should have assigned his programs to alleviate the depression to established departments such as Agriculture, Labor, Commerce, and Treasury. But he recognized, as many commentators in public administration have not, that even with new chiefs, the old-line agencies would not be likely to generate the enthusiasm and vigor that the gravity of the situation warranted. [19] To circumvent the power of established groups and agencies, Roosevelt made it part of his strategy to create new administrative bodies when he wanted creative attacks on the problems at hand. He was determined not to lose in the process of administration what he had previously won in the legislative arena. Similarly, Johnson deliberately refrained from asking the traditional-line agencies to administer his war on poverty. Not only did he insist that OEO be established as an independent agency, he also sought to shield it from hostile interests by locating it in the executive office of the president. The war on poverty might have turned out very differently if he had succumbed to the wishes of big city mayors and placed OEO in the Department of Housing and Urban Development, which has been oriented primarily to the needs of metropolitian government. If HUD had been given responsibility for administering OEO programs, OEO might never have become an advocate agency seeking to challenge the actions of municipal governments. [20] Even though polyarchists and populists often argue that an untidy, pluralistic administrative system is wasteful and inefficient, they fail to realize that it may serve other important purposes. Some degree of creative disorder in the overall organization of the federal bureaucracy may be necessary to protect new programs against hostile interests.

For related reasons, pluralists believe that administrative overlap is important in fostering interagency competition in the implementation of federal programs. While a degree of organizational disorder is necessary to protect the establishment of new or controversial programs, it also serves to guarantee that bureaus do not abuse their powers of discretion in carrying out their tasks. As indicated earlier, the fact that many present-day political problems cut across traditional boundaries is in large part responsible for the blurring of agency jurisdictions, but the granting of overlapping jurisdictions may have an added virtue. If agencies like OEO, HUD, HEW, or the Department of Labor have related responsibilities, each can scrutinize the others' activities that might have some impact on its own constituents. In the process they can make certain that policies designed to benefit certain groups are not subtly altered in the process of administration. For instance, as James Sundquist had noted, once OEO was established, it successfully put pressure on state employment agencies to launch outreach programs to find work for the urban poor. [21] While the internal norms of the state employment agencies that Blau studied often led them to discourage residents of the inner city from seeking their help, the external pressure of OEO stimulated other employment agencies to redouble their efforts to assist the poor.

Finally, if government bureaus are given only incomplete grants of authority and overlapping jurisdictions in the running of their programs, they cannot conceal their operations from the scrutiny of outside interests. In the same manner that group competition can insure more rational policy making, interest-group as well as interagency competition can insure that government agencies do not alter the original objectives of a policy in the process of administering it. When agencies do not have a monopoly over any particular issue or program, they face greater pressure to justify their activities and to improve the performance of their tasks. While the report of the Ash Commission testifies to the lack of popularity of this view, the record of the Roosevelt administration indicates that it can work. More than any other president, Roosevelt attempted to administer his policies in a pluralistic, competitive, overlapping fashion. As Arthur Schlesinger has noted, jurisdictional overlap "was sloppy and caused much trouble," but at the same time he recognized that the resulting administrative competition helped to keep the bureaucracy "forever on its toes."[22]

NOTES

1. See Arthur M. Schlesinger, Jr., *The Age of Roosevelt*, Vol. II: *The Coming of the New Deal*, pp. 535-52, for a description of Roosevelt's view of administration; and Harold Seidman, *Politics, Position, and Power*, pp. 3-37, for an analysis of the Hoover Commission's administrative proposals.

2. Theodore J. Lowi, *The End of Liberalism*, pp. 101-57; Michael Harrington, *Toward a Democratic Left*, pp. 3-56.

3. Max Weber, *From Max Weber*; Luther H. Gulick and L. Urwick, eds., *Papers on the Science of Administration*.

4. Peter Blau and Richard Schoenherr, *The Structure of Organizations*.

5. Paul R. Lawrence and Jay W. Lorsch, *Organization and Environment*; Charles Perrow, *Complex Organizations*; Charles Perrow, "A Framework for the Comparative Analysis of Organizations," pp. 194-208; James D. Thompson, *Organizations in Action*.

6. Charles Perrow, *Organizational Analysis*, p. 81.

7. Lawrence and Lorsch, *Organizations and Environment*.

8. James L. Sundquist, *Making Federalism Work*, pp. 1-32.

9. Warren Bennis, *Changing Organizations*.

10. Seidman, *Politics, Position, and Power*, p. 281.

11. Robert K. Merton, *Social Theory and Social Structure*; Peter Blau, *The Dynamics of Bureaucracy*.

12. Merton, *Social Theory and Social Structure*, p. 197. See also Amitai Etzioni, *Modern Organizations*, p. 12.

13. Blau, *Dynamics of Bureaucracy*, pp. 1-100.

14. Francis E. Rourke, *Bureaucracy, Politics, and Public Policy*; Mathew Holden, "Imperialism in Bureaucracy," pp. 943-51; Philip Selznick, *Leadership in Administration*; Richard Neustadt, *Presidential Power*.

15. Holden, "Imperialism in Bureaucracy," p. 945.

16. Seidman, *Politics, Position, and Power*, p. 16.

17. Selznick, *Leadership in Administration*, pp. 119-30.

18. Seidman, *Politics, Position, and Power*, p. 15.

19. Schlesinger, *The Age of Roosevelt*, Vol. II: *The Coming of the New Deal*, p. 534.

20. Seidman, *Politics, Position, and Power*, p. 19.

21. Sundquist, *Making Federalism Work*, pp. 49-54.

22. Schlesinger, *The Age of Roosevelt*, Vol. II, p. 535.

Chapter

11

Conclusion

The preceding chapters have suggested that the literature on democratic theory suffers from two serious problems. First, much of the commentary lacks a comparative focus. Instead of systematically weighing the advantages and disadvantages of alternative models of democratic government, many studies have examined the weaknesses or strengths of only one or two approaches. Such a circumspect and partial view can often lead to incomplete and distorted assessments; the merits of a particular variety of democratic government can never be fully appreciated or discounted until we know the costs and benefits associated with deciding policy in an alternative fashion.

Moreover, very few studies have made any serious effort to deal with criticism that is hostile to their own position. In *The End of Liberalism*, Lowi devotes over three hundred pages to the alleged defects of pluralism, yet he spends a scant thirteen pages discussing his own suggestions for reform.[1] Bachrach devotes 90 percent of his book, *The Theory of Democratic Elitism*, to a critique of polyarchy and pluralism while he defends a participatory form of democracy in a brief fourteen pages.[2] Likewise, Wolff spends roughly fifty pages in his article "Beyond Tolerance" criticizing pluralism but only one or two pages detailing his plans for small, intensive communities.[3] Many participatory democrats have argued that because the pluralistic interplay of groups fails to provide a sense of community, it is inherently inferior to more decentralized forms of democracy. But unfortunately, the same participatory democrats have merely assumed—rather than proven—that communal forms of participation are always desirable. Before we can make any statements about the need to go "beyond tolerance" and pluralistic democracy, we must carefully consider whether the participatory option is actually superior to a pluralistic form of government. Participatory democrats like Wolff and Bachrach often do not provide us with that kind of balanced assessment. With a similar lack of systematic analysis, many polyarchists have assumed that by showing how an allegedly pluralistic form of decision making failed to work adequately in a particular instance, they have thereby proved the opposite case for centralized planning. Such reasoning is both bad logic as well as bad political science. Before we can argue that a pluralistic form of government cannot get anything done, we need to compare the performance of pluralism with more centralized patterns of decision making. The recent literature on democratic government, whether it is written from a polyarchal, populist, or participatory perspective, seems better as political criticism than as positive political philosophy. While Lowi or Bachrach or Wolff have written subtle, sustained critiques of pluralism, their suggestions for reform neither confront nor convincingly refute the arguments against both more centralized and more decentralized patterns of democracy.

The second major shortcoming of the literature on democratic theory lies in its failure to distinguish among different types of pluralism. Many commentators have assumed that there is a single type of interest-group democracy and have therefore failed to see that the criticisms they have made of pluralism often apply to only one particular form of the doctrine. Similarly, because the critics have not distinguished among various types of pluralism, they have failed to realize that their proposed reforms can often be easily incorporated within a pluralistic framework. Many of the reforms proposed by commentators like Kariel constitute modifications of a laissez-faire version of pluralism rather than radical alternatives to pluralism in general. For instance, Kariel argues that it is necessary for the federal government to regulate the internal affairs of groups dominated by self-serving elites, but he believes that such policies constitute an attack on pluralism rather than simply a modification of one form of the doctrine. [4] A public pluralist would argue that if the government refrains from dictating policy objectives to an organization but insures that the rank and file have the final say over the group's goals, the integrity of a pluralistic system need not be compromised.

The failure to distinguish among different varieties of pluralism has led Lowi and McConnell to insist that the problems that plague a laissez-faire form of economics are analogous to those that trouble a pluralistic form of decision making. Both Lowi and McConnell attack pluralism for failing to see that competition between groups can break down and that the equilibrium point established by the interplay of groups—even if competition is maintained—may not necessarily be the optimal decision-making point. "One of the major Keynesian criticisms of market theory," Lowi points out, "is that even if pure competition among factors of supply and demand did yield an equilibrium, the equilibrium could be at something far less than the ideal of full employment."[5] By analogy, Lowi argues that even if a pluralistic system were competitive, the resulting policies might not necessarily be desirable from the viewpoint of society as a whole. While Lowi and McConnell may be correct in drawing a comparison between laissez-faire economics and certain varieties of pluralistic democracy, they fail to see that their arguments do not readily apply to all forms of pluralism, especially public pluralism. By organizing marginal interests from the bottom up, by expanding the size of the decision-making arena, and by fostering competition among government agencies, a public form of pluralism attempts to prevent any set of groups or agencies from establishing semi-monopolies. Likewise, by having political elites supervise the give-and-take of group bargaining, public pluralism seeks to insure that the equilibrium point established between interest groups and agencies is also the optimal decision-making point.

Because Lowi fails to distinguish among several different types of pluralism, he overlooks the fact that the reforms of laissez-faire economics in the twentieth century have more in common with public pluralism's recommendations for change than with his own calls for more centralized planning. Many economists, like Keynes, who were critical of the laissez-faire model of the economy nonetheless felt that the market system would work well if it were properly stimulated and regulated. Even though they had limited faith in the invisible hand of Adam Smith, they were equally wary of a completely controlled economy. They believed that the market system was basically an effective mechanism for deciding economic issues and that active state intervention was necessary only when monopolies appeared or when the economy failed to achieve full employment. In place of a command system, they favored a dual structure in which the government intervened in the workings of the market system only when the latter failed to work effectively by itself.

In a similar vein, a public pluralist would insist that it is unnecessary to restrict the participation of interest groups merely because in the past certain interests have established semi-monopolies or because the decisions reached through group bargaining have not necessarily been socially desirable. If, as Lowi argues, the workings of a laissez-faire economy and the operations of pluralism are comparable, then the reforms of Keynesian economics and the proposals of public pluralism are likewise analogous. Just as Keynesian economists do not wish to substitute government planning for the operations of the market system, so public pluralists do not wish to see the curtailment of pluralistic bargaining. Like a market economy, which can function well if the state regulates the workings of the price system, a pluralistic system of government can function well if the state guides and supervises the process of interest-group bargaining. The pluralistic interplay of groups may not be self-sustaining, but if it is properly regulated, it may be far superior to the alternatives from which we have to choose.

NOTES

1. Theodore J. Lowi, *The End of Liberalism*, pp. 297-309.

2. Peter Bachrach, *The Theory of Democratic Elitism*, pp. 93-106.

3. Robert Paul Wolff, Barrington Moore, Jr., and Herbert Marcuse, *A Critique of Pure Tolerance*, pp. 51-52.

4. Henry S. Kariel, *The Decline of American Pluralism*, pp. 179-87.

5. Lowi, *End of Liberalism*, pp. 294-95.

Bibliography

Aberbach, Joel, and Walker, Jack. "The Meaning of Black Power: A Comparison of White and Black Interpretations of a Political Slogan." *American Political Science Review* 64, no. 2 (June 1970): 367-88.

Adizes, Ichak. *Industrial Democracy: Yugoslav Style.* New York: Free Press, 1971.

Aiken, Michael. "The Distribution of Community Power: Structural Bases and Social Consequences." In *The Structure of Community Power,* edited by Michael Aiken and Paul Mott, pp. 487-525. New York: Random House, 1970.

Aiken, Michael, and Alford, Robert. "Community Structure and Innovation: The Case of Public Housing." *American Political Science Review* 64, No. 3 (September 1970): 843-64.

———. "Community Structure and Mobilization: The Case of the War on Poverty." Discussion Paper, Institute for Research on Poverty, Madison: University of Wisconsin, October 1968.

Almond, Gabriel, and Powell, Bingham. *Comparative Politics.* Boston: Little, Brown & Co., 1966.

Almond, Gabriel, and Verba, Sidney. *The Civic Culture.* Boston: Little Brown & Co., 1963.

Altshuler, Alan A. *Community Control.* New York: Pegasus, 1970.

Anderson, Martin. *The Federal Bulldozer: A Critical Analysis of Urban Renewal, 1949-1962.* Cambridge, Mass.: M.I.T. Press, 1964.

Apple, R. W., Jr. "The GOP Fears November Will Be No Grand Old Picnic." *New York Times,* the Week in Review, 3 March, 1974, p. 1.

Apter, David, and Eckstein, Harry, eds. *Comparative Politics.* New York: Free Press, 1963.

Arrow, Kenneth. *Social Choice and Individual Values.* New York: John Wiley & Sons, 1951.

Bachrach, Peter. *The Theory of Democratic Elitism.* Boston: Little, Brown & Co., 1967.

Bachrach, Peter, and Baratz, Morton S. "Decisions and Nondecisions." *American Political Science Review* 57, no.3 (September 1963): 641-51.
———. *Power and Poverty: Theory and Practice.* New York: Oxford University Press, 1970.
———. "Two Faces of Power." *American Political Science Review* 56, no. 4 (December 1962): 947-52.
Banfield, Edward C. *Political Influence: A New Theory of Urban Politics.* New York: Free Press, 1965.
Banfield, Edward C. and Wilson, James Q. *City Politics.* New York: Random House, 1963.
Barkai, Haim. *The Kibbutz: An Experience in Microsocialism.* Jerusalem: Hebrew University Press, 1971.
Barry, Brian M. *Political Argument.* London: Routledge & Kegan Paul, 1965.
———. *Sociologists, Economists and Democracy.* London: Collier-Macmillan, 1970.
Barss, Rietzel, and Associates. "Community Action and Institutional Changes." Unpublished report to OEO, July 1969.
Baskin, Darryl. *American Pluralistic Democracy: A Critique.* New York: Van Nostrand Reinhold Co., 1971.
Bauer, Raymond A.; Pool, Ithiel de Sola; and Dexter, Lewis Anthony. *American Business and Public Policy.* New York: Atherton Press, 1963.
Baumol, William J. *Economic Theory and Operations Research.* Englewood Cliffs, N. J.: Prentice-Hall, 1961.
———. *Welfare Economics and the Theory of the State.* London: G. Bell & Sons, 1965.
Ben-Yosef, Avraham. *The Purest Democracy in the World.* New York: Herzel Press, 1963.
Bennis, Warren. *Changing Organizations: Essays on the Development and Evolution of Human Organizations.* New York: McGraw-Hill, 1966.
Bentley, Arthur F. *The Process of Government.* Chicago: University of Chicago Press, 1908.
Berelson, Bernard; Lazarsfeld, Paul F.; and McPhee, William N. *Voting: A Study of Opinion Formation in a Presidential Campaign.* Chicago: University of Chicago Press, 1954.
Berlin, Isaiah. *Four Essays on Liberty.* London: Oxford University Press, 1966.
Bettelheim, Bruno. *Children of the Dream.* London: Collier-Macmillan, 1969.
Birch, Anthony Harold. *Small Town Politics.* London: Oxford University Press, 1959.

Bish, Robert L., and Nourse, Hugh O. *Urban Economics and Policy Analysis*. New York: McGraw-Hill, 1975.

Black, Duncan. *The Theory of Committees and Elections*. Cambridge: At the University Press, 1958.

Blau, Peter M. *Bureaucracy in Modern Society*. New York: Random House, 1956.

———. *The Dynamics of Bureaucracy*. Chicago: University of Chicago Press, 1955.

Blau, Peter M., and Meyer, Marshall W. *Bureaucracy in Modern Society*. 2d ed. New York: Random House, 1971.

Blau, Peter M., and Schoenherr, Richard. *The Structure of Organizations*. New York: Basic Books, 1971.

Blumberg, Paul. *Industrial Democracy*. Cambridge, Mass.: Schenkman Publishing Co., 1972.

Boyd, Richard W. "Popular Control of Public Policy: A Normal Vote Analysis of the 1968 Election." *American Political Science Review* 66, no. 2 (June 1972): 429-49.

Braybrooke, David, and Lindblom, Charles. *A Strategy of Decision Making*. New York: Free Press, 1963.

Brody, Richard A., and Page, Benjamin I. "Comment: The Assessment of Policy Voting." *American Political Science Review* 66, no.2 (June 1972): 451-58.

Brown, Steve R., and Taylor, Richard W. "Objectivity and Subjectivity in Concept Formation: Problems of Perspective, Partition, and Frames of Reference." Paper delivered at the 66th annual meeting of the American Political Science Association, Los Angeles, September 1970.

Buchanan, James, and Tullock, Gordon. *The Calculus of Consent*. Ann Arbor: University of Michigan Press, 1969.

Bunzel, John H. "The National Federation of Independent Business." In *Interest Group Politics in America*, edited by Robert Salisbury, pp. 106-19. New York: Harper & Row, 1970.

Burtt, Everett Johnson, Jr. *Labor Markets, Unions, and Government Policies*. New York: St. Martin's Press, 1963.

Campbell, Angus; Converse, Philip E.; Miller, Warren E.; and Stokes, Donald E. *The American Voter*. New York: John Wiley & Sons, 1960.

———. *Elections and the Political Order*. New York: John Wiley & Sons, 1966.

Campbell, Angus; Gurin, Gerald; and Miller, Warren E. *The Voter Decides*. Evanston, Ill.: Row & Peterson, 1954.

Cassinelli, C. W. "The Law of Oligarchy." *American Political Science Review* 47, no. 3 (September 1953): 773-84.

Clark, Kenneth B. *Dark Ghetto*. New York: Harper & Row, 1965.

Clark, Kenneth B., and Hopkins, Jeannette. *A Relevant War Against Poverty*. New York: Harper & Row, 1968.

Clark, Terry. "Community Structure, Decision Making, Budget Expenditures, and Urban Renewal in Fifty-one American Cities." *American Sociological Review* 33, no. 3 (August 1968): 576-91.

Cobb, Roger W., and Elder, Charles. *Participation in American Politics: The Dynamics of Agenda Building*. Boston: Allyn & Bacon, 1972.

Cohen, Sanford. *Labor Law*. Columbus, Ohio: C. F. Merrill Books, 1964.

Coleman, James. *Community Conflict*. New York: Free Press, 1957.

————. "The Possibility of a Social Welfare Function." *American Economic Review* 56, no. 5 (December 1966): 1105-23.

Connolly, William E., ed. *The Bias of Pluralism*. New York: Atherton Press, 1969.

Converse, Philip E. "The Nature of Belief Systems in Mass Publics." In *Ideology and Discontent*, edited by David E. Apter, pp. 206-61. New York: Free Press, 1964.

Cook Philip J. "Robert Michels' *Political Parties* in Perspective." *Journal of Politics* 33, no. 3 (August 1971): 773-96.

Cook, Terrence, and Morgan, Patrick. *Participatory Democracy*. San Francisco: Canfield Press, 1971.

Coser, Lewis. *The Functions of Social Conflict*. New York: Free Press, 1956.

Crain, Robert L. *The Politics of School Desegregation*. New York: Aldine, 1968.

Crain, Robert L.; Katz, Elihu; and Rosenthal, Donald. *The Politics of Community Conflict: The Fluoridation Decision*. Indianapolis: Bobbs-Merrill Co., 1969.

Crick, Bernard. *In Defense of Politics*. Baltimore: Penguin Books, 1964.

Dahl, Robert A. *After the Revolution*. New Haven: Yale University Press, 1970.

————. "Democracy and the Chinese Boxes." In *Frontiers in Democratic Theory*, edited by Henry S. Kariel, pp. 370-74. New York: Random House, 1970.

————. *Pluralistic Democracy in the United States: Conflict and Consensus*. Chicago: Rand McNally & Co., 1967.

————. *A Preface to Democratic Theory*. Chicago: University of Chicago Press, 1956.

————. *Who Governs?* New Haven: Yale University Press, 1961.

Dahl, Robert A., and Lindblom, Charles E. *Politics, Economics, and Welfare*. New York: Harper Torchbooks, 1963.

Darin-Drabkin, H. *The Other Society.* London: Victor Gollancz, 1962.

Derthick, Martha. *The Influence of Federal Grants: Public Assistance in Massachusetts.* Cambridge, Mass.: Harvard University Press, 1970.

————. *Between State and Nation: Regional Organizations of the United States.* Washington, D.C.: The Brookings Institution, 1974.

Downs, Anthony. *An Economic Theory of Democracy.* New York: Harper & Row, 1957.

Duncan, Graeme, and Lukes, Steven. "Democracy Restated." In *Frontiers in Democratic Theory,* edited by Henry S. Kariel, pp. 188-213. New York: Random House, 1970.

Dye, Thomas R., and Zeigler, L. Harmon. *The Irony of Democracy: An Uncommon Introduction to American Politics.* Belmont, Calif.: Wadsworth Publishing Co., 1970.

Eckstein, Harry. *Pressure Group Politics.* Stanford: Stanford University Press, 1960.

Edelman, Murray. *The Symbolic Uses of Politics.* Urbana: University of Illinois Press, 1967.

Eldersveld, Samuel V. *Political Parties.* Chicago: Rand McNally & Co., 1964.

Ellerman, David. "Capitalism and Workers' Self Management." In *Workers' Control,* edited by Gerry Hunnius et al., pp. 3-20. New York: Random House, 1973.

Elliot, W. Y. *The Pragmatic Revolt in Politics.* New York: Macmillan Co., 1928.

Etzioni, Amitai. *Modern Organizations.* Englewood Cliffs, N. J.: Prentice-Hall, 1964.

Fenno, Richard. *Congressmen in Committee.* Boston: Little, Brown & Co., 1973.

Field, John O., and Anderson, Ronald E. "Ideology in the Public's Conceptualization of the 1964 Election." *Public Opinion Quarterly* 33, no. 3 (Fall 1969): 380-93.

Fine, Keitha Sapsin. "Worker Participation in Israel." In *Workers' Control,* edited by Gerry Hunnius et al., pp. 226-67. New York: Random House, 1973.

Finer, S. E. "Groups and Political Participation." In *Participation in Politics,* edited by Geraint Parry, pp. 58-79. Manchester: Manchester University Press. 1972.

French, David, and French, Elena. *Working Communally.* New York: Russell Sage Foundation, 1975.

Gable, Richard. "NAM, Influential Lobby or Kiss of Death?" *Journal of Politics* 15, no. 2 (May 1953): 250-66.

Galbraith, John Kenneth. *American Capitalism.* Boston: Houghton Mifflin Co., 1956.

Gans, Herbert J. *The Urban Villagers.* New York: Free Press, 1962.

George, Alexander L. "The Case for Multiple Advocacy in Making Foreign Policy." *American Political Science Review* 66, no. 3 (September 1972): 751-86.

Gittell, Marilyn. *Participants and Participation: A Study of School Policy in New York City.* New York: Praeger, 1967.

Greenblatt, Milton, ed. *Poverty and Mental Health.* Psychiatric Research Reports, no. 21. New York: American Psychiatric Association, January 1967.

Greenstone, J. David, and Peterson, Paul E. *Race and Authority in Urban Politics.* New York: Russell Sage Foundation, 1973.

Grove, Walter, and Costner, Herbert. "Organizing the Poor: An Evaluation of a Strategy." *Social Science Quarterly* 50, no. 3 (December 1969): 643-56.

Gulick, Luther H., and Urwick, L., eds. *Papers on the Science of Administration.* New York: Institute of Public Administration, Columbia University, 1937.

Hamilton, Richard. *Class and Politics in the United States.* New York: John Wiley & Sons, 1972.

Hampden-Turner, Charles. "The Factory as an Oppressive and Non-Emancipatory Environment." In *Workers' Control,* edited by Gerry Hunnius et al., New York: Random House, 1973, pp. 30-45.

Hanson, Donald. "What is Living and What is Dead in Liberalism." *American Politics Quarterly* 2, no. 1 (January 1974): 3-37.

Harrington, Michael. *Toward a Democratic Left.* New York: Harper & Row, 1970.

Hastings, Philip K. "The Nonvoter in 1952: A Study of Pittsfield, Massachusetts." *Journal of Psychology,* 38 (October 1954): 301-12.

————. "The Voter and Nonvoter." *American Journal of Sociology* 62, no. 3 (November 1956): 302-307.

Hawley, Amos H. "Community Power Structure and Urban Renewal Success." *American Journal of Sociology 68, no. 4 (January 1963): 422-31.*

Heilbrun, James. *Urban Economics and Public Policy.* New York: St. Martin's Press, 1974.

Heinz, John. "The Political Impasse in Farm Support Legislation." In *Interest Group Politics in America,* edited by Robert Salisbury, pp. 186-98. New York: Harper & Row, 1970.

Hilsman, Roger. *To Move a Nation.* Garden City, N. Y.: Doubleday & Co., 1967.

Hine, Robert. *California's Utopian Colonies.* San Marino, Calif.: Huntington Library, 1953.

Hirsch, Werner. *The Economics of State and Local Government.* New York: McGraw-Hill, 1970.

Hirschman, Albert O. *Exit, Voice, and Loyalty: Responses to Decline in Firms, Organizations, and States.* Cambridge, Mass.: Harvard University Press, 1970.

Holden, Mathew. "Imperialism in Bureaucracy." *American Political Science Review* 60, no. 4 (December 1966): 943-51.

Hunnius, Gerry. "Workers' Self Management in Yugoslavia." In *Workers' Control,* edited by Gerry Hunnius et al., pp. 268-324. New York: Random House, 1973.

———. "Yugoslavia." In *Workers' Control,* edited by Gerry Hunnius et al., pp. 265-67. New York: Random House, 1973.

Huntington, Samuel P. *Political Order in Changing Societies.* New Haven: Yale University Press, 1968.

Jacobs, Paul and Landau, Saul, eds. *The New Radicals.* New York: Random House, 1966.

James, Dorothy B. *Poverty, Politics, and Change.* Englewood Cliffs, N. J.: Prentice-Hall, 1972.

Janis, Irving L. *Victims of Groupthink.* Boston: Houghton Mifflin Co., 1972.

Johnson, Hugh. *The Blue Eagle.* New York: Alfred A. Knopf, 1935.

Kanter, Rosabeth Moss. *Commitment and Community.* Cambridge, Mass.: Harvard University Press, 1972.

Kariel, Henry S. *The Decline of American Pluralism.* Stanford: Stanford University Press, 1961.

———, ed. *Frontiers of Democratic Theory.* New York: Random House, 1970.

Kaufman, Arnold S. "Human Nature and Participatory Democracy." In *The Bias of Pluralism,* edited by William E. Connolly, pp. 178-201. New York: Atherton Press, 1969.

Kendall, Willmore, and Carey, George W. "The 'Intensity Problem' and Democratic Theory." *American Political Science Review* 62, no. 1 (March 1968): 5-24.

Key, V. O. *Politics, Parties, and Pressure Groups.* 4th ed. New York: Thomas Y. Crowell Co., 1958.

———. *Public Opinion and American Democracy.* New York: Alfred A. Knopf, 1961.

———. *The Responsible Electorate.* Cambridge, Mass.: Harvard University Press, 1966.

Klatzky, S. R. "Relationship of Organizational Size to Complexity and

Coordination." *Administrative Science Quarterly* 15, no. 4 (December 1970): 428-38.

Kolaja, Jiri. *Workers' Councils: The Yugoslav Experience.* New York: Praeger, 1965.

Kornhauser, William. *The Politics of Mass Society.* Glencoe, Ill.: Free Press, 1959.

Kotler, Milton. *Neighborhood Government.* Indianapolis: Bobbs-Merrill Co., 1967.

Kramer, Daniel. *Participatory Democracy.* Cambridge, Mass.: Schenkman Publishing Co., 1972.

Kramer, Ralph M. *Participation of the Poor.* Englewood Cliffs, N. J.: Prentice-Hall, 1969.

Lane, Robert E., and Sears, David O. *Public Opinion.* Englewood Cliffs, N. J.: Prentice-Hall, 1964.

Laski, Harold J. *The State in Theory and Practice.* New York: Viking Press, 1935.

Lasswell, Harold; Lerner, Daniel; and Rothwell, C. Easton. *The Comparative Study of Elites.* Stanford: Stanford University Press, 1952.

Lawrence, Paul R., and Lorsch, Jay W. *Organization and Environment.* Cambridge, Mass.: Harvard University Press, 1967.

Lazarsfeld, Paul F.; Berelson, Bernard; and Gaudet, Hazel. *The People's Choice: How the Voter Makes up his Mind in a Presidential Campaign.* 2d ed. New York: Columbia University Press, 1948.

Leiserson, William M. *American Trade Union Democracy.* New York: Columbia University Press, 1959.

Leon, Don. *The Kibbutz.* London: Pergamon Press, 1969.

Leuthold, David. *Electioneering in a Democracy.* New York: John Wiley & Sons, 1968.

Levitan, Sar A., and Taggart, Robert. *The Promise of Greatness.* Cambridge, Mass.: Harvard University Press, 1976.

Lindblom, Charles E. *The Intelligence of Democracy.* New York: Free Press, 1965.

———. "Policy Analysis." *American Economic Review* 48, no. 3 (June 1958): 288-312.

———. "The Science of Muddling Through." *Public Administration Review* 19, no. 4 (Spring 1959): 79-88.

Lineberry, Robert L., and Fowler, Edmund P. "Reformism and Public Policies in American Cities." *American Political Science Review* 61, no. 3 (September 1967): 707-709.

Linz, Juan. "Robert Michels." *International Encyclopedia of the Social Sciences*, vol. 10, pp. 264-71, 1968.

Lipset, Seymour Martin. *Agrarian Socialism.* Berkeley and Los Angeles: University of California Press, 1959.

――――. Lipset, Seymour Martin; Trow, Martin A.; and Coleman, James S. *Union Democracy: The Internal Politics of the International Typographical Union.* Glencoe, Ill.: Free Press, 1956.

Lockard, Duane. *The Politics of State and Local Government.* New York: Macmillan Co., 1969.

Lowi, Theodore J. "American Business, Public Policy, Case Studies, and Political Theory." *World Politics* 16, no. 4 (July 1964): 677-715.

――――. *The End of Liberalism.* New York: W. W. Norton & Co., 1969.

――――. "The Public Philosophy: Interest Group Liberalism." *American Political Science Review* 61, no. 1 (March 1967): 5-24.

Luttbeg, Norman. "The Structure of Beliefs Among Leaders and the Public." *Public Opinion Quarterly* 32, no. 3 (Fall 1968): 398-409.

McClosky, Herbert. "Consensus and Ideology in American Politics." *American Political Science Review* 58, no. 2 (June 1964): 361-82.

McConnell, Grant. *The Decline of Agrarian Democracy.* Berkeley and Los Angeles: University of California Press, 1953.

――――. *Private Power and American Democracy.* New York: Alfred A. Knopf, 1966.

McFarland, Andrew S. *Power and Leadership in Pluralistic Systems.* Stanford: Stanford University Press, 1969.

McKean, Roland. *Public Spending.* New York: McGraw-Hill, 1968.

MacPhearson, C. B. *The Real World of Democracy.* New York: Oxford University Press, 1966.

Madison, James. "Federalist 10." In *The Federalist Papers,* by Alexander Hamilton, James Madison, and John Jay. New York: New American Library, 1961.

Mahood, H. R., ed. *Pressure Groups in American Politics.* New York: Charles Scribner's Sons, 1967.

Markovic, Dragan, et al. *Factories to Their Workers.* Belgrade; Prirredni Pregled, 1965.

Marris, Peter, and Rein, Martin. *Dilemmas of Social Reform.* New York: Atherton Press, 1967.

Masters, Nicholas A.; Salisbury, Robert H.; and Eliot, Thomas H. "The School Men in Missouri." In *Interest Group Politics in America,* edited by Robert Salisbury, pp. 216-43. New York: Harper & Row, 1970.

Matthews, Donald. *U.S. Senators and Their World.* New York: Vintage Books, 1960.

May, John. "Democracy, Organizations, Michels." *American Political Science Review* 59, no. 2 (June 1965): 417-29.

Mayo, H. B. *An Introduction to Democratic Theory.* New York: Oxford University Press, 1960.

Merton, Robert K. *Social Theory and Social Structure.* Glencoe, Ill.: Free Press, 1957.

Michels, Robert. *Political Parties: A Sociological Study of the Oligarchical Tendencies of Modern Democracy.* Translated by Eden Paul and Cedar Paul. 1915. Reprint. Glencoe, Ill.: Free Press, 1958.

Miller, Warren E., and Stokes, Donald E. "Constituency Influence in Congress." *American Political Science Review* 57, no. 1 (March 1963): 45-56.

Miner, Horace. *St. Denis, A French Canadian Parish.* Chicago: University of Chicago Press, 1963.

Moley, Raymond. *The First New Deal.* New York: Harcourt, Brace & World, 1966.

Moynihan, Daniel Patrick. *Maximum Feasible Misunderstanding.* New York: Free Press, 1969.

Mueller, John E. "Voting on the Propositions: Ballot Patterns and Historical Trends in California." *American Political Science Review* 63, no. 4 (December 1969): 1197-1212.

Musgrave, Richard A., and Musgrave, Peggy B. *Public Finance in Theory and Practice.* New York: McGraw-Hill, 1973.

Neal, Fred. *Titoism in Action.* Berkeley and Los Angeles: University of California Press, 1958.

Neuberger, Richard. "Governments by the People." *Survey* 86, no. 11 (November 1950): 490-93.

Neustadt, Richard. *Presidential Power.* New York: John Wiley & Sons, 1960.

Newfield, Jack, and Greenfield, Jeff. *A Populist Manifesto.* New York: Praeger, 1972.

Nie, Norman; Verba, Sidney; and Petrocik, John. *The Changing American Voter.* Cambridge, Mass.: Harvard University Press, 1976.

Niemi, Richard. "Majority Decision Making with Partial Unidimensionality." *American Political Science Review* 63, no. 2 (June 1969): 488-97.

Obradovic, Josip. "Participation and Work Attitudes in Yugoslavia." *Industrial Relations* 9, no. 2 (February 1970): 161-69.

Office of Economic Opportunity, Office of Operations. "Utilization Test Survey Data for 591 CAA's."

Olson, Mancur, Jr., *The Logic of Collective Action.* New York: Schocken Books, 1968.

Ostrom, Elinor, et al. *Community Organization and the Provision of Police Services.* Beverly Hills, Calif.: Sage Professional Papers in Administration and Policy Studies, 1973.

Page, Benjamin I., and Brody, Richard A. "Policy Voting and the Electoral Process: The View Nam War Issue." *American Political Science Review* 66, no. 3 (September 1972): pp. 979-96.

Parry, Geraint, ed. *Participation in Politics.* Manchester: Manchester University Press, 1972.

————. *Political Elites.* London: George Allen and Unwin, 1969.

Pateman, Carole. *Participation and Democratic Theory.* Cambridge: At the University Press, 1970.

Perrow, Charles. *Complex Organizations.* Glenview, Ill.: Scott, Foresman & Co., 1972.

————. "A Framework for the Comparative Analysis of Organizations." *American Sociological Review* 32, no. 2 (April 1967): 194-208.

————. *Organizational Analysis: A Sociological Review.* Belmont, Calif.: Brooks/Cole Publishing, 1970.

————. "Technology and Organizational Structure." In *Proceedings of the Nineteenth Annual Meeting of the Industrial Relations Research Association,* pp. 156-63, Madison, Wis., 1967.

Pitkin, Hanna F. *The Concept of Representation.* Berkeley and Los Angeles: University of California Press, 1967.

Piven, Frances Fox, and Cloward, Richard. *Regulating the Poor.* New York: Vintage Books, 1971.

Polsby, Nelson. *Community Power and Political Theory.* New Haven: Yale University Press, 1963.

Pomper, Gerald M. *Elections in America: Control and Influence in Democratic Politics.* New York: Dodd, Mead & Co., 1974.

Popper, Karl. *The Logic of Scientific Discovery.* New York: Harper & Row, 1968.

Prewitt, Kenneth. "Political Ambitions, Voluteerism, and Electoral Accountability." *American Political Science Review* 64, no. 1 (March 1970): 5-18.

Rabin, A. I. *Growing Up in the Kibbutz.* New York: Springer Publishing Co., 1965.

Ranney, Austin, and Kendall, Willmore. *Democracy and the American Party System.* New York: Harcourt, Brace & Co., 1956.

Rayack, Elton. *Professional Power and American Medicine.* New York: World Publishing Co., 1967.

RePass, David E. "Issue Salience and Party Choice." *American Political Science Review* 65, no. 2 (June 1971): 389-400

Ricci, David M., and Keynes, Edward. *Political Power, Community and Democracy.* Chicago: Rand McNally & Co., 1970.

Riker, William H., and Brams, Steve J. "The Paradox of Vote Trading." *American Political Science Review* 67, no. 4 (December 1973): 1235-47.

Riley, Patrick, "A Possible Explanation of Rousseau's General Will." *American Political Science Review* 64, no. 1 (March 1970): 86-93.

Rourke, Francis E. *Bureaucracy, Politics, and Public Policy.* Boston: Little, Brown & Co., 1969.

Rousseau, Jean Jacques. *The Social Contract.* In *Political Writings.* Translated by F. Watkins. Edinburgh: Thomas Nelson & Sons, 1953.

Rus, Veljko. "Influence Structure in Yugoslav Enterprise." *Industrial Relations* 9, no. 2 (February 1970): 148-60.

Sartori, Giovanni. *Democratic Theory.* New York: Praeger, 1958.

Sayre, Wallace S., and Kaufman, Herbert. *Governing New York City: Politics in the Metropolis.* New York: Russell Sage Foundation, 1960.

Schattschneider, Elmer Eric. *The Semi-Sovereign People.* New York: Holt Rinehart & Winston, 1960.

Schlesinger, Arthur M., Jr. *The Coming of the New Deal.* Vol II of *The Age of Roosevelt.* Boston: Houghton Mifflin Co., 1958.

Schumpeter, Joseph A. *Capitalism, Socialism and Democracy.* New York: Harper & Brothers, 1950.

Seidman, Harold. *Politics, Position, and Power.* New York: Oxford University Press, 1970.

Selznick, Philip. *Leadership in Administration: A Sociological Interpretation.* New York: Harper and Row, 1957.

———. *TVA and the Grass Roots.* Berkeley and Los Angeles: University of California Press, 1949.

Simon, Herbert A., and March, James G. *Organizations.* New York: John Wiley & Sons, 1958.

Simpson, Richard, and Gulley, William. "Goals, Environmental Pressures, and Organizational Characteristics." *American Sociological Review* 27, no. 3 (June 1962): 344-50.

Spiro, Melford. *Children of the Kibbutz.* New York: Schocken Books, 1965.

———. *Kibbutz: Ventures in Utopia.* Cambridge, Mass.: Harvard University Press, 1956.

Stern, Boris. *The Kibbutz That Was.* Washington, D. C.: Public Affairs Press, 1965.

Sullivan, John L., and O'Connor, Robert E. "Electoral Choice and Popular Control of Public Policy: The Case of the 1966 House Elections." *American Political Science Review* 66, no. 4 (December 1972): 1256-68.

Sundquist, James L. *Making Federalism Work.* Washington, D.C.: The Brookings Institution, 1969.

Talmon, J. L. *The Origins of Totalitarian Democracy.* New York: Praeger, 1960.

Talmon, Yonina. *Family and Community in the Kibbutz.* Cambridge, Mass.: Harvard University Press, 1972.

Thompson, James D. *Organizations in Action.* New York: McGraw-Hill, 1967.

Tiebout, Charles. "A Pure Theory of Local Expenditures." *Journal of Political Economy* 64 (October 1956): 416-24.

Tornquist, David. *Look East, Look West: The Socialist Adventure in Yugoslavia.* New York: Macmillan Co., 1966.

Truman, David. *The Governmental Process.* New York: Alfred A. Knopf, 1951.

U. S. Department of Commerce. *Annual Report of the Secretary.* Washington, D.C.: Government Printing Office, 1922.

Verba, Sidney, and Nie, Horman H. *Participation in America.* New York: Harper & Row, 1972.

Vidich, Arthur J., and Bensman, Joseph. *Small Town in Mass Society: Class, Power and Religion in a Rural Community.* Garden City, N.Y.: Doubleday & Co., 1960.

Wagner, Hardy. *Erfahr ungen mit dem Betriebsverfassungsgesetz.* Cologne: Bund-Verlag, 1960.

Walker, Jack L. "A Critique of the Elitist Theory of Democracy." *American Political Science Review* 60, no. 2 (June 1966): 285-95.

Weber, Max. *From Max Weber: Essays in Sociology.* Translated and edited by H. H. Gerth and C. Wright Mills. London: Oxford University Press, 1946.

Weingarten, Murray. "The Individual and the Community." In *Man Alone,* edited by Eric Josephson and Mary Josephson, pp. 516-32. New York: Dell Publishing Co., 1962.

Wilson, James Q. *The Amateur Democrat.* Chicago: University of Chicago Press, 1962.

―――. "Innovation in Organizations: Notes towards a Theory." In *Approaches to Organizational Design,* edited by James D. Thompson, pp. 193-218. Pittsburgh: University of Pittsburgh Press, 1966.

―――. *Political Organizations.* New York: Basic Books, 1973.

Wolff, Robert Paul. *In Defense of Anarchism.* New York: Harper & Row, 1970.

―――. *The Poverty of Liberalism.* Boston: Beacon Press, 1968.

Wolff, Robert Paul; Moore, Barrington, Jr.,; and Marcuse, Herbert. *A Critique of Pure Tolerance.* Boston: Beacon Press, 1965.

Wolfinger, Raymond E., and Greenstein, Fred I. "The Repeal of Fair Housing Legislation in California: An Analysis of Referendum Voting." *American Political Science Review* 62, no. 3 (September 1968): 753-69.

Wolfinger, Raymond E.; Wolfinger, Barbara Kay; Prewitt, Kenneth; and Rosenhach, Sheilah. "America's Radical Right: Politics and Ideology." In *Ideology and Discontent*, edited by David E. Apter, pp. 262-93. New York: Free Press, 1964.

Yates, Douglas. *Neighborhood Democracy*. Lexington, Mass.: D. C. Heath & Co., 1973.

Zeigler, Harmon. *Interest Groups in American Society*. Englewood Cliffs, N.J.: Prentice-Hall, 1964.

Zukin, Sharon. *Beyond Marx and Tito*. London: Cambridge University Press, 1975.

Zupanov, Josip, and Tannenbaum, Arnold S. "The Distribution of Control in Some Yugoslav Industrial Organizations as Perceived by Members." In *Control in Organizations*, edited by Arnold Tannenbaum, pp. 91-109. New York: McGraw-Hill, 1958.

Index

About the Author

William Kelso, assistant professor of political science at the University of Florida, has specialized in American political theory and public administration. His articles have appeared in *The Bureaucrat, Midwest Review of Public Administration,* and other journals.